THE ROCK CANON

To my parents

The Rock Canon
Canonical Values in the Reception of Rock Albums

CARYS WYN JONES

ASHGATE

Published by
Ashgate Publishing Limited
Gower House
Croft Road
Aldershot
Hampshire GU11 3HR
England

Ashgate Publishing Company
Suite 420
101 Cherry Street
Burlington, VT 05401-4405
USA

Ashgate website: http://www.ashgate.com

British Library Cataloguing in Publication Data
Jones, Carys Wyn
  The rock canon : canonical values in the reception of rock
  albums. – (Ashgate popular and folk music series)
  1. Rock music 2. Music – Philosophy and aesthetics
  I. Title
  781.6'6'01

Library of Congress Cataloging-in-Publication Data
Jones, Carys Wyn, 1978–
  The rock canon : canonical values in the reception of rock albums / by Carys Wyn Jones.
    p. cm. – (Ashgate popular and folk music series)
  Includes bibliographical references.
  ISBN 978-0-7546-6244-0 (alk. paper)
  1. Musical canon. 2. Rock music–History and criticism. I. Title.

ML3890.J66 2008
781.66'117–dc22

2008008222

ISBN 978-0-7546-6244-0

Printed and bound in Great Britain by MPG Books Ltd, Bodmin, Cornwall.

Contents

Contents of Appendix

General Editor's Preface

The upheaval that occurred in musicology during the last two decades of the twentieth century has created a new urgency for the study of popular music alongside the development of new critical and theoretical models. A relativistic outlook has replaced the universal perspective of modernism (the international ambitions of the 12-note style); the grand narrative of the evolution and dissolution of tonality has been challenged, and emphasis has shifted to cultural context, reception and subject position. Together, these have conspired to eat away at the status of canonical composers and categories of high and low in music. A need has arisen, also, to recognize and address the emergence of crossovers, mixed and new genres, to engage in debates concerning the vexed problem of what constitutes authenticity in music and to offer a critique of musical practice as the product of free, individual expression.

Popular musicology is now a vital and exciting area of scholarship, and the *Ashgate Popular and Folk Music Series* presents some of the best research in the field. Authors are concerned with locating musical practices, values and meanings in cultural context, and may draw upon methodologies and theories developed in cultural studies, semiotics, poststructuralism, psychology and sociology. The series focuses on popular musics of the twentieth and twenty-first centuries. It is designed to embrace the world's popular musics from Acid Jazz to Zydeco, whether high tech or low tech, commercial or non-commercial, contemporary or traditional.

Professor Derek B. Scott
Professor of Critical Musicology
University of Leeds, UK

Acknowledgements

I would like first of all to thank Dr Kenneth Gloag for his invaluable comments and guidance throughout the project. I would also like to thank the following people for their kind and various assistance along the way: Dr David Wyn Jones, Dr David Beard, the library and support staff at Cardiff University, John Davies, Professor Derek B. Scott and Heidi May at Ashgate. Finally I would like to thank my parents, Tom and Dilys, my sister Kathryn and my partner David for their unswerving love and support from beginning to end.

Introduction

In March 2003 the *NME* introduced their list of the *NME* writers' 'NME's 100 Best Albums of All Time!' by saying, 'This isn't a boring attempt to create some kind of canon of "classics" – just an honest account of what continues to rock our world.'[1] Yet the selection of albums in this poll (including albums by the Beatles, the Beach Boys and the Velvet Underground) suggests not only that a canon of 'great' artists and albums is emerging in rock music – but also that, for some reason, the writers of the *NME* are keen to deny it. This book asks the question of whether rock music is in fact in the process of creating a canon of classics, and in doing so, will investigate the extent to which canonical models from literature and classical music have informed the structures and values of the reception of rock music albums.

Simply put, the canon comprises the works and artists that are generally considered to be the greatest in their field. Yet such an apparently simple construct embodies a complicated web of values and mechanisms. The oldest and most venerated canon comprises the books of the Bible, and this canon has remained largely unquestioned over the centuries. The oldest and most established secular canon is that of literature, and canonical debate originated primarily within this field. However, the canon is also an increasingly important issue in the academic study of music, as it absorbs different styles and traditions of music into its orbit.

Indeed, the study of canons in general is a growing concern as our culture becomes increasingly multicultural. We struggle to find a way to reconcile the plurality of today's culture with the canon and yet the idea of the canon still holds authority over many areas of our lives. Traditionally canons have existed only in the rarefied spheres of high art; however, today the values embodied by these canons have filtered into the reception of popular culture. It is perhaps not surprising that popular culture inherits many of its structures of value from high culture, but that is not to say that such inheritance is not problematic. Canonical models from literature and classical music will therefore be used to explain patterns of reception in popular music, particularly the reception of rock music albums, which displays marked echoes of canons in its guiding logic.

Until now canons in popular music have not been explored in detail in academic literature, and the general position of the academic study of popular music towards canons has been ambivalent. Subjects related to canonicity in rock music (such as value judgement and marginalization of certain perspectives) have so far been discussed separately but not as part of a discussion of canons.[2] Some academics have privileged certain artists (especially the Beatles and Bob Dylan) in their research

---

1   Various Contributors, 'NME's 100 Best Albums of All Time!', *New Musical Express*, 8 March 2003, 35–42 (35).

2   For example, value judgement in the reception of popular music forms the central concern of Simon Frith, *Performing Rites: On the Value of Popular Music* (Oxford and New York: Oxford University Press, 1996). Perspectives of women in rock are discussed in *Sexing*

and have thus started a tentative canon of works apparently considered worthy of academic study.[3] However, by contrast, Allan Moore states quite unequivocally in his book *Rock: The Primary Text* that he is trying to 'subvert the growth of an accepted "canon" of popular music (which already accepts the Beatles, "punk" and Bob Dylan, at the very least)'.[4] The publication of a special issue of the journal *Popular Music* on 'Canonisation in Popular Music' (January 2006) demonstrates the growing interest in the role of canons in popular music, but as the diverse articles in this edition make clear, there is little consensus as of yet over the field and values under discussion.[5] This book therefore aims to present an in-depth discussion of one particular aspect of canons in popular music and therefore to form part of the growing dialogue surrounding the issue.

For reasons of clarity and convenience, the music under study will be consistently referred to as 'rock' music in this book. However, this is indubitably an unsatisfactory term to apply on the whole. Bob Dylan's music is often characterized as folk, and *Never Mind the Bollocks: Here's the Sex Pistols* is regarded as the epitome of punk, while the music of both the Beatles and the Beach Boys is more frequently referred to as 'pop' than 'rock'. Arguably the most jarring discrepancy in this use of the label 'rock' is in the discussion of Marvin Gaye's *What's Going On*, which is widely recognized as soul music. There is perhaps room here to argue that a new term is needed to describe music that is defined primarily by albums, one that transcends the different styles of soul, punk, pop and folk but that creates a more satisfying umbrella term than 'rock' (which has its own set of connotations).[6] I will come to argue, however, that while Gaye's music itself is not necessarily 'rock', the values by which it is judged in popular reception are rock values (albeit ones inherited from the high arts). Therefore, in the absence of a more suitable term, the word 'rock' will be employed throughout the book in its most general meaning in that it is defined primarily by the album (for the most part incorporating other terms such as rock 'n' roll, pop, folk-rock and so on). Where the term 'popular music' is employed later in the book, it indicates the field in its widest possible conception.

The majority of this study will deal with the possibility of an emerging canon of albums within the field of 'popular' rock music reception, and so a distinction is also drawn between 'popular' rock music reception and 'academic' rock music reception. Non-academic authors are defined as those who are not recognized primarily as academics (in any field) and whose works are published by non-academic publishers.

the Groove: Popular Music and Gender, ed. by Sheila Whiteley (London and New York: Routledge, 1997).

3   See for example Yrjö Heinonen and others, '(Being a Short Diversion to) Current Perspectives in Beatles Research', in *Beatlestudies 1: Songwriting, Recording, and Style Change*, ed. by Yrjö Heinonen and others (Jyväskylä: University of Jyväskylä Press, 1998), pp. i–iv.

4   Allan F. Moore, *Rock: The Primary Text, Developing a Musicology of Rock*, 2nd edn (Aldershot: Ashgate, 2001), p. 7.

5   *Popular Music*, Special Issue on Canonisation, 25/1 (January 2006).

6   Perhaps the most obvious term for music defined primarily by albums is 'album music'; however, the immediate clumsiness and ambiguity of this term may explain why it has never come into use. Other terms, such as 'art rock' and 'classic rock', are also problematic in this respect, and this subject will be revisited later in the book.

However, some grey area inevitably arises, most notably in the case of Greil Marcus (a serious non-academic critic) and Simon Frith (an academic who also writes for non-academic publications).

Chapter 1 presents a general overview of the concept of the canon. It explores theories and definitions of the canons of literature and classical music in order to create a model of the canon that can then be applied to and compared with rock music reception in later chapters. Theorizations of the canon employed in this section include those of Harold Bloom, John Guillory and Charles Altieri in the field of literature and William Weber and Marcia Citron in the field of classical music.

Chapters 2 and 3 then demonstrate where these canonical ideas and ideals have filtered into the reception of rock music by focusing on ten albums: Bob Dylan's *Highway 61 Revisited*, the Beach Boys' *Pet Sounds*, the Beatles' *Revolver*, the Velvet Underground's *The Velvet Underground & Nico*, Van Morrison's *Astral Weeks*, Marvin Gaye's *What's Going On*, the Rolling Stones' *Exile on Main St.*, Patti Smith's *Horses*, The Sex Pistols' *Never Mind the Bollocks: Here's the Sex Pistols*, and Nirvana's *Nevermind*. These albums and artists routinely appear in histories of rock music, feature highly in lists of 'greatest albums of all time' and have been the focus of books and articles describing their creation and influence. This part of the book therefore searches for canonical values, criteria and mechanisms in their reception. It also covers issues of secondary literature, aesthetic criteria, author/genius, and the album as a work of art. The focus is then redirected to common narrative strands of canons, the imagined structure of the canon and the perception of canonically excluded identities. Finally this section addresses canonical mechanisms present in rock reception, including the test of time, reissues and 'canonizers'.[7]

Chapter 4 explores the reception of the same ten albums for evidence of other canonical values and criteria specific to rock music that are generally absent from the canons of literature and classical music. Chapter 5 then turns to the problem of authority in rock music, and explores the position of academic study in relation to a canon of popular music. In conclusion, Chapter 6 puts forth a case for and against a canon in rock and then finally returns to the concept of the canon itself in order to question its future in an increasingly democratized and globalized culture.

---

7   The term 'canonizer', relating to those whose actions serve to create and perpetuate canons, is used by John Guillory in 'Canon', in *Critical Terms for Literary Study*, ed. by Frank Lentricchia and Thomas McLaughlin (Chicago: University of Chicago Press, 1990), pp. 233–49 and also Philip Bohlman in Philip V. Bohlman, 'Ethnomusicology's Challenge to the Canon; The Canon's Challenge to Ethnomusicology', in *Disciplining Music: Musicology and Its Canons*, ed. by Katherine Bergeron and Philip V. Bohlman (Chicago and London: University of Chicago Press, 1992), pp. 116–36 (p. 203).

Chapter 1

Defining the Canon

In the last thirty years there has been much interest, conflict and uncertainty created by the word 'canon'. The concept of the canon is unfamiliar to many, especially those outside of academia; however, the idea of the canon is embodied in every reference to 'a classic', in lists of 'all-time greats' and in the habitual reverence of hallowed and ancient wisdom.

Put simply, a canon is the collection of works and artists that are widely accepted as the greatest in their field. These are the works and artists that are studied in schools and universities, performed in concert halls and displayed in galleries. These works are passed down from one generation to the next, and the artists are celebrated in histories and honoured with centennials. In Western literature the canon includes the works of Chaucer, Shakespeare and Tolstoy; in art, Botticelli, Rembrandt and Picasso; and in classical music, Bach, Beethoven and Brahms. However, such a reductive account of history and culture masks a complex and contradictory set of values and mechanisms that have been passed down over the years in the form of the canon.

The word 'canon' has meant many things over the years (including 'reed' or 'rod' or 'rule'), but as John Guillory recounts, it first came to signify a 'list of texts or authors, specifically the books of the Bible and of the early theologians of Christianity', in the fourth century AD. This early canon determined what was worthy of attention; in effect 'early Christianity had to decide what its "truths" were, what it was going to teach its followers.'[1] Once these 'truths' were established, the biblical canon became highly resistant to change; and much of the weight, authority and power of the word 'canon' can be traced back to these roots in religion. Therefore canons retain a residual aura of morality and unquestionable greatness.[2]

However, today's canons are no longer primarily those of religion. Since the twentieth century, use of the word canon has become more generally secular, but also more loosely defined. Rather than one (religious) canon, today we have many. As Charles Altieri comments:

> There are personal canons and official canons, canons for what one needs to know and canons for undermining all one is told one needs to know – and each of these classes has

---

1   John Guillory, 'Canon', in *Critical Terms for Literary Study*, ed. by Frank Lentricchia and Thomas McLaughlin (Chicago: University of Chicago Press, 1990), pp. 233–49 (p. 233).

2   See Richard Tristman, 'Canon: Historical and Conceptual Overview', in *The Encyclopaedia of Aesthetics*, ed. by Michael Kelly (Oxford: Oxford University Press, 1998), I, pp. 331–4 (pp. 332–4).

several subdivisions. There are probably even canons for bathroom reading. Canons, then, reveal the same diversity and flexibility we find in the self's affairs.[3]

Yet this multitude of modern canons cannot hope to serve a similar social role, nor engender the same unquestioning respect, as the early canon of Christianity. Any comparison made between today's canons and the now closed biblical canon therefore requires a degree of caution.

Some of the uncertainty surrounding the concept of the canon is attributable to the term itself. Although the concept of the 'great' artist and the 'classic' work (or 'masterwork') has been around for centuries, the term 'canon' is a relatively recent addition to the vocabulary of literary criticism, and so its varied and often confused usage (especially outside of academia) is understandable. General use of the word 'canon' as a collection of prized works has only become common in the last 30 years, and even now this is only one possible understanding of the word.[4]

Adding to the confusion is the fact that the canon in any one discipline is not a fixed set of works (like the Bible), but is instead a forever shifting collocation of works that represents its greatest achievements; what Guillory has referred to as 'an *imaginary* totality of works'.[5] Given the vagueness associated with the idea of the canon, it is a concept that always requires (re)definition or qualification. The rest of this chapter will therefore seek to define the canon by focusing on the canons of two disciplines, those of Western literature and Western classical music, in order to crystallize the shared characteristics of these canons into a model that will then be employed throughout the rest of the book.

Of the various secular canons now in existence, the canon of Western literature is the oldest and most venerated. It is also the canon that has attracted the most criticism in the last 20 years, since the publication of *Canons* (1984), a collection of essays edited by Robert von Hallberg that was highly influential in raising the issue of canons in literary and music criticism.[6] Most of the issues pertaining to the canon as a concept have been raised with regard to the specific canon of Western literature.

The canon of Western classical music has been influenced by that of literature and yet remains wholly separate, and is therefore an invaluable model for the study of more recent canon formation, especially in the field of music. The musical canon is in its infancy compared to that of literature, and it was only properly established with the rise of musicology and the cult of Beethoven in the nineteenth century.[7] However, criticism

---

3   Charles Altieri, 'An Idea and Ideal of a Literary Canon', in *Canons*, ed. by Robert von Hallberg (Chicago and London: Chicago University Press, 1984), pp. 41–64 (p. 63 n. 6).

4   Even within the discipline of musicology, the word 'canon' is more usually recognized as a form of contrapuntal composition rather than a collocation of great works; alternatively, 'canon' is employed to denote the collected works of a single composer (for example, 'Symphony no. 9 is one of the greatest in the Beethoven canon').

5   John Guillory, *Cultural Capital: The Problem of Literary Canon Formation* (Chicago and London: University of Chicago Press, 1993), p. 30. [Emphasis in the original.]

6   *Canons*, ed. by Robert von Hallberg (Chicago and London: University of Chicago Press, 1984).

7   William Weber has explored the rise of the musical canon in various articles and books, most notably William Weber, *The Rise of Musical Classics in Eighteenth-Century*

of the canon in classical music has risen simultaneously with that of the literary canon, with the inclusion of Joseph Kerman's article 'A Few Canonic Variations' in von Hallberg's *Canons*.[8] This overview of canons will firstly explore why we have canons, then look at how canons are made and what makes a work canonical, before finally addressing the problems surrounding canons in our culture today.

Why Do We Have Canons? – Stories, Influence and the Test of Time

Canons underpin our culture, and yet many people are unaware of what canons are, much less how they came to take their current form. Yet their prevalence today suggests that, if not inevitable, then canons are at least extremely useful. In as much as canons are loosely defined and always require qualification, they are also flexible in their many applications.

A primary function of canons is their ability to bring order to chaos, to essentially tell a story of our cultural history and present it in its most awe-inspiring light. Canons reduce fields down to their essence, thus selecting for us works that are worthy of our attention; this is a necessary function given the vast numbers of works of literature or classical music in existence. In music, Joseph Kerman draws a line between canon and repertory, claiming that 'a canon is an idea, a repertory a plan of action'; however, there is inevitably some overlap between the two.[9] We cannot possibly absorb all the writing and music, not to mention art and dance, ever created, and the canon presents, in effect, a collocation of 'greatest works' to experience before you die.

However, although canons can be considered as simplified stories, they are also narratives of some complexity.[10] Hugh Kenner makes the point that 'our canon … is something we shape by our needs and our sense of what is complexly coherent.'[11] Or, as Frank Kermode comments, 'There is … a powerful notion, perhaps one could even call it a myth, that somehow everything hangs together and that one can at least begin to show how.'[12] The inherently closed structure of stories (and, by extension, canons) runs counter to the current conception of postmodern pluralities, relativism and the fragmentation of culture. Yet such an ordered perspective of history still holds great appeal.

As a collection of exemplary works, canons draw attention to the possibilities of a medium. They also implant the desire to struggle under the weight of the past to achieve comparable greatness. Minor figures in the arts are seen to use canonical

---

England: A Study in Canon, Ritual, and Ideology (Oxford: Clarendon Press, 1992).

8   Joseph Kerman, 'A Few Canonic Variations', in *Canons*, ed. by Robert von Hallberg (Chicago and London: University of Chicago Press, 1984), pp.177–95. This article was first published in 1983 in *Critical Inquiry*, 10/1, 107–25.

9   Ibid., p. 177.

10 Narratives are structures that underpin stories but do not present stories in themselves.

11 Hugh Kenner, 'The Making of the Modernist Canon', in *Canons*, ed. by Robert von Hallberg (Chicago and London: University of Chicago Press, 1984), pp. 363–75, p. 375.

12 Frank Kermode, *Forms of Attention* (Chicago and London: University of Chicago Press, 1985), p. 83.

works as models; major figures use them as a point of departure. The canon can therefore be regarded as both a model of greatness and a site of 'conflict between past genius and present aspiration'; in other words a battleground for representation in history.[13]

The guiding narrative of the canon is therefore usually one of evolution and progress made visible in the progression of its key works. The narrative is dictated by the perceived course of artistic influence over the centuries, history reduced to the story of its greatest artists passing on the torch of inspired invention. However, as Anita Silvers observes, this narrative presents one of the greatest underlying struggles facing the canon, since this story of progress and change is embodied in a concept that promotes stability and stasis.[14] While presenting a narrative of progressive evolution, the canon is also used to preserve traditional knowledge and values 'against the erosion of time and influences from outside the culture', and to endow a society with a sense of heritage, roots, pride, unity and cultural wealth.[15] The literary canon in particular also has a normative semantic role, through which it is capable of sustaining and disseminating complex languages.[16] The canon therefore insulates its works and the knowledge and values they represent against change.

Yet this stasis is illusory: every age is (apocalyptically) assumed to be the last, and the most definitive, and so the past shifts time and time again under the hands of new generations of canonical curators (or canonizers) to accommodate the present. Contemporary artists and works that succeed in challenging the hegemony of the canon are invariably subsumed by it over time, and the appearance of stasis is retrospectively restored. However, with such contradictory pressures at work, the canon is ultimately a complex and contradictory structure that is far from stable.[17]

The Test of Time

Canonical works are revered for their ability to survive the so-called 'test of time', a familiar expression that cloaks the very human decisions that go into the survival of any work.[18] This test supposedly functions by eliminating ephemeral works, those that are of poor quality or those too specific to their time to be of lasting value. Once a work becomes recognized as part of a canon, its survival is far more assured, since the collective value of the canon is reflected back onto its constituent works in a self-perpetuating cycle. As time passes, the works themselves become more problematically complex as they are taken out of their original context and accrue

---

13 Harold Bloom, *The Western Canon: The Books and School of the Ages* (London and New York: Harcourt Brace & Company, 1994), pp. 8–9.

14 See Anita Silvers, 'The Canon in Aesthetics', in *The Encyclopaedia of Aesthetics*, ed. by Michael Kelly (Oxford: Oxford University Press, 1998), I, pp. 334–8 (p. 338).

15 See George A. Kennedy, 'The Origin of the Concept of a Canon and its Application to the Greek and Latin Classics', in *Canon vs Culture: Reflections on the Current Debate*, ed. by Jan Gorak (New York and London: Garland, 2001), pp. 105–16 (p. 105).

16 Altieri, 'An Idea and Ideal of a Literary Canon', p. 54.

17 For further discussion, see Bloom, *The Western Canon*, p. 37.

18 For an in-depth discussion of the 'test of time', see Anthony Savile, *The Test of Time: An Essay in Philosophical Aesthetics* (Oxford: Clarendon Press, 1982).

other meanings and significances, not least through their association with other 'great' works in the canon.

The longer a work remains in the canon, the less likely its presence and value is to be questioned, and thus its own deficiencies (by whatever criteria) played down. To this effect, Bloom describes how Shakespeare's anti-Semitism and patriarchal values, which would have been acceptable at the time, today tend to be glossed over or explained away in discussions of his work.[19]

In addition, to survive the test of time a work must usually become 'timeless'. Timeless works must appear to speak to successive generations, and, to this effect, time-contingent elements of works are glossed over or explained in more universal terms. Gradually this leads to the works becoming unpinned from their own time and increasingly associated instead with the other great works in the canon. The canon, therefore, is not formed by contemporary audiences, but is instead crystallized by every new generation that reasserts the value of its constituent works.

This ability of a work to appeal to successive generations with different social values has been memorably termed as 'omnisignificance' by Frank Kermode; by becoming timeless, works can achieve 'perpetual value' and 'perpetual modernity'. 'To be inside the canon', Kermode maintains, 'is to be protected from wear and tear, to be credited with indefinitely large numbers of possible internal relations and secrets, to be treated as a heterocosm … It is to acquire magical and occult properties that are in fact very ancient.'[20] As a consequence of this omnisignificance, the work's greatness is seen to rest in some intrinsic worth, which is itself untouched by the changing values of society.

The test of time also incorporates the test of random survival, for as Kermode observes, 'Chance may act before opinion can, taking a hand in determining the survival of whatever it is that we may hold opinions about.'[21] To survive the physical test of time it is also necessary for canonical works to exist in a form that is easily reproduced, disseminated and preserved (such as the book, the preserved image or the musical score or recording) in order for cultural activity to be frozen into an idealized canon. Only when oral culture is notated does it usually achieve canonical status, which is one reason why music lacked a canon until the idea of music-as-score rose to prominence in the nineteenth century (and more recently with the recording-as-definitive-interpretation). There may be shadow-canons of what we know to have once existed, but these are less powerful than those of works that have survived.

The belief that time is a natural and neutral test that allows taste to govern selection can be traced at least as far back as the eighteenth-century philosopher David Hume, and his essay 'On the Standard of Taste'.[22] Hindsight, therefore, has long been believed to bestow better judgement than any contemporary audience response. There is a beguiling side to leaving the fate of works to the test of time,

---

19 See Bloom, *The Western Canon*, p. 51.

20 Kermode, *Forms of Attention*, pp. 62 & 90.

21 Ibid., p. 73.

22 See Silvers, 'The Canon in Aesthetics', p. 337. David Hume, 'Of the Standard of Taste', included in *Art and Its Significance: An Anthology of Aesthetic Theory*, ed. by Stephen David Ross (Albany, NY: SUNY Press, 1994).

absolving contemporary critics of ultimate wisdom, and enticing artists with the possibility of immortality, seemingly regardless of the reception of contemporary audiences. In reality, however, the test of time is located in the decisions made by individuals (canonizers) in the context of cultural institutions.

How Are Canons Made? – Institutions and Canonizers

Canons do not exist in a vacuum; they are supported and perpetuated by institutions. The earliest canons, both sacred and secular, were pedagogic in nature, and today a person's initial (and usually main) interaction and contact with canonical texts will be through school. Academic institutions are responsible for exposing each new generation to the key works of the canon while also introducing them to the set of values that maintain esteem for these particular works. Within the setting of the school, the values, terms and mechanisms of the canon are reinforced in the minds of future generations.

Scholars and institutions are repeatedly called upon to justify their selection of works worthy of study, and by extension the tastes and values of the wider community. Therefore cultural (or academic) institutions not only select and preserve canonical texts, upholding them as models of wisdom, but also mediate their contents and meaning. Canons and institutions have a mutually reliant symbiotic relationship; institutions rely on canons for curriculum and prestige, while canons rely on institutions for their survival. As Herrnstein Smith notes in *Contingencies of Value*, it is the 'normative activities of ... the literary and aesthetic academy' that are largely responsible for the stabilizing of labels and expectations of classified objects in a community.[23] Such labels and expectations dictate the contents of canons, and by extension curricula at schools and the boundaries of academic disciplines.

However, schools are not the only institutional settings for canons: libraries, theatres, museums, publishing and printing houses, editorial boards and prize-awarding bodies all use canons to invoke high ideals and bring order to a field. Echoes of canons in cultures outside school are only to be expected, since the values represented in the canonical works taught at school are internalized by the students. As Guillory comments, 'structures of tastes may be formed by particular social communities outside the school', and the site (or social and cultural context) of a canon will determine certain of its characteristics; hence, we 'cannot simply speak about a history of reception, of canon-formation.'[24]

The collocation of works in the canon also presents common questions, problems and interests for both readers and writers, resulting in shared values that underpin a society's thinking as a whole. Teachers most often use the same anthologies, textbooks and histories, both for reasons of examination syllabus and copyright, and this creates a common set of objects for study.[25] Indeed, as Barbara Herrnstein Smith

---

23 Barbara Herrnstein Smith, *Contingencies of Value: Alternative Perspectives for Critical Theory* (Cambridge, MA and London: Harvard University Press, 1988), p. 43.

24 Guillory, 'Canon', p. 239.

25 See Marcia Citron, *Gender and the Musical Canon* (Cambridge: Cambridge University Press, 1993), pp. 24 & 25.

states, canonical works are simply used more and are more familiar to us than other works. They are

> more frequently read or recited, copied or reprinted, translated, imitated, cited, commented upon and so forth – in short, culturally re-produced ... by professors, scholars, critics, poets, and other elders of the tribe; for all these acts have the effect of drawing the work into the orbit of potential readers and, by making the work more likely to be experienced at all, they make it more likely to be experienced as "valuable" ... Value creates value.[26]

As a consequence of being uniformly taught in schools, canons can promote nationalism and a sense of unity in a given society.[27]

Aside from reinforcing these canonical values, reference to canonical texts can be regarded as a form of cultural capital.[28] Guillory believes the school operates as a 'system of credentialization by which it produces a specific *relation* to culture'; this contributes to an individual's cultural capital, although cultural capital is determined over the whole of society, not just the school, and so includes other factors such as race, gender and class.[29] However, while the full meaning of the canonical work is only thought to be understood by an elite minority of people, the value of the canon is supposed to apply to all.

Traditionally, another related function of the canon has been the separation of high and low culture. For example, canons preserve hierarchies within language, separating high, written language from everyday speech, and by extension the educated elite from the uneducated or illiterate.[30] However, more recently there has been a blurring of the lines drawn between high and popular culture and this in turn has had repercussions on the status of the canon. Rather than being a distinguishing feature between high and low culture, canons today are emerging in popular culture itself; this contradiction will form the central concern of this book.

Canons in Literature and Classical Music

While the canon in literature has its roots in antiquity and the teachings of Plato and Aristotle, the canon in classical music arose as recently as the eighteenth century. William Weber, who has studied the rise of the canon in classical music in depth, describes the ways in which the separation of theory and practice in classical music prevented the formation of a canon until well into the seventeenth century. As a consequence, classical music was long denied the high art status of literature and art.[31] However, as the literary

---

26 Herrnstein Smith, *Contingencies of Value*, pp. 21 & 10.

27 For example, Citron notes that nationalism played a role in the revival of old classics in classical music, see Citron, *Gender and the Musical Canon*, pp. 36–7. Guillory suggests that one consequence of a unified 'Western' canon is the perpetuation of the myth of a homogenized Western culture. Guillory, *Cultural Capital*, p. 42.

28 John Guillory describes this in depth in his book *Cultural Capital: The Problem of Literary Canon Formation*.

29 Ibid., p. 56.

30 Guillory, 'Canon', pp. 240 & 242.

31 See Weber, *The Rise of Musical Classics in Eighteenth-Century England*, p. 2.

canon shifted to include Shakespeare, whose work had become an inescapable influence, so the perception of greatness migrated from antiquity to the near-contemporary. At the beginning of the eighteenth century, as the literary canon therefore became more fragmented and popularized and thus lost hold of some of its elitist authority, it allowed the possibility of canons in less ancient arts to rise up around it.[32]

Accordingly, until the eighteenth century music lacked a canon of acknowledged works and figures from the past and it was more common for pieces to be composed for specific occasions and then discarded.[33] It follows that before the rise of the canon in classical music, composers were concerned with immediate rather than enduring success. Those works that were not discarded were either assimilated into the rituals of an annual feast (viewed as a 'custom' rather than a classic) or used as pedagogical models but not performed. However, as literature loosened its bonds with the past, music now began to build for itself a history and tradition by redefining the concept of what constituted 'ancient' works to include far more recent compositions. For example, orchestral–choral pieces that had previously been discarded began to be performed as major civic events, the (new) 'antiquity' of the works adding to the grandeur of the occasion. Musical theory evolved from speculative thought on the music of (actual) antiquity to 'musical criticism, aesthetics, and social commentary upon musical life' which formed the basis of the growing canon.[34] These changes brought about the potential for the multitude of canons now in existence.

Changing social and cultural structures in eighteenth-century England after the Reformation created a 'public sphere' in which these changes in the perception, and reception, of music took place.[35] In *Gender and the Musical Canon* Marcia Citron describes how the shift of social power from the church to the general public saw a gradual trend towards commercialization, with its associated 'music publishing, music magazines, concert series, instrument makers, critics, entrepreneurial composers, and independent performers and performing groups.'[36]

The intellectual basis of the canon, in music as in literature, was shaped primarily by empiricism, through journalism, criticism, history, pedagogy and social commentary, legitimizing the study of music by claiming it as a science.[37] The ideas of empiricism brought enduring hierarchies to music, by establishing the ear as superior to the eye and the composer superior to the theorist. Weber states that these

32 William Weber, 'The Intellectual Origins of Musical Canon in Eighteenth-Century England', *The Journal of the American Musicological Society*, 47 (1994), 488–520 (493–6). The process of canon formation in music has a complex and little-explored relationship with that of literature, although William Weber asserts that earliest canonical tendencies in music bore little resemblance to the literary canon. William Weber, 'Canon and the Traditions of Musical Culture', in *Canon vs Culture: Reflections on the Current Debate*, ed. by Jan Gorak (New York and London: Garland, 2001), pp. 135–50 (p. 140).

33 Weber, *The Rise of Musical Classics in Eighteenth-Century England*, p. 2. The rest of the paragraph draws from Weber's 'Canon and the Traditions of Musical Culture', pp. 140–43 unless otherwise stated.

34 Weber, 'The Intellectual Origins of Musical Canon in Eighteenth-Century England', 493.

35 Weber, 'Canon and the Traditions of Musical Culture', p. 142.

36 Citron, *Gender and the Musical Canon*, p. 33.

37 Weber, 'The Intellectual Origins of Musical Canon in Eighteenth-Century England', 517.

principles 'established classics as the ultimate authority in musical taste. The canon was essential to musical empiricism; the new manner of writing on music demanded its own authority.'[38] This authority was bestowed on and maintained by the new discipline of musicology that grew over the course of the nineteenth century.

The Canonizers of Literature and Classical Music

Although the canon itself is perceived as an objective, unchanging collocation of works, it was formed and is now maintained by the values and choices of people in positions of influence, referred to here as 'canonizers'. These are the individuals who have the power, within certain institutional settings, to ensure the reproduction of the works, and the perpetuation of their perceived value.

Harold Bloom illustrates this point by posing the question 'who canonized Milton?' His conclusion is that the first to canonize Milton was Milton himself, through his unprecedented ambitions of literary posterity; next are his fellow and succeeding 'great' poets (Marvell and Wordsworth), who find him to be an inescapable influence; and finally critics (Dr Johnson and Hazlitt), who explicitly state and explain the importance of Milton.[39] Beyond this, the power to reproduce these judgements belongs to teachers, publishers and authors of histories of anthologies.

There have been only a few individual 'master critics' over the years, notably Dr Samuel Johnson and later T.S. Eliot, Matthew Arnold and F.R. Leavis.[40] The 'ideal critic' is described by Herrnstein Smith in these impossible terms as

> one who, in addition to possessing various exemplary natural endowments and cultural competencies, has, through exacting feats of self-liberation, freed himself of all forms of particularity and individuality, all special interests (or, as in Kant, all interests whatsoever), and thus of all bias – which is to say, one who is "free" of everything in relation to which any experience or judgement of value occurs.[41]

Given this, it is understandable that Bloom contends that 'no one has the authority to tell us what the Western Canon is, certainly not from about 1800 to the present day', although his book *The Western Canon* is itself an attempt to define the canon of literature, and so Bloom himself is one of the most prominent canonizers today.[42] When disagreements about the value of individual works arise, the intangibility of canons is invoked: 'Disagreements about value ... tend not to be resolved but simply

---

38 Ibid., 506.

39 Bloom, *The Western Canon*, p. 28.

40 Altieri names Samuel Johnson as being the most 'canonical figure' in relation to discussion of canons. Altieri, 'An Idea and Ideal of a Literary Canon', p. 41. F.R. Leavis's *The Great Tradition* is a notable attempt to construct a canon of English literature according to Leavis's ideas and ideals of the English novel: F.R. Leavis, *The Great Tradition: George Eliot, Henry James, Joseph Conrad* (London: Chatto and Windus, 1948).

41 Herrnstein Smith, *Contingencies of Value*, p. 42.

42 Bloom, *The Western Canon*, p. 37.

aborted by a secret appeal to ... [a] higher court of judgement, which knows no time or place, which judges for every time and place.'[43]

With regard to more recent canons, Hugh Kenner suggests that the modernist literary canon has been formed mainly by the canonized artists themselves, through mutual referencing and an awareness of the mechanisms of canonicity.[44] The public plays a relatively small role in the transmission of canons in literature, as they tend to focus on contemporary publications and relate to the canon as an already established body of works.

By contrast, the location of authority in musical life has changed dramatically over the last four centuries. During the eighteenth century, musical connoisseurs or critics were respected figures in society, more usually commenting on the quality of performance or voice rather than the work. Some composers were also critics, and could therefore promote their own aesthetic.[45] However, the general public were seen to have the greatest authority in value judgement, despite being divorced from the central theory and learning of classical music.[46]

During the nineteenth century, connoisseurs grew in stature and gradually gained ultimate authority over the public, but Citron suggests that the public played a role in the late twentieth-century shift from modernism to postmodernism in music (since modernism severed the line of communication between composer and audience, while postmodernism sought absolution). Today, as in literature, the public has far more immediate influence over contemporary repertoire rather than the canon, which is less susceptible to the whims of the general public and is more resistant to rapid change.[47] The canonizers of music, as in literature, are those critics, academics and publishers who are in a position to reproduce the works and their validations of the works of the canon; these musical canonizers include Donald Grout for his seminal *A History of Western Music*, and more recently Richard Taruskin for his six-volume *The Oxford History of Western Music* (2005).[48]

What is a Canon? – Canonical Criteria, Secondary Material, and the Structure of the Canon

Canonical Criteria and Secondary Material

Drawing up an inventory of canonical criteria is potentially misleading since canons rely on a nexus of perceived greatness rather than a list of rules for canonicity. For one thing, works can be regarded as canonical and important for quite contradictory reasons, depending on the context (for instance, the canon of Western classical music

---

43 Guillory, 'Canon', p. 236.

44 Kenner, 'The Making of the Modernist Canon, p. 374.

45 Citron, *Gender and the Musical Canon*, p. 35.

46 Weber, 'Canon and the Traditions of Musical Culture', pp. 142 & 148.

47 Citron, *Gender and the Musical Canon*, p. 28.

48 Donald J. Grout, *A History of Western Music* (New York and London: W.W. Norton & Company, 1960); Richard Taruskin, *The Oxford History of Western Music* (Oxford and New York: Oxford University Press, 2005).

includes both large-scale symphonies and aphoristic chamber pieces). Criteria of value and greatness can change over time, and once a canon is reduced to a simple set of rules, it loses much of its authority. Anita Silvers emphasizes this point when she states that great works of art 'originate their own value', and so 'canons rather than rules have been adopted as the embodiment of aesthetic standards.'[49] However, canonical works tend to share similar qualities, which both help them to survive and give them a common bond of perceived greatness.

Canonical works are generally believed to possess great aesthetic strength. In the case of literature, Bloom asserts that such strengths include 'mastery of figurative language, originality, cognitive power, knowledge, exuberance of diction'; also, 'In strong writing there is always conflict, ambivalence, [and] contradiction between subject and structure.'[50] However, since each artwork is seen to originate its own value, critical analysis is required to identify such aesthetic strength. Given that aesthetic strength is difficult to quantify, it will always be open to interpretation and, by extension, debate. As Barbara Herrnstein Smith points out, given that values change over time, 'Any theory of aesthetic value [in canons] must be able to account for continuity, stability, and apparent consensus as well as for drift, shift, and diversity.'[51]

Aesthetic value is privileged in canons above practical value, sentimental value, ornamental value, hedonistic value, historical value and financial worth, and the canon is seen to exist in a rarefied plane above such base concerns.[52] In music, this privileging of aesthetic value is reflected in the aforementioned superiority of the ear over the eye and the suspicion of 'flashy virtuosic technique' that has been evident since the eighteenth century.[53] Music created for intellectual engagement is still largely privileged over functional music created for dance, film or other extra-musical reasons.

The quality of truth has also long been regarded as an important element of literary works; it was a criterion of great importance in the selection of the texts in the medieval literary canon, and truth has remained important in all its subsequent manifestations.[54] Yet truth is by its very nature temporary, contingent and subjective, and so no single standard of truth can be drawn by which to measure canonicity. However, perceived truths, and associated authenticity, remain important markers of value in canons.

Certain works will be upheld as great because they represent certain genres or national canons. Therefore our expectations of a canonical work may rely to a degree on our preconceived notion of ideals of genre and national styles. As the canon gained hold in the reception of classical music, complex instrumental music, proper reverence

---

49 Silvers, 'The Canon in Aesthetics', p. 338.

50 Bloom, *The Western Canon*, pp. 27–9.

51 Barbara Herrnstein Smith, 'Contingencies of Value' in *Canons*, ed. by Robert von Hallberg (Chicago and London: University of Chicago Press, 1984), pp. 5–39 (p. 19).

52 Herrnstein Smith, *Contingencies of Value*, p. 33.

53 Charles Avison, *An Essay on Musical Expression* (London: C. Davis, 1752) quoted and summarized in Weber, 'The Intellectual Origins of Musical Canon in Eighteenth-Century England', 511–12.

54 Guillory, *Cultural Capital*, p. 72.

at concerts and scholarly writings were upheld as moral alternatives to the pagan social scene of opera, singing and dancing. These more 'serious' genres gradually became valued over the hedonic. Following this, the string quartet, symphony, concerto and the overture were valued most of all in the nineteenth-century canon.[55]

The value of craft in musical composition has remained a constant throughout the history of the canon, engendering the idea of a single, continuous tradition in music. In the latter part of the nineteenth century, through the Romantic ideas of the artist/genius and personal transcendence (largely inherited from literature), the generalized idea of musical craft was distilled to just a great few men rather than a whole pool of composers. A Romantic genius is an idiosyncratic individual who resists the rules of art or society and possesses an unconventional spirit. William Weber's account of the genius figure in classical music suggests 'a man with a boundless comprehending imagination', who looks deep within himself for his art.[56] By these measures, Beethoven and Mozart are valued above all others.[57] Indeed, Beethoven is arguably the most canonical composer in classical music, and his reputation has built to the point that the myth of his life bears scant relation to the reality. However, such individuals are still regarded as being part of a continuing tradition of musical craft, albeit exceptionally gifted or influential members.

The rise of the composer-centred view of music coincided and correlated with the rising idea of the work-concept around the beginning of the nineteenth century, rendering the composer the most powerful figure in music and notated music more important than oral or improvised forms. Therefore, the single unit of any canon is usually either the artist/genius or 'the work'. The idea of the work-concept in music has been the subject of growing discussion in recent years.[58] Although definitions vary, much as definitions of the canon are always contingent to their context, Michael Talbot summarizes that a work must be 'discrete, reproducible and attributable', but also tends to be attributed with 'status, originality and "aura"'.[59] The idea of the work also contains the implicit suggestion of a single ideal interpretation of a piece of music that performers must strive to recreate; this has brought rise to issues of authenticity of performance and a reverence for the score and a composer's intention.

In literature the work does not usually require performance to be realized (beyond the element of performance involved in reading). The work will still, however, be primarily associated with first editions and the intentions of the author. This is especially true in the case of translated texts, where subtle meaning is lost in the transformation from one language to another, and the act of translation becomes more of an art than

55 Weber, *The Rise of Musical Classics in Eighteenth-Century England*, p. 21.

56 Weber, 'The Intellectual Origins in Eighteenth-Century England', 512–13.

57 See Weber, 'Canon and the Traditions of Musical Culture', p. 141.

58 See especially Lydia Goehr, *The Imaginary Museum of Musical Works: An Essay in the Philosophy of Music* (Oxford and New York: Oxford University Press, 1992); and *The Musical Work: Reality or Invention?*, ed. by Michael Talbot (Liverpool: Liverpool University Press, 2000).

59 Michael Talbot, 'Introduction', *The Musical Work: Reality or Invention?*, ed. by Michael Talbot (Liverpool: Liverpool University Press, 2000), pp. 1–13 (pp. 3–5).

an exact science.[60] The words and intentions of the author in their original language are usually valued over subsequent edited versions or translations.

Perhaps the most important and unifying criterion of all canons is that canonical works must above all be original; they must stand apart from all others as discrete entities that are in some way different from all other preceding works. This quality of originality may be perceived in different ways. Bloom for instance suggests that works are canonized for their 'sublimity' or their 'strangeness', and authors' works can either be celebrated for their 'weirdness' (Milton) or their exceptionally accurate portrayal of the familiar (Shakespeare). However, great authors are always considered to be 'subversive of all values, both ours and their own', and their spark of originality is what makes canonical authors inescapable influences.[61]

Despite this expectation of originality and difference, canonical works are treated as a collective group, sharing the bond of enduring excellence. Therefore, while the canon is struggling under the dual roles of representing progress and stasis, it is also facing the struggle to maintain a common identity for a collocation of unique works. Such contradictions ensure that the canon is always dialectical in nature rather than an inert body of works.

As well as originality, complexity is also a valued quality in a canonical work. The more complex the work, the more potential for discussion it creates, and the more latent interpretations it holds for successive generations to unearth. As the potential to be described, analysed and discussed in secondary material over successive generations is necessary to the mechanisms of the canon's passage through time, works that are partially coded (with sublimated meanings), that naturally lend themselves to multifaceted dissection, and that demand multiple readings fare better than more one-dimensional texts with simple, overt meanings that can be satisfactorily read and then discarded. Indeed, Bloom asserts that 'one ancient test for the canonical remains fiercely valid: unless it demands rereading, the work does not qualify.' For Bloom, the purpose of canonical works is not to give immediate pleasure, but rather a more difficult pleasure or even a 'high unpleasure'.[62]

This preference for complexity in the canon is reflected in the importance of polyphony in the canon of classical music. Polyphony was used as a marker of value in Charles Avison's *An Essay on Musical Expression* (1752) and the music of J.S. Bach was central to the early formation of the canon in classical music. Joseph Kerman has suggested that the music we choose to analyse and privilege through canons tends to be that which is best illuminated by our methods of analysis (in effect presenting a musical 'chicken or egg' conundrum, whereby it must be asked if the analysis arose to describe the music or the music was chosen to accommodate the method of analysis).

---

60 For example, translations of Hans Christian Andersen's *Fairy Tales* have been notoriously variable over the years, due in part to his idiosyncratic style but also because Danish was a relatively obscure language for translation in the nineteenth century; yet his original texts remain important for their originality and power of invention. See Tiina Nunnally's translator's note to Hans Christian Andersen, *Fairy Tales* (London and New York: Penguin, 2004).

61 Bloom, *The Western Canon*, pp. 13–41 (p. 29) & p. 548. Bloom has written in depth on influences in Harold Bloom, *The Anxiety of Influence* (New York: Oxford University Press, 1973).

62 Bloom, *The Western Canon*, p. 30.

This, he reckons, has led to a canonical preference for the Germanic instrumental tradition, and an analytic focus on seeking out organicism, coherence and unity in a large-scale work, and a preference for the large scale (in both work and performance forces and space) in line with the notions of genius and the work discussed above.[63] Consequently, such preferences and methods of analysis further serve to emphasize the centrality of Beethoven to the canon of Western classical music.

The demand for complexity in its works is one way in which canons have traditionally separated high culture from low. Anthony Easthope explores the boundaries drawn between high and low culture in his book *Literary into Cultural Studies*, and he suggests that popular culture has long been iconic and visually predisposed, possessing a 'will-to-transparency', whereas high culture is remarkable for its 'will-to-difficulty'. Ultimately, he claims, it is the complexity of textuality that separates high (canonical) from low cultural texts.[64]

The amount of interpretation and degree of engagement (or work) required of the reader therefore becomes a means by which to measure canonical value. A work needs to be structurally complex and information-rich to sustain a depth of commentary surrounding it, but must also suit a wide variety of needs and interests. Therefore, the work must have the potential to be reconfigured many times to satisfy the interests of different subjects and a growing body of secondary material.[65]

Secondary literature (or secondary material in its broadest sense) plays a vital role in canon formation and perpetuation, as it forms a secondary discourse, and a secondary collocation of works that can be considered a canon in its own right. Kermode describes the canon as a 'metacommentary', itself sustained by secondary, interpretive commentary.[66] Canonical works require secondary material to support their position of greatness in the ongoing debate of value judgement in the arts. This is as true for music as it is in literature, and it was a necessary stage for the canonization of music for it to acquire a literary dimension and accrue a body of secondary literature in order to privilege and preserve its greatest works. When these debates are distilled and absorbed into a canon (which is presented as a story of originality and influence), the texts are better insulated against potential threats to their continued existence, since each work becomes a vital piece of the whole.

This secondary material asserts and supports the value of the primary works and is therefore essential to the teachings of the canon in schools and universities. Secondary material includes commentaries and analyses, anthologies, catalogues of works, edited editions of seminal texts, biographies of authors, centenary

---

63 This is the subject of Joseph Kerman's 1980 article 'How We Got into Analysis, and How to Get Out', where he suggests how this has lead to a focus on the Germanic instrumental tradition, and an analytic focus on seeking out organicism, coherence and unity in a large-scale work, in line with the notions of genius and the work discussed above. Joseph Kerman, 'How We Got into Analysis, and How to Get Out', *Critical Inquiry*, 7 (Winter 1980), 311–31.

64 Anthony Easthope, *Literary into Cultural Studies* (London and New York: Routledge, 1991), pp. 67–95.

65 See Herrnstein Smith, *Contingencies of Value*, p. 51–2.

66 Kermode, *Forms of Attention*, p. 76.

festivals and celebrations, and the translation of works into other languages.[67] In music especially, contemporary journals have also played a role in reinforcing the values of the canon.[68]

The quality and complexity of secondary material on a work reflects back onto the reputation of the original. When combined, this secondary material forms a constellation that revolves around, supports and protects the original work. Kermode explains that secondary literature 'is primarily concerned with fact, with correct attribution and description, with offering the world [the] authentic'; in order to achieve this, secondary material will tend to be clinical and objective in manner. All this has the effect of gradually eroding the difference between knowledge and opinion.[69] However, this quasi-scientific approach to the works of the canon is misleading. Value-neutral scholarship may now be employed to defend the greatness of canonical works, but it is value-laden, humanistic pedagogy that originally placed them in the canon. Therefore, an overly close analysis of the values and criteria underpinning canons reveals a wealth of contradictions that can threaten the cohesion of the whole.

The Structure of the Canon and the Non-canonical

The canon is not a rigidly defined collocation of works in the manner of the periodic table of elements; rather, it is an imaginary collocation of great works and artists that no one person has the authority to define. Therefore, the canon is incorporeal, forever changing and nebulous, but for this reason enduring since it is made perpetually relevant through constant modernization.

Few have attempted to suggest a shape to such an incorporeal concept. For instance, Bloom rather ambiguously suggests that 'the greatest authors take over the role of "places" in the Canon's theater of memory, and their masterworks occupy the position filled by "images" in the art of memory.'[70] However, given that the canon is ultimately imaginary, it is necessarily a subjective mental image of greatness, albeit one that is heavily influenced by ideas of canonical greatness as instilled by the school.

This is one reason why, as stated at the beginning of this chapter, the canon is both simple and complex. The idea of the canon that comes instantly to mind is that of the core figures of any field (Chaucer, Shakespeare, Tolstoy; Bach, Beethoven, Mozart, and so on). Yet the canon contains far more works and artists than can be presented in this highly reduced image and is (however loosely) structured via hierarchies of value, works and artists. Some works and composers will be more canonical than others; and canonical figures may have more canonical periods of work. Therefore,

---

67 For texts to appear in the same language, whether originally written so or in translation, creates a sense of unity within a canon (see Guillory, *Cultural Capital*, p. 43). A shared language is also important in promoting shared nationalism. However, translation removes some of the difference between canonical texts, but also distances the text from its original context and meanings. Such decontextualization is imperative to the sense of unity within the canon.

68 See Citron, *Gender and the Musical Canon*, p. 34.

69 Kermode, *Forms of Attention*, p. 12.

70 Bloom, *The Western Canon*, p. 39.

many people's perception of the canon will echo Bloom's structure for *The Western Canon* in which one central figure, Shakespeare, is orbited by other lesser canonical figures and works.

For Bloom, Shakespeare is the centre, the past, the present and the future of the canon, the most canonical canonical figure. Shakespeare's influence radiates onto all subsequent canonical writing as well as reflecting back onto the writing that came before, and he even goes so far as to suggest that 'Shakespeare is the center of the embryo of a world canon'. His work is also in the unusual position of being both 'difficult and popular art', giving the canon a complex yet widely known centre. Shakespeare also makes an ideal centre to the canon because of his neutrality as a person; little is known about the life of Shakespeare, our knowledge of him is mostly gleaned from interpretation of his works, but Bloom believes that this very neutrality gives him more strength as a canonical centre.[71]

A similarly central role has been occupied by Beethoven in the field of Western classical music. Although more is known of the life of Beethoven compared to that of Shakespeare, the fact that most of his canonical work is instrumental lends him a verbal neutrality that is impossible for canonical authors of literature. Beethoven's work also combines complexity with popularity (for instance, his symphonies and concerti are played regularly on both BBC Radio 3 and Classic FM). He is also uniquely given his own chapter in Donald Grout's seminal *A History of Western Music*, one of the most influential textbooks of the twentieth century. In this book certain styles and genres are privileged and named in chapter headings (including polyphony, sonata, symphony and opera) and other chapters are organized according to nationality, geography or stylistic era (including the familiar divisions of Baroque, Classical and Romantic).[72] However, the only other composers featured in depth are Haydn and Mozart, who share the previous chapter and who, with Beethoven, have long formed a central trinity in the canon of classical music.

While the structure of the canon must remain somewhat incorporeal, the idea of the canon is strengthened by the identification of the non-canonical. The authority of the canon relies on the notion that certain works throughout history are more worthy of our attention than others. However, this implicitly suggests that certain people, situations and types of creativity are more artistically worthy than others. Barbara Herrnstein Smith argues that the idea and ideal of the canon involves the

> tacit assumption of canonical audiences experiencing those works under canonical conditions plus the tacit exclusion of noncanonical (that is, non-Western, non-academic, non-adult or non-high-culture) *audiences* and noncanonical (for example, folk, tribal or mass-mediated) *conditions of production and reception*.[73]

---

71 Bloom, *The Western Canon*, pp. 24–62.

72 Curiously, more recent editions were expanded to include a fleeting mention of popular music in the guise of 'rock and roll', suggesting tentatively that this music is part of the same tradition. However, after naming and describing Bill Haley, Elvis Presley and the Beatles, no further mention is made of this music, and we are left to fill in the rest of that strand of history for ourselves. Donald J. Grout and Claude V. Palisca, *A History of Western Music*, 6th edn (New York and London: W.W. Norton & Company, 2001).

73 Herrnstein Smith, *Contingencies of Value*, p. 37. [Emphasis in the original.]

The non-canonical may be a passive category of texts that fall short of the demands of canons, or it may refer to texts that are created in full awareness of the canon and actively undermine it (in this case more anti-canonical than non-canonical). Non-canonical music or texts may be celebrated precisely because they are outside the dominant canon, and then form part of a new, wholly separate collocation of works that become a sub-canon in their own right. Taking the broadest definition of the non-canonical, however, would simply suggest that any work not in the canon is non-canonical, whether because it is perceived as being of poor quality, unoriginal, composed in a non-canonical genre, overtly commercial or difficult to assimilate into the overall 'story' of the canon. Aside from the negative judgement of not having been selected for the canon, there is a slight, residual overtone of heresy associated with the non-canonical.

The Problem of Canons Today

Although canons fulfil many positive roles, they also transmit biases in culture and society over generations that are becoming increasingly hard to sustain. The canons of Western classical music and literature are now subject to increasing debate as society becomes increasingly fragmented and multicultural. Canons do not exist in a cultural vacuum; although a canon of great works and great composers (of mostly dead, white men) still exerts a strong influence on musical scholarship and practice, many other canons have arisen both to complement and challenge it. Thus musical life today is organized through plural, coexisting contexts and perspectives, including those of repertory, musicology, pedagogy, feminism, ethnomusicology and various genres and styles. A similar framework of plural perspectives is in place in the reception of literature, and even the centrality of Shakespeare is now a matter of debate.[74]

The relative lack of canon and widely known classics in music until comparatively recently has been regarded as both detrimental and beneficial to classical music as a whole. On the one hand, an absence of highly venerated works from antiquity restricted the social status of the classical music, and theoretically limited composers' levels of aspiration. However, on the other hand, it also left musicians free of the burdens of influence and the pressures of emulating the great masters, and new music was celebrated far more than old, a fact which seems appealing in light of today's apparently static canon of Western classical music.

The long-established literary canon on the other hand has witnessed canonic rejection and revision throughout the centuries in a constant succession of affirmation and attack on established 'canonical' figures. Defenders of the canon believe that the great works and artists are unquestionably great and it is our duty to protect, revere and study them in order to preserve the richness of our culture. Critics of the canon, however, believe that the selection and preservation of works in the canon has been a far from neutral process, and suggest instead that the manner and criteria of selection are highly political processes of exclusion. Feminist, class-based and multiculturalist perspectives are often

---

74 See for example John Drakakis, *Alternative Shakespeares* (London: Routledge 1985), pp. 23–4.

at the forefront of such debates.[75] The positive roles of canons – including cultural and social unity, a sense of heritage and educational uniformity – are pitted against the negative aspects such as the replication of prejudices and limitations on artistic freedom in the ongoing debate about canons.

Part of the problem involved in canonical debate is the fact that the canon is not a clearly defined entity and the territory being fought over is constantly shifting as a result. Critics and defenders are united in their goal of making the canon universal. However, critics seek to achieve this by 'opening up the canon', by democratizing its contents and including previously excluded figures and works, while defenders of the canon claim that its universality is as a result of it being an elite collocation of works whose value applies to the whole of society. Indeed, conservative defenders of canons regard it as a mistake to try and map the ideals of social democracy onto the values of canons. Charles Altieri believes that negative detraction from canons can have far-reaching effects, for 'Once we emphasise disbelief, we cannot maintain traditional notions of the canon … Works we canonize tend to project ideals, and the roles we can imagine for the canon require us to consider seriously the place of idealization in social life.'[76] Harold Bloom is a similarly staunch defender of the canon, having branded liberal critics of the canon (including feminist, multicultural and historicist perspectives) as the 'School of Resentment'. However, even he concedes with regret that the canon is now a place of nostalgia, and that the 'great canon' of literature has not withstood the attack of the modern world.[77] Canons may have a unifying effect on society, but if their universality is under question, then this function will undoubtedly diminish.

The debate over canons today has no clear means of resolution. The canon represents not only works and artists but also the cultural values and social inequalities of our past. It is where these values conflict with our own that the canon is most strongly debated, and yet it is not possible to change the canon retrospectively without changing the values on which it was based, and performing a fairly radical revision of history. Equality of gender, race and class is a modern goal that cannot easily be applied retrospectively to the canon since women, non-whites and the lower classes were for the most part not in a position (educationally, socially or financially) to create canonical works or be in a position to dictate the values on which canons are based. Democracy is required at the site of production before it can be reflected at the site of reception. The clearest way around this problem might be to abolish all canons and radically reassess our valuation of history and culture. Certainly the unquestioning superiority of high culture over low is regarded with increasing suspicion in today's society. However, far from leading to the abolition

---

75 Prominent texts in this debate include Marcia Citron's *Gender and the Musical Canon*, which discusses many different, often hidden, ways that the canon is biased in terms of gender; and John Guillory's *Cultural Capital*, which explores the role of the canon in maintaining hierarchies in society. Also *Disciplining Music: Musicology and Its Canons*, ed. by Katherine Bergeron and Philip V. Bohlman (Chicago and London: University of Chicago Press, 1992) for various perspectives in music, including those of ethnomusicology and jazz reception.

76 Altieri, 'An Idea and Ideal of a Literary Canon', pp. 42 & 46.

77 Bloom, *The Western Canon*, pp. 1–4.

of all canons, this democratization seems rather to have resulted in a hitherto unprecedented proliferation of canons in our culture.

The consensus among academics today is generally that the only possibility is to accept an ever-changing number of different (but not necessarily equal) canons that interact with each other but at the same time maintain separate identities. This would necessitate a new approach to the reception of canonical works, and to this end Gary Tomlinson propounds a more discursive type of canon that shifts the focus from the centre to the margins; in Tomlinson's conception, as Katherine Bergeron comments, 'The canon, quite contrary to its nature, becomes an open question.'[78] This open question now creates a space for the consideration of the possible formation of a canon of popular music, a possibility that becomes the central concern of this book.

---

78 Katherine Bergeron, 'Prologue: Disciplining Music', in *Disciplining Music: Musicology and Its Canons*, pp. 1–9 (p. 6).

Chapter 2

Aesthetic Criteria and the Work of Art in the Reception of Rock Albums

Although the canon is an inherently elitist concept, from the mid-1990s onwards there has been a growing suggestion of a canon in the reception of rock music. This potential canon has grown with the swell in the number of rock music histories, lists (and books) of greatest albums, and the decision to re-release certain deleted records as compact discs. One such example of the growing number of books appraising the albums of the past is the (somewhat expansive) *All Time Top 1000 Albums*, first published by Guinness in 1994 and subsequently published by Virgin Books in two further revised editions in 1998 and 2000.[1] The lists contained in the three editions of this book are compiled from the opinions of about 200,000 various voters, but the book as a whole is 'conceived, written, edited and produced' by Colin Larkin.

The *All Time Top 1000 Albums* is fairly typical of lists of this type in that the music of the Beatles, the Beach Boys and Bob Dylan routinely appears in the upper reaches of the list (see Appendix). Writing in response to the second edition of this book, published in 1998, Simon Frith commented that:

> It's in these titles that the ideology of rock is laid out: white male music made in Britain and the US since 1965 … guitar-based, indie, with recent entries echoing the earliest in a circle of self-congratulation ...
>
> From this perspective, the most interesting aspect is … its confirmation that a rock canon is now in place. It has less to do with sales … than constant citations by critics – hence Van Morrison's *Astral Weeks*, Velvet Underground's *Velvet Underground*, Love's *Forever Changes*.[2]

Frith's remarks in this article confirm earlier comments made by musicologist Dai Griffiths in an article written by John Davies on the subject of canons in music that appeared in the *Times Higher* in 1995. Griffiths notes the irony that popular music, which 'began as a way of undermining certain ideas of a fixed canon is forever generating lists.' He continues by contending that when the *NME* and *Mojo* magazine

---

1   Colin Larkin, *All Time Top 1000 Albums* (Enfield: Guinness, 1994); Colin Larkin, *All-Time Top 1,000 Albums*, 2nd edn (London: Virgin, 1998); Colin Larkin, *All-Time Top 1,000 Albums*, 3rd edn (London: Virgin, 2000).

2   Simon Frith, 'Our Favourite Rock Records Tend to Go Round and Round', *The Observer*, 6 September 1998. Copyright Guardian News & Media Ltd 1998. This article was written as a response to Colin Larkin, *All-Time Top 1,000 Albums*, 2nd edn (London: Virgin, 1998), which polled 200,000 people to create its list of 'best albums'. See Appendix.

both 'come up with a critics' Top 20 albums headed by *Revolver* and *Pet Sounds*, a canon is clearly established.'[3]

Superficially, the increasing numbers of magazine articles and books on 'the greatest albums of all time' suggest a collocation of works that are generally considered to be the greatest in their field and might therefore be called, albeit loosely, the canon of rock albums. But there is also plenty of evidence that the influence of canonic terms and mechanisms runs deep in the reception of rock albums today. The introduction to *VH1's 100 Greatest Albums*, edited by Jacob Hoye, echoes many of the canonic ideals outlined in the first chapter of this book, including the necessity of re-reading, exceptional greatness, the 'test of time', expression of human experience, and direct comparison with the high arts (novels, plays and paintings):

> You can love a song, but you can form a bond with an album, a relationship that evolves as organically and beautifully as a marriage. Like people, there aren't all that many great ones, and few stand the test of time. But they're out there … albums that tackle the human experience … Like novels, plays, and paintings, they help us understand ourselves.[4]

In order to explore exactly how deep the influence of canons runs in the reception of rock albums, the following two chapters of the book will therefore explore the presence of individual canonical facets in the popular reception of rock music. The present chapter investigates the presence of canonical aesthetic criteria and conceptions of the artist/genius and the work in the reception of rock music. Chapter 3 addresses the issue from the perspective of canonical narratives of influence and evolution, before exploring the idea of the non-canonical in the context of rock albums. It will then turn to the idea of the 'test of time' in the reception of these albums and address the question of potential canonizers in rock.

At this point is necessary to reduce the field of study down to some of its most representative works. For this purpose, ten albums have been selected from *Mojo* magazine's 'The 100 Greatest Albums Ever Made' feature from August 1995.[5] Although lists are only, at best, problematic shorthand manifestations of canons, they do serve as a microcosm of values (this subject will be revisited in Chapter 5). This list in particular includes many of the albums that have been widely accepted as the greatest in their field:

---

3   John Davies, 'Baroque and Roll', *Times Higher*, 15 December 1995, 13–14 (13).

4   *VH1's 100 Greatest Albums*, ed. by Jacob Hoye (New York and London: MTV Books/ Pocket Books, 2003), pp. xiv–xv.

5   Various Contributors, 'The Hundred Greatest Albums Ever Made', *Mojo*, 21 (August 1995), 50–87. This is one of the lists Dai Griffiths referred to in Davies' *Time Higher* article mentioned above.

1. The Beach Boys, *Pet Sounds* (1966)
2. Van Morrison, *Astral Weeks* (1968)
3. The Beatles, *Revolver* (1966)
4. The Rolling Stones, *Exile on Main St.* (1972)
5. Bob Dylan, *Highway 61 Revisited* (1965)
6. Marvin Gaye, *What's Going On* (1971)
7. The Rolling Stones, *Let It Bleed* (1969)
8. Bob Dylan, *Blonde on Blonde* (1966)
9. The Velvet Underground & Nico, *The Velvet Underground & Nico* (1967)
10. Patti Smith, *Horses* (1975)

Given that two of the albums in this list are by the same artists, only the first of each will be used, and so the reception of *Highway 61 Revisited* and *Exile on Main St.* will be studied, but not *Let It Bleed* or *Blonde on Blonde*.

The importance of these albums in polls is corroborated by the list compiled by statistician Henrik Franzon of all the 'greatest albums' polls up to the year 2005 (presented on his Internet site www.acclaimedmusic.net).[6] Two other albums featured in the *Mojo* poll of 1995 will also be discussed, namely *Never Mind the Bollocks: Here's the Sex Pistols* (1977) by the Sex Pistols, and *Nevermind* (1991) by Nirvana. These two albums have risen to great prominence since 1995 (a fact corroborated by Franzon's ongoing poll of polls). The ten albums featured in this book are therefore:

- Bob Dylan, *Highway 61 Revisited* (1965)
- The Beach Boys, *Pet Sounds* (1966)
- The Beatles, *Revolver* (1966)
- The Velvet Underground & Nico, *The Velvet Underground & Nico* (1967)
- Van Morrison, *Astral Weeks* (1969)
- Marvin Gaye, *What's Going On* (1971)
- The Rolling Stones, *Exile on Main St.*(1972)
- Patti Smith, *Horses* (1975)
- The Sex Pistols, *Never Mind the Bollocks: Here's the Sex Pistols* (1977)
- Nirvana, *Nevermind* (1991)

Secondary Material and Canonical Criteria

The Secondary Material of Rock

As discussed in the first chapter of this book, canons are formed when potentially canonical works are supported by secondary material, including articles, histories, biographies, anniversary celebrations and anthologies that will be passed down

---

6   http://www.acclaimedmusic.net, accessed 05/08/07, see Appendix. With the exception of Patti Smith's *Horses*, all ten albums feature high in this statistical compilation of 'greatest albums'. The role of the Internet in disseminating and preserving such lists will be revisited in Chapter 4.

to successive generations; over time this secondary material supports the work's position of importance, and helps ensure its continued presence in the canon.

The quality and complexity of secondary material written about a work reflects back onto the reputation of the work itself, and a quasi-objective approach to presenting facts and descriptions is favoured in the canonical secondary writings of the high arts. However, the secondary material of rock tends to reflect its subject matter and therefore its tone ranges between the determinedly lowbrow and the ambitiously highbrow. The Beatles have without doubt inspired more matter of this type than any other artist, and the secondary material generated by their work includes biographies, illustrated lyric books, guitar tab books, photo books, special editions of music magazines (including *NME* and *Mojo*), plastic and ceramic memorabilia, Beatles clothing, Beatles wigs, cover bands, festivals, various commemorative television programmes, and an assortment of CD and DVD releases (including the mid-1990s *Anthology* series of television programmes, DVDs and sound recordings). Such attention is given in varying degrees to the other nine artists under study. For the purposes of canon formation, certainly within the context of this study, it is the secondary literature (histories, polls and biographies) that is of most interest.

While all ten albums are discussed in magazine polls of 'greatest albums' and privileged for their influence on new music, most of the ten have also been the subject of a book. Increasingly, publishers are drawn to the idea of a series of books, each based on a different rock album, with its own pre-established fan base. For instance, Schirmer Books have published a *Classic Rock Albums* series that includes books on *Never Mind the Bollocks: Here's the Sex Pistols* (1998)*, Nevermind* (1998) and *Exile on Main St.* (1999). Their aim, according to the back cover of the *Nevermind* volume, is to create 'a series of books highlighting the albums that changed rock history. Including behind-the-scenes interviews, documentation, and new information, each volume tells a compelling story of rock and roll history.'[7]

Continuum Press also has an ongoing series of books, each based on a single album. Of the ten albums studied in this book, books on *The Velvet Underground & Nico* (2004), *Pet Sounds* (2005), *Exile on Main St.* (2005), *Highway 61 Revisited* (2006) and *Horses* (2008) have so far been published.[8] These vary in style and content according to album and author (the three books are authored respectively by a critic/writer, record producer and a singer/songwriter), showing the variety of approach both possible and evident in commentaries on rock albums.

These books, along with general histories of rock (including *The Rolling Stone Illustrated History of Rock & Roll, The Rough Guide to Rock*, and magazine

7   Jim Berkenstadt and Charles Cross, *Nevermind: Nirvana* (London and New York: Schirmer Trade Books, 1998), back cover; Clinton Heylin, *Never Mind the Bollocks: Here's the Sex Pistols – The Sex Pistols* (New York: Schirmer Books, 1998); John Perry, *Exile On Main St.* (New York: Schirmer Books, 2000) and Philip Shaw, *Horses* (New York and London: Continuum, 2008). This series also includes books on the Beatles' *Let it Be/Abbey Road*, David Bowie's *The Rise and Fall of Ziggy Stardust and the Spiders of Mars*, the Who's *Meaty, Beaty, Big and Bouncy*, and *Disraeli Gears* by Cream.

8   Jim Fusilli, *Pet Sounds* (New York and London: Continuum, 2005); Joe Harvard, *The Velvet Underground & Nico* (New York and London: Continuum, 2004); Bill Janovitz, *Exile on Main St.* (New York and London: Continuum, 2005); and Mark Polizzotti, *Highway 61 Revisited* (New York and London: Continuum, 2006).

special editions such as *Q* magazine's '50 Years of Rock 'n' Roll 1954–2004'), and 'greatest albums' polls and books (such as *The Mojo Collection: The Ultimate Music Companion* and the previously discussed *All Time Top 1000 Albums* series) will therefore be analysed for the canonic implications they hold. This is not an exhaustive survey of all material relating to these ten albums, much less the ten artists or bands involved, but is rather an overview of the opinions, judgements and descriptions that the albums have accrued over time.

Canonical Words

The most immediate way in which rock writing displays canonic tendencies is in the language used to describe its subject matter. Canonical words mingle with more vivid, everyday spoken language; the terms 'masterpiece', 'classic', 'genius', 'artist', 'test of time' and 'sublime' all appear regularly in descriptions of these albums.

For instance, *Nevermind* is described in the *Mojo Collection* as '[swinging] from moments of skull-crushing intensity to passages of sublime beauty.'[9] The albums in the *NME* '100 Greatest Albums of All Time' poll of 2003 are described as '75 hours of ear-shagging genius.'[10] The word genius is often applied to the ten artists, for instance, '[Cobain's] songwriting and performing genius was commemorated on the *UNPLUGGED IN NEW YORK* (1994) session, recorded in late 1993.'[11] *The Rough Guide to Rock* describes the Beach Boys' *PET SOUNDS* in these terms: 'Sublime tracks distilling the essence of the Californian dream … The new maturity was crystallized on the masterpiece *Pet Sounds* (1966).'[12] And Jim Fusilli, in his book on the same album, asserts that 'more than a wonderful work that has withstood the test of time, *Pet Sounds* raises pop to the level of art.'[13] Many further examples of this kind are quoted throughout the following two chapters, and this undercurrent of canonically redolent terms in the reception of these albums serves to incrementally support the idea that this music is now being situated in a canonical dialogue by a series of rock writers and commentators.

Just as classical music found itself changing its perception of what constituted 'old' and venerated music in order to give its works an added sense of importance and create favourable conditions for its canonization, the reception of rock albums tends to focus on the relatively new (such as the music of the 1960s) as if it were old, and imbue it with a sense of history. Albums can now be almost instant classics; for instance, *The Rough Guide to Rock* claims that '*Horses* was the first "new underground" rock album to break through into the mainstream … and it has

---

9   *The Mojo Collection: The Ultimate Music Companion*, ed. by Jim Irvin and Colin McLear, 3rd edn (Edinburgh and New York: Canongate, 2003), p. 558.

10   Various Contributors, 'NME's 100 Best Albums of All Time!', *New Musical Express*, 8 March 2003, 35–42 (front cover).

11   *Rock: The Rough Guide*, ed. by Jonathan Buckley and others, 2nd edn (London: Rough Guides Ltd, 1999), p. 693. Reproduced by permission of Penguin Books Ltd.

12   Ibid., p. 60.

13   Fusilli, *Pet Sounds*, pp. 116–17. Excerpts from *Pet Sounds* by Jim Fusilli © 2005, reprinted by permission of the publisher, The Continuum International Publishing Group.

remained a genuine classic.'[14] Canonical concepts are woven into this notion of an extended history to give a sense of weight, gravitas and permanence to its subject matter as this statement from the *Mojo* poll of 1995 demonstrates: 'The rest, as the man said, is history, and despite several attempts at negative reassessment, What's Going On stands as a template of achievement in popular music.'[15] In the reception of rock the 1960s and early 1970s constitutes its past, its heritage, and its history, and by the timescale of the canon of Western literature, the patently new is considered reverently old.

Aesthetic Strengths

Although rock albums are clearly commercial works, the reception of these albums often makes a point of emphasizing their aesthetic strengths above any commercial success. Originality, in its various different guises, is as much a hallmark of greatness in rock music as in literature and classical music, and reference to it is littered throughout accounts of the albums. For instance, *Mojo* claims that 'of the accolades accorded Nevermind upon its release, "startlingly original" was often top of the heap, and the only real question was how Nirvana had come up with such a remarkable album on the heels of their unremarkable first.'[16] The Beatles are attributed with having invented a whole 'new sound that could not be exhausted in the course of one brief flurry on the charts.'[17] *Astral Weeks* on the other hand has been described as possibly 'the best record of original thought that anyone's ever made ... completely unlike anything that went before it.'[18] Originality is also perceived in the detail of a recording; for example Ben Edmonds views the 'deep and varied use of percussion' on *What's Going On* as a 'strikingly original signature'.[19] Indeed, any way in which an album is perceived as different from other albums – before or since – is usually seized upon by commentators as a marker of value.

Originality can also be expressed in the perceived subversion of previous rules, and this notion finds a natural home in the ideology of rock, where rule-breaking is celebrated as an aesthetic in its own right. Quite contrary to the perceived commercial nature of popular music as a whole, 'greatest albums' are often celebrated for breaking the 'rules' of immediate commercial appeal and conventional songwriting (and recording) techniques. Bob Dylan is attributed with having 'redefined pop

---

14   *Rock: The Rough Guide*, Buckley and others, p. 910.

15   Various Contributors, 'The Hundred Greatest Albums Ever Made', *Mojo*, 21 (August 1995), 85.

16   Ibid., 74.

17   Greil Marcus, 'The Beatles', in *The Rolling Stone Illustrated History of Rock & Roll*, ed. by Anthony DeCurtis and James Henke with Holly George-Warren, 2nd edn (London: Straight Arrow, 1992), pp. 209–22 (p. 218). From *The Rolling Stone Illustrated History Of Rock And Roll* by Rolling Stone, edited by Jim Miller, © 1976, 1980 by Rolling Stone Press. Used by permission of Random House, Inc.

18   Elvis Costello quoted in *VH1's 100 Greatest Albums*, Hoye, p. 98.

19   Ben Edmonds, *What's Going On?: Marvin Gaye and the Last Days of Motown Soul* (Edinburgh: Canongate, 2002), p. 166.

music' with *Highway 61 Revisited*;[20] while Marvin Gaye is described as having 'dared to push popular music beyond its proscribed boundaries'.[21] The Sex Pistols, on the other hand, according to *The Rough Guide to Rock*, took 'a sledgehammer to the definition of rock music'.[22] Patti Smith's *Horses* is described as having 'attacked preconceptions and declared innovation to great effect'.[23] Similarly we are told that the Velvet Underground 'set about rewriting the rock rule book';[24] and that after *The Velvet Underground & Nico,* 'all maps had to be thrown out and all borders redrawn'.[25] This perceived breaking of the rules feeds into dialectical narratives of tradition and progress, a subject which will be revisited in the following chapter.

As discussed in Chapter 1, Harold Bloom has located a form of originality in the perception of 'strangeness' and the weird. Strangeness in rock music is often perceived through new sounds and recording techniques and a general feeling of unfamiliarity that the album provoked from its audience when first released. The writer Kingsley Abbott, in his (suggestively titled) book *The Beach Boys' Pet Sounds: The Greatest Album of the Twentieth Century*, makes a point of the unusual instrumentation, including a theremin, drinks cans, a harpsichord, a 'rockin'' accordion and a chamber orchestra, that he claims give *Pet Sounds* a distinctive 'strange sound'.[26] Echoing this, David Leaf suggests that *Pet Sounds* 'evoked feelings in the listener with unfamiliar sounds'.[27] This attraction to unfamiliar sounds is echoed by *Revolver*'s sound engineer Geoff Emerick saying that 'the group encouraged us to break the rules... [They told me] that every instrument should sound unlike itself: a piano shouldn't sound like a piano, a guitar shouldn't sound like a guitar.'[28]

'Strangeness' and unfamiliarity is also a quality identified in the lyrics of these albums, lending them an element of mystery and difference that marks the albums apart. *Astral Weeks* in particular is noted for its lyrical strangeness. Greil Marcus describes the album as a 'set of songs about childhood, initiation, sex and death ... a strange, disturbing, exalting album for which there was little precedent in rock & roll history when it was released in November 1968.'[29] In a later poll compiled by the

20   Larkin, *All-Time Top 1,000 Album*, 3rd edn, p. 46.

21   *100 Albums That Changed Music: and 500 Songs You Need to Hear*, ed. by Sean Egan (London: Robinson, 2006), p. 185.

22   *Rock: The Rough Guide*, Buckley and others, p. 870.

23   Larkin, *All-Time Top 1,000 Albums*, 3rd edn, p. 123.

24   *Rock: The Rough Guide*, Buckley and others, p. 1057.

25   Harvard, *The Velvet Underground & Nico*, p. 8. Excerpts from *The Velvet Underground & Nico* by Joe Harvard © 2004, reprinted by permission of the publisher, The Continuum International Publishing Group.

26   Kingsley Abbott, *The Beach Boys' Pet Sounds: The Greatest Album of the Twentieth Century* (London: Helter Skelter Publishing, 2001), p. 65.

27   David Leaf, 'Landmark Albums: Pet Sounds', in *Back to the Beach: A Brian Wilson and the Beach Boys Reader*, ed. by Kingsley Abbott (London: Helter Skelter, 1997), pp. 40–42 (p. 41).

28   Interview with Geoff Emerick quoted in *The Mojo Collection,* Irvin and McLear, p. 66.

29   Greil Marcus, 'Van Morrison', in *The Rolling Stone Illustrated History of Rock & Roll*, ed. by DeCurtis and Henke with George-Warren, pp. 442–7 (p. 444).

Observer, Astral Weeks is admired for its 'transcending' and obscure lyrics: '[Even] if the words don't add up, the voice goes places most rock singers can only dream of. Morrison repeats phrases, words, syllables, dismantling language in an attempt to express the unsayable, to transcend the limits of mere words.'[30] For some, the meanings generated by this confusion of meaning is more valuable than any overt lyric: '"After all these years I still don't know what Van Morrison is singing about," Arnd Schirmer shrugs when naming *Astral Weeks* his top album. "It's strange and beautiful."'[31]

Kurt Cobain's affinity to this lyrical ambiguity is encapsulated in this account of his approach to writing the lyrics for *Nevermind*:

> Most of the lyrics are just like contradictions. I'll write a few sincere lines and then I'll have to make fun of it with another line. I don't like to make things too obvious. Because if it is too obvious, it gets really stale. We don't mean to be really cryptic or mysterious. But I just think that lyrics that are different and kind of weird paint a nice picture. It's just the way I like art.[32]

Bob Dylan's work especially is celebrated for its lack of transparency, treading the fine line between rock lyric and poetry, and we are told that with the release of *Highway 61 Revisited*, 'Rivals gasped in astonishment at the endless waves of expressionistic lyrics woven deep into the music's bluesy after-hours groove.'[33] Similarly, *Exile on Main St.* is described as being 'shrouded in a bleary, narcotic haze that was sometimes so thick that it sounded like Charlie Watts was recorded under water.'[34] Such strangeness and ambiguity has enduring appeal in a canon for the multiple interpretations it affords and can result in the kind of complexity in a work that ensures its perpetual modernity, since each new generation will approach the work afresh and most likely find some new facet to explore and some resonance with the modern world.

Complexity, therefore, is a valued criterion in the selection of these 'greatest' albums; but such complexity is often defined using slightly different parameters to those of classical music and literature. Albums are very different from the score-based works of classical music in that they do not require performance by a third party. However, compared to the compositions of classical music, rock music is often basic in terms of structure and harmony. Therefore musical complexity in rock albums is usually situated in sonic originality and lyrics rather than the craft tradition of polyphony and harmonic complexity of classical music. Although polyphony is a feature often noted of *Pet Sounds*, this is the exception rather than the rule in the ten albums. In his book on *Pet Sounds*, Jim Fusilli uses some fairly traditional musical

---

30   Sean O'Hagan, 'Astral Weeks', in Various Contributors, 'The 100 Greatest British Albums', *Observer Music Monthly*, 10 (June 2004), 17.

31   Paul Gambaccini, *Paul Gambaccini Presents the Top 100 Albums* (GRR/Pavilion: London, 1987), p. 17.

32   Excerpt from an interview with Kurt Cobain quoted in Berkenstadt and Cross, *Nevermind*, p. 64.

33   *Rock: The Rough Guide*, Buckley and others, pp. 305–306.

34   Ibid., p. 833.

analysis to support his points, such as his claim that 'the sense of disorientation in "Wouldn't It Be Nice" is derived in part from a key change, from A major to C major, and then the F at the word "nice" as the intro becomes the verse.'[35] However, such analyses of harmony and structure feature less than descriptions of the sounds achieved, such as this exceptionally detailed account of 'Rocks Off' from Bill Janovitz's book on *Exile on Main St.*: 'Listen to the four bar-long fill around 3:33–3:40 … The guitars, drums, and percussion hold the fort down while horns slur, Jagger drawls, and a bunch of backing vocal tracks from Richards and Jagger slip and slide all over the place, rarely crisp or on the beat.'[36]

Originality, complexity and enduring appeal are therefore all sought in the sounds on the album, which can be interpreted again and again by successive critics. The whole album, or even just a moment of the album can be analysed in detail repeatedly and meanings layered onto the original sound, such as this description of *The Velvet Underground & Nico* that features in *VH1's 100 Greatest Albums*: 'The squealing feedback that ends "Heroin", which sounds like subway brakes and is, in its way, the record's defining moment, retain both a thrilling, rockin' primitivism as well as a forward-looking, form-shattering originality.'[37] The perception of originality and the location of value in the sound and production on these albums is a subject that will be revisited in Chapter 4.

Discrete Entities with a Common Identity

Canons are comprized of individual, discrete works that struggle under the dual forces of difference and unity. Similarly, albums in the lists of 'greatest albums' and histories of rock are usually marked out as distinctive or different in some way, while retaining a position in the ongoing 'story' of rock. This difference may be a quality of the album, the artists, or more often both.

It is often the case that albums chosen as great represent an artist at their peak, and so the album is different not only from the work of others but also other work by that artist. For instance, Ben Edmonds contends that though *What's Going On* 'has inspired multiple tribute albums and its individual songs have been covered with regularity over the years, nothing in the annals of pop music since – including the illustrious catalog of Mr Gaye himself – has sounded quite like it.'[38] *Astral Weeks* is similarly described as sounding 'like nothing before or since', or alternatively, 'not exactly Celtic Soul, but not exactly anything else either'.[39]

Although *Revolver* is not the only album by the Beatles to feature prominently in lists of greatest albums or general histories, this idea of difference still prevails

---

35 Fusilli, *Pet Sounds*, p. 42.

36 Janovitz, *Exile on Main St.*, p. 71. Excerpts from *Exile on Main St.* by Bill Janovitz © 2005, reprinted by permission of the publisher, The Continuum International Publishing Group.

37 *VH1's 100 Greatest Albums*, Hoye, p. 53.

38 Edmonds, *What's Going On?*, p. 2.

39 Sean O'Hagan, 'Astral Weeks', in Various Contributors, 'The 100 Greatest British Albums', *Observer Music Monthly*, 17; Various Contributors, 'The 100 Greatest Albums of All Time According to *Time Out*', compiled by Nick Coleman and Steve Malins, *Time Out*, 21–28 June 1989, 18–23, p. 18.

and so we find it described as 'an album that sounds quite unlike anything else, even prior or subsequent work by the Beatles. *Revolver* exists in its own universe.'[40] However, the sonic originality of the Beatles is generally considered to have left its mark on all their recordings; or, as John Lennon stated in a later interview, 'We didn't sound like anybody else, that's all.'[41]

In other cases it is the artists who are celebrated as unique, and their most celebrated albums are attributed with this quality by extension. The Rolling Stones' *Exile on Main St.* is regarded as a definitive statement of the band's musical aesthetic, and therefore a worthy representative of a band central to the story of rock but not known primarily for any single album.[42] Alternatively, an album may be seen to represent the peak of a particular style, unique in its achievement rather than difference. The Sex Pistols are seen to represent punk as much as they represent themselves in the lists and histories of greatest albums; according to the *All-Time Top 1,000 Albums*, 'In the same way that *Sgt. Pepper* ... and *Revolver* are cast in stone at the top of the pop/rock genre, so this milestone [*Never Mind the Bollocks – Here's the Sex Pistols*] stands above any other punk record of its kind.'[43] Similarly Marvin Gaye's music represents Motown in such lists, and *What's Going On* stands as 'the last great Motown record from Detroit and their first political soul album'.[44] In each case, these albums are chosen as the greatest example of their kind – whether of a style or genre or particular artist. Once selected, their difference from (or superiority over) other albums is emphasized until they stand as monuments of their type.

The Romantic Artist/Genius and Notions of Truth

Echoing the towering centrality of the great figures in the canons of Western literature and classical music, the idea of the Romantic artist/genius is one of the strongest elements uniting the ten albums under study. The primary creators of each album are perceived as different or separate from those around them. In this they fit the template of the figure, taken directly from canons of literature and classical music, of the struggling, tortured, Romantic genius, characterized by William Weber as 'idiosyncratic, perhaps odd ... an unconventional spirit, seeing a virtue in resisting the rules of art or society.'[45]

Each album has its own associated genius or geniuses, and the mythologizing of these figures contributes to the aura of the work. Bob Dylan's persona is regarded as especially mysterious; for instance, his entry in *The Rough Guide to Rock* reveals that 'his obliquely revelatory lyrics, combined with a reclusive attitude to the press, and industrial-strength sunglasses, led to the creation of an enigmatic persona unique

---

40   *VH1's 100 Greatest Albums*, Hoye, p. 3.

41   John Lennon in 1970, quoted in Marcus, 'The Beatles', p. 209.

42   See for example *Rock: The Rough Guide*, Buckley and others, p. 833.

43   Larkin, *All-Time Top 1,000 Albums,* 3rd edn, p. 48.

44   *The Mojo Collection*, Irvin and McLear, p. 254.

45   William Weber, 'The Intellectual Origins of Musical Canon in Eighteenth-Century England', *The Journal of the American Musicological Society*, 47 (1994), 488–520 (512).

in popular music.'[46] This idea of the man as myth is regularly applied to Dylan, and he is regarded as a contradictory figure in rock:

> Dylan has probably spent more time in the spotlight than any other figure in rock & roll. Yet in all those years, the most influential songwriter of the rock era has only become more of an enigma; unlike such celebrated recluses as Thomas Pynchon and J.D. Salinger, Dylan doesn't have to hide to increase the mystery surrounding him. He is hidden in plain sight.[47]

Brian Wilson is a natural candidate as a Romantic hero with his partial deafness and troubled past, and thus he has been similarly mythologized through statements such as this:

> You wonder if some god said, "I'll create a being whose work will mean so much to so many people, a being whose work will enrich people, put sun in their lives, show them a way to express themselves, to understand themselves, to find their place in the world. And yet I'll make him suffer terribly. I'll remove him from his own gifts and I'll make the world he improved a foreboding cell for him."
> "Beat that, Shakespeare", said the demented god, pointing through the clouds at a little boy in Hawthorne, California, born June 20, 1942.[48]

Stephen Holden goes further to suggest that such mythologizing is actually part of the creative process of composition, by stating that '[Van] Morrison (in his groundbreaking 1968 acoustic album *Astral Weeks*), and later Tom Waits and Rickie Lee Jones, were romantic visionaries who mythologised their personal experience in often private stream-of-consciousness lyrics.'[49]

The importance of perceived truth is as noticeable in the reception of rock albums as it is in the canons of literature and classical music. However, in the case of rock music, this idea of truth tends to be located in the work as it relates to the identified author/genius. Canonical artists are expected to look deep inside themselves for their art and this is another familiar theme in the reception of rock music. This is a concept of authenticity that wearies certain academics and rock critics, but is still rife in the reception of rock albums.[50]

Bob Dylan, with his roots in the folk music tradition, is regarded as the ultimate example of the authentic, autonomous singer-songwriter in rock: 'After Dylan ...

46　*Rock: The Rough Guide*, Buckley and others, p. 305.

47　Alan Light, 'Bob Dylan', in *The Rolling Stone Illustrated History of Rock & Roll*, ed. by DeCurtis and Henke with George-Warren, pp. 299–308 (p. 299).

48　Fusilli, *Pet Sounds*, p. 40.

49　Stephen Holden, 'The Evolution of the Singer-Songwriter' in *The Rolling Stone Illustrated History of Rock & Roll*, ed. by DeCurtis and Henke with George-Warren, pp. 480–91 (p. 482).

50　See for example Simon Frith, '"The Magic That Can Set You Free": The Ideology of Folk and the Myth of the Rock Community', *Popular Music*, 1 (1981), 159–68; for authenticity and reflexivity, Johan Fornäs, *Cultural Theory and Late Modernity* (London: Sage 1995), pp. 274–9; for a summary of authenticity in popular musicology, Allan F. Moore, 'Authenticity as Authentication', *Popular Music*, 21/2 (2002), 209–25; and a general discussion of different types of authenticity perceived in rock music, Lawrence Grossberg, *We Gotta Get Out Of This Place: Popular Conservatism and Postmodern Culture* (London: Routledge, 1992).

instead of a polished interpreter, the writer became the definitive exponent of his or her work. The recording medium, through which idiosyncratic voices could be distinctively showcased in custom-designed settings, also encouraged a greater intimacy in both songwriting and performance.'[51]

Again and again albums are regarded as direct expressions of the artists who made them, cast in the role of troubled Romantic genius, and perceived truths and honesty of expression become markers of value. The *Rolling Stone* '500 Greatest Albums' poll claims that '*Astral Weeks* is Morrison going deep inside himself, to the far corners of his life and art, without a net or fear. He was never this open, and naked, again.'[52] The *Observer* list of '100 Greatest British Albums' likewise claims that '[*Astral Weeks*] may be the closest a pop record has come to expressing adolescent desire in all its confusions.'[53] This album is so successful as a perceived unadulterated expression of the individual that it is used as a benchmark against which others are compared; for example, Ben Edmonds declares that 'as personal meditation, *What's Going On* is as deep as Van Morrison's *Astral Weeks*.'[54]

Artists are expected to find truth not outside but within, and so Marvin Gaye's account of war and social crisis in *What's Going On* is considered to have remained relevant precisely because he 'outlin[ed] these concerns in terms that were at once all-encompassing and universal, yet deeply, elementally personal.'[55] In his book on the album, Edmonds maintains that 'his songs were about how things emotionally affected him, and he wanted to let others who might feel the same know they weren't alone. That's how a personal feeling becomes universal.'[56]

Brian Wilson is described by Fusilli as having gone 'deep, deep, deep into his heart and mind for his music' to create *Pet Sounds*, which is as a result 'a miraculous and often painful expression of a young man's desire to find love, acceptance, and tranquillity.' Later in the same book, Fusilli claims that 'what Brian Wilson did was capture a time that we all pass through, that we all experience ... And he did so honestly, without hyperbole.'[57] In a similar vein it is suggested in Berkenstadt and Cross's book on *Nevermind* that 'anyone who ever listened to this album ... knew the real Kurt Cobain. There was no line between who he was and what his music was, no artifice, no posing, no false front.'[58]

Artists, especially solo artists such as Bob Dylan, Van Morrison or Marvin Gaye, are attributed with great autonomy of vision and creation in accounts of the albums. The consensus, especially for music derived in part from the folk music tradition, is that there's 'something more trustworthy about an individual than a band. The

---

51   Holden, p. 482.

52   Various Contributors, 'The 500 Greatest Albums of All Time', *Rolling Stone*, 11 December 2003, 98.

53   Sean O'Hagan, 'Astral Weeks', in Various Contributors, 'The 100 Greatest British Albums', *Observer Music Monthly*, 17.

54   Edmonds, *What's Going On?*, pp. 208–209.

55   *100 Albums That Changed Music*, Egan, p. 185.

56   Edmonds, *What's Going On?*, pp. 208–209.

57   Fusilli, *Pet Sounds*, pp. 11 & 120.

58   Berkenstadt and Cross, *Nevermind*, p. 143.

singer who sets forth his or her own emotions and ideas in their own words to their own accompaniment just seems somehow more honest than a group prancing about playing roles.'[59]

This ideal of autonomous vision is played out in descriptions of these albums that suggest that the singer/songwriter is in truth an auteur, responsible for all aspects of its creation. *Pet Sounds* is considered to be primarily the work of Brian Wilson, who wrote the music, co-wrote the lyrics, produced the album and sang the majority of the songs while the rest of the Beach Boys were away on tour. Van Morrison is also cast in the role of singer/songwriter/producer on *Astral Weeks*, albeit unofficially: 'In all fairness to Van he was the one who was directing the taping ... Lew and I [the producers] were in the control room but Van was the real producer.'[60] A similar artistic autonomy is also attributed to Marvin Gaye within the context of Motown where the roles of performer, writer and producer were more usually enacted by different individuals.[61] Kurt Cobain's autonomy and individual vision is also highlighted in accounts such as this from Berkenstadt and Cross: 'Though a man of few words, Kurt knew what he wanted his music to sound like, and he approached recording with a self-assurance that few people working on their second album bring into the studio.'[62]

Such assertions contribute to the power and integrity of the singer/songwriter, and we find that in the reception of rock, as in classical music, there is an 'exaltation of the persona of the composer'.[63] Alongside, complementing and usually supporting the potential canon of albums in rock and the core idea of artist/genius are various other '100 greatest...' lists. Prominent among these are the polls of '100 greatest' stars or artists. For example, nine of the ten singer/songwriters from the albums under study feature in *Q* magazine's '100 Greatest Stars of the 20th Century' feature of August 1999 (John Lennon, Paul McCartney, Kurt Cobain and Bob Dylan were placed first, second, third and fourth respectively).[64] These statements are loaded with the canonical terms outlined in Chapter 1. The mythologized genius, originality, influence, musical craft, complexity, honesty and truth, personal conflict and struggle, the wisdom of hindsight, the progress of history, the test of time, and even a residual air of sanctity (represented by Cobain's 'martyrdom') are all implied in this sequence of highly canonical statements:

> [Bob Dylan, #4]: Just as The Beatles changed the way rock sounded, Dylan changed how it thought ...
>
> Self-publicist and self-mythologiser, Dylan hid his arrogance and vulnerability behind reclusiveness, and spun mumbo-jumbo to confuse the facts.

---

59 'Bob Dylan and the Folk Rock Boom', ed. by Steve Sutherland, *NME Originals*, 2/5 (2005), 4.

60 *The Mojo Collection*, Irvin and McLear, p. 182.

61 See Chapter 5, 'What's Happening, Brother?' in Edmonds, *What's Going On?*, pp. 95–126.

62 Berkenstadt and Cross, *Nevermind*, p. 31.

63 Marcia J. Citron, *Gender and the Musical Canon* (Cambridge: Cambridge University Press, 1993), p. 202.

64 Various Contributors, '100 Greatest Stars of the 20th Century', *Q*, 159 (August 1999), 43–74. See Appendix for list. Van Morrison does not feature.

[Kurt Cobain, # 3]: Martyrdom has elevated him to the pantheon, but even before his suicide, there was always a sense that Kurt Cobain would ascend/descend to rock god status. Fame and fortune were his for the taking: his musical talent and lyrical honesty ensured that ...

His genius was to illuminate and darken Nirvana's primal roar with a sacred intensity, that hoarse, rasp which was both universal and utterly maverick. Once heard, literally, he could never be forgotten ... What made this troubled man so unique, was that he articulated the anguish of personal despair better than any other figure in music history. Fact: no Nirvana song ever ended on a fade-out.

[Paul McCartney, #2]: One hundred years from now they'll find it difficult to believe, but for much of the late 20th Century it was fashionable to scorn Paul McCartney ...

By instinct, growing up on the BBC Light Programme and his Dad's 78s, he absorbed harmonic fluency. The only licks he studied were by Eddie Cochran and Scotty Moore, but by the age of 20 he was the musical equal of long-dead maestros who'd worn tights and white wigs ... He wrote Yesterday, Hey Jude, Blackbird and Penny Lane, to name but four Beatles classics; after that came lesser-known beauties (My Love, Waterfalls, No More Lonely Nights) that will outlive us all.

[John Lennon, #1]: John Lennon, the greatest recording artist of the 20th Century, remains more difficult to pin down than mercury ... His art and public actions alike reflected a battle raging within ...

As a conceptual musician, however, he was untouchable, the catalyst for a host of innovations (Tomorrow Never Knows from Revolver and A Day in the Life from Sgt. Pepper's Lonely Heart's Club Band are still being unpicked by contemporary musicians over 30 years later). Until Lennon, rock 'n' roll had rarely been so abrasive, confessional, otherworldly, primal, political or so deeply moving and thought provoking (and certainly never all at once). No political record has caused more fuss than Revolution #1 ... and there's never been a manifesto as universal as Imagine.

More than this, he single-handedly brought a surreal twist to pop music, mixing the Goons with LSD and widening the parameters for the generations that followed ...[65]

The value of the album is confirmed by such acclaim for the songwriter, and *Q* magazine's later 'The Greatest Songwriters of All Time' feature of 2004 also includes Lennon and McCartney, Bob Dylan, Brian Wilson, Lou Reed and Kurt Cobain.[66] Such accolades of greatness all add to the constellation of value surrounding each work.

What these accounts tend to ignore is the division of labour involved in making albums, even for solo artists (this subject will be revisited in more detail in Chapter 4). However, the concept of the authenticity of music written by the performer based on his (or her) own experiences is such familiar trope in rock music reception that accounts of albums by groups as opposed to individual artists are often reduced to accounts of the

---

65   Various Contributors, '100 Greatest Stars of the 20th Century' *Q*, 159 (August 1999), 71.

66   Various Contributors, 'Greatest Songwriters of All Time', *Q*, 219 (October 2004), 73–99. The accompanying articles include tributes from fellow musicians – in the case of Lennon and McCartney, Ozzy Osbourne stating that 'to me, they're the Mozarts of our time', (p. 74). The list is not rank ordered, and features 21 songwriters in total.

main singer-songwriter. Accounts of Kurt Cobain alone tend to dominate descriptions of Nirvana's music, just as Brian Wilson dominates the reception of the Beach Boys.

Alternatively, unable to ignore the fact that the Rolling Stones (like the Beatles) comprise more than one notable singer-songwriter, authenticity or truth is sought in their ability to portray a generalized notion of mankind as opposed to the truth of one single artist/genius.[67] Bill Janovitz regards *Exile on Main St.* as a form of mythology that ultimately conveys truth, claiming 'these are our shared myths, not lies. We want to subscribe to it all, because myths have always helped us make sense of the world, appealing to some universal, ephemeral sensation that is present in us.'[68]

Seriousness and ambition are both associated with the canon, along with the residual moral overtones of its roots in religion. In accordance once more with the Romantic notion of tortured artist/genius, the more an artist has to suffer for their art, the more truth tends to be perceived. Therefore accounts will often relate crises, extreme experiences, daring or suffering they have undergone in their lives and in the process of creating these albums. This description of the early experiences of the Beatles in Hamburg is typical of stories that focus on early hardship and later triumph: 'The living was rough and wild, with the fresh-faced Liverpool teens exposed overnight to the pleasures of speed, existentialism, all night drinking, fighting and the Reeperbahn's notorious red-light zone.'[69]

Accounts of the albums are riddled with stories of hardship or artistic crisis that went into their making. Bob Dylan is said to have been on an aeroplane, on the verge of abandoning his musical career, when he was suddenly inspired to write 'Like a Rolling Stone'. We are told that this song emerged from 'an unstoppable stream of frustrated psychobabble … With inspiration running on overdrive … he kept recording throughout July and August and came up with the fabulous *HIGHWAY 61 REVISITED*, surely his creative high watermark.'[70] Marvin Gaye's life is typically portrayed as one long tale of personal hardship, such as this account in the *All Music Guide*: 'Divorces, financial woes, and record-label troubles conspired to send Gaye, never an emotionally strong or stable man anyway, into a tailspin that ended tragically when he was shot by his father in 1984.'[71] Taking the idea of struggle for art to its logical extreme, Charles R. Cross asserts that '*Nevermind* made Kurt Cobain, yet it was also a record that destroyed him.'[72]

Hardly any of the ten albums seem to have been created without some degree of struggle or sacrifice. Stories surrounding the albums describe Brian Wilson unravelling under the influence of drugs, Marvin Gaye facing opposition from his own record label and also struggling with drugs, the Velvet Underground working with primitive equipment, accommodating individual egos and under time pressure

---

67   See for example *VH1's 100 Greatest Albums*, Hoye, p. 34, which claims that *Exile on Main St.* is 'a really great portrait of the inside of a man …'.

68   Janovitz, *Exile on Main St.*, p. 161.

69   *Rock: The Rough Guide*, Buckley and others, p. 65.

70   Ibid., p. 306.

71   *All Music Guide: the Best CDs, Albums & Tapes*, ed. by Michael Erlewine with Chris Woodstra and Vladimir Bogdanov (San Francisco: Miller Freeman Books, 1994), p. 138.

72   *100 Albums That Changed Music*, Egan, p. 311.

in the studio, the Beatles creating *Revolver* in the shadow of their immensely pressuring world tours and the Rolling Stones 'struggling' to record the album while in tax exile in the basement of a villa in France. Such struggle translates into value attributed to the album that is not tarnished by subsequent commercial success.

Value Beyond Commerce

Since canonical works are meant to be made of pure artistic motivation, the canon is based on values other than commerce. Yet that is not to say that the canon is non-commercial. In reality commerce has long been a strong reason for creating a canon, since it is capable of supporting a whole industry that publishes, performs and writes about the canon.[73] In the field of rock music it is harder to separate art from commerce since wealth visibly attaches itself to successful artists and albums are clearly commercial products. However, the reception of this music underplays such a connection as much as the reception of literature and classical music has long exorcized commercial aspects.

Accordingly, the reception of these rock albums tends to reflect the non-commercial, aesthetic ambition of canons more than the ephemeral disposability of rock music, thus creating one of the most glaring contradictions between canonic and rock ideology (a subject that will be revisited at greatest length in Chapter 4). To uphold this (shaky) difference between high and low in popular music, rock is sometimes presented as the more artistically serious counterpart of pop; or, alternatively, these albums are seen to represent the serious side of popular music.[74]

For instance, *Pet Sounds* is upheld as an unprecedented benchmark of artistic achievement. Fusilli claims that before *Pet Sounds*, 'people who made pop records weren't expected to reach into their souls in order to create a work that would last forever.'[75] Meanwhile, *Astral Weeks* is described as 'as serious an album as could be imagined, but it soared like an old Drifters 45'.[76] In order to distance rock albums from the visibly commercial mass media industry, the act of composition is often mystified and the musicians depicted as wholly separate from the industry's machinations.[77] Kingsley Abbott abandons all attempts to explain the value of *Pet Sounds* by describing it as 'a miracle, and therefore unfathomable'.[78] And artistic decisions are usually depicted as having been made independently of, or even in flat defiance of, industry logic.[79]

Even Bloom's notion that canonical works should create a 'high unpleasure' rather than instant gratification is echoed (albeit faintly) in the valorization of complexity

---

73   See Citron, *Gender and the Musical Canon*, p. 36.

74   The unease of terminology in the field of popular music will be revisited shortly in this chapter.

75   Fusilli, *Pet Sounds*, p. 112.

76   Marcus, 'Van Morrison', p. 444.

77   See John Stratton, 'Between Two Worlds: Art and Commercialism in the Record Industry', *The Sociological Review*, 30 (1982), 267–85 (273).

78   Abbott, *The Beach Boys' Pet Sounds*, p. viii.

79   See for example Chapter 6, 'Stubborn Kinda Fella', in Edmonds, *What's Going On?*, pp. 127–52.

over immediacy in these albums. Moreover, the ambition to create difficult, challenging, complex and original music is actually expected to reduce the numbers in the audience. To this effect, John Harris notes that 'much like Dylan, The Beatles could not move forward without alienating some of those whose adoration had placed them on their towering pedestal'[80] The information that *Astral Weeks* was initially afforded only a small-scale commercial release now lends it an air of exclusivity;[81] and the fact that '*Pet Sounds*' sales were a relatively damp squib' is now considered something of a badge of honour.[82] Stories abound that *Pet Sounds* was considered too challenging for the Beach Boys' fans and was therefore rushed out

> before Good Vibrations could be completed for inclusion and with at least one track (Let's Go Away For a While) left unintentionally instrumental. Even though it edged into the US Top Ten and made it to Number 2 in England (behind The Beatles' Revolver), just eight weeks after its release Capitol issued Best of the Beach Boys. All the label's promotional efforts were diverted to this collection, which quickly went gold and stayed on the Billboard chart for 78 weeks. But if Best of the Beach Boys won the most sales, Pet Sounds won the most souls.[83]

The Velvet Underground & Nico is also celebrated for its lack of commerciality when it was first released, and Joe Harvard claims that 'it's a contradiction so glaring it approaches paradox: a band that left its mark on rock music and musicians in a profound way, but whose music was purposefully snubbed by the major outlets.' He goes on to say that 'industry inertia was nearly comprehensive: record stores, radio stations, the music press, promoters, the marketing personnel and bean counters of the record labels who controlled the crucial distribution networks.'[84]

The implication here is that if the industry, whose motivations are famously commercial, rejects an album, the motivation of the album itself must be non-commercial. Although *Nevermind* was highly popular and commercially successful from the time of its release, the band are distanced from this commercial success with reports of their dislike towards their new-found popularity; 'Nirvana', it seems, 'were appalled by their broad appeal' to 'jocks, misogynistic metalheads, racist, homophobic rednecks … and none of their new-found audience seemed to appreciate the degree of hate they inspired in their new idols.'[85] This raises the interesting proposition that artists are not only measured by perceived authenticity of motivation but also authenticity of intended audience.

Nevermind's mass appeal is also offset by accounts of its musical authenticity and artistic merit. To this end Berkenstadt and Cross attempt to clearly delineate aesthetic

---

80 John Harris, 'Out of Their Heads', in *From Elvis to the Beatles*, Q Special Edition: 50 Years of Rock 'N 'Roll 1954–2004, (London: EMAP, 2004), 62.

81 *Astral Weeks*' producer Lewis Merenstein quoted in *The Mojo Collection*, Irvin and McLear, p. 182.

82 *100 Albums That Changed Music*, Egan, p. 66.

83 Various Contributors, 'The Hundred Greatest Albums Ever Made', in *Mojo*, 21 (August 1995), 87.

84 Harvard, *The Velvet Underground & Nico*, p. 2.

85 *Rock: The Rough Guide*, Buckley and others, p. 692.

and commercial value in their appraisal of the album's success, claiming that 'even if it had sold only a single copy, *Nevermind* would still rank as one of the greatest albums of the '90s, if only because of the artistic high water mark it represented. But that is something to be considered apart from commercial concerns.'[86] Such opinions are supported by comments such as Krist Novoselic's that *Nevermind* is a 'milestone in its honesty … "They made an absolutely honest-sounding record that was also in its way commercial … They earned it. It wasn't a manufactured thing".'[87]

Inevitably, if perhaps a little ironically, some of these albums have become commercially successful today more or less entirely because of their rarefied 'canonic' status. They can now be celebrated for their initial lack of commerciality but embraced by today's audience who feel they are endowed with the wisdom of hindsight. This is especially true of *The Velvet Underground & Nico*, *Astral Weeks*, and to a certain extent, *Pet Sounds*. However, their popularity today need not detract from the integrity achieved by the original obscurity or relative lack of contemporary success, and their perceived authenticity remains intact.

The Album as a Work of Art

The Album (as Canonical Work)

A canon is the collection of works and artists that are widely accepted as the greatest in their field, and the selection of these canonical works is inevitably dictated by preconceived hierarchies of genre and style. Most works of art have in effect been pre-classified by the canon. As discussed in Chapter 1, in the field of classical music the string quartet, symphony, concerto and the overture have largely been privileged over other genres. In the field of rock music albums, far more than individual songs, have the potential to satisfy the criteria of 'the work' as described in Chapter 1. Not only are they 'discrete, reproducible and attributable', and can be attributed with 'status, originality and "aura"', but they are also relatively large-scale and complex, and organicism, unity, coherence, completeness and self-sufficiency can all potentially be located in these albums.

In this potential canon of rock albums, the ideal work can be conceived of as an album that is a coherent body of work as a whole (not singles with 'filler'), that possesses the canonical criteria of originality, complexity and truth and that is associated with an autonomous artist/genius. This idealized 'canonical' album demands repeated listening and can sustain multiple interpretations, has withstood the test of time and influenced subsequent albums, but it is also complete in itself, forming an object of endless study and value. In practice this constructed ideal of the album is reflected in the reception of the ten albums under study.

Where albums display a lack of unity, this is usually glossed over with suitable explanations. This description of *Exile on Main St.* presents the album as an organic

---

86 Berkenstadt and Cross, *Nevermind*, p. 122.
87 Krist Novoselic quoted in ibid., p. 138.

whole while glossing over the presence of an unoriginal song, regarding it as a marker of musical authenticity rather than a disruption of the band's authorial autonomy:

> Mood and overall feel is important to the pacing and tone of *Exile*. This album is not concerned with serving up an endless parade of singles, but rather it is a collection that offers the opportunity to throw in a well-executed cover like ['Shake Your Hips'] to establish the vibe ... [*Exile on Main St.*] works as a piece, wherein such songs are appropriated the attention they deserve, as pieces of a whole ...
>
> If nothing else, on such cover versions the Stones solidify their roots and their musicianship, displaying an authoritative air of authenticity and a comfort in blues vernacular.[88]

The genre in classical music the rock album most resembles (and is compared to) is that of the song cycle rather than the symphony or string quartet. Holden even regards the two as synonymous, claiming that 'the notion of the pop song cycle or "concept album", which had been refined by the Beatles ... proved to be an ideal format for the singer-songwriter, whose characteristic product was a confessional self-portrait comprised of a dozen or so thematically related pieces.'[89] Accordingly, *Astral Weeks* is reported as having been initially conceived as a song cycle and other accounts of the albums also reflect this idea of a unified cycle of songs.[90]

The presence of *What's Going On* in lists of 'greatest albums' underlines the importance of the album-as-work more than any other. Prior to this, Motown recordings tended to be more akin to 'singles with fillers' and therefore have been denied the 'great album' status so readily attributed to Marvin Gaye's more unified album. Conversely, *What's Going On* has been variously described as 'one of the great soul albums, it was one of the first to be organized as a flowing, wall-to-wall statement', a 'moving and masterful suite' and 'a seamless suite of songs.'[91] This album is always presented as special, and as representing great artistic ambition; according to Ben Edmonds, 'The mission this time was not to make a record, it was to create a sonic environment and then extend it.'[92] Paul Gambaccini is not alone in describing *What's Going On* as 'the first major Black concept album'.[93] It is also compared to other 'great albums' as much as it is with other soul music, and Edmonds asserts that '[*What's Going On* is] something more than the "black *Sgt Pepper*" it is often described as. In its musical maturity and stylistic cohesion it can be better compared to the Beach Boys' *Pet Sounds*.'[94]

Many of the ideals noted above in regard to the 'ideal album' are associated with the idea of the 'concept album' that arose from the late 1960s onwards. The term 'concept album' was first applied to albums that were a cohesive whole; only later did

---

88 Janovitz, *Exile on Main St.*, pp. 79–80.

89 Holden, 'The Evolution of the Singer-Songwriter', p. 482.

90 Sean O'Hagan, '*Astral Weeks*', in Various Contributors, 'The 100 Greatest British Albums', *Observer Music Monthly*, 17.

91 *Rock: The Rough Guide*, Buckley and others, p. 400; *VH1's 100 Greatest Albums*, Hoye, p. 11; Larkin, *All-Time Top 1,000 Albums*, 3rd edn, p. 53.

92 Edmonds, *What's Going On?*, p. 197.

93 Gambaccini, *Paul Gambaccini Presents the Top 100 Albums*, p. 14.

94 Ibid., p. 218.

it accrue negative connotations of excess and (now embarrassing) artistic pretensions. *Pet Sounds* and *Revolver* amongst others (including the Beatles' *Sgt. Pepper's Lonely Hearts Club Band* and the Who's *Tommy*) are variously cited as the first concept album, and their position of importance in rock is related to the perceived unity of the albums. These earlier instances of concept albums are usually distanced from the more high-concept albums of the 1970s, and their 'concept album' description usually rests on their uniform excellence rather than some lyrical theme or underlying musical motif. Brian Wilson reinforced this notion in an interview in 1976 when he stated that he 'felt the production was a masterpiece ... It wasn't really a *song* concept album, or *lyrically* a concept album: it was really a *production* concept album'.[95] The importance of production in the reception of rock albums will be revisited later.

The pioneering nature of these early albums-as-works is often noted in their reception. The general perception (clearly articulated in *VH1's 100 Greatest Albums*) is that before *Pet Sounds*, albums 'consisted of hit singles surrounded by obvious filler', and therefore '*Pet Sounds* was a giant step toward artistic freedom in the name of rock 'n' roll'.[96] Kingsley Abbott even suggests that 'the use of the word "album" can be dated from the conceptual approach [Brian Wilson] introduced' with the recording of *Pet Sounds*.[97] And in a more recent assessment of the making of the album, Charles L. Granata claims that 'while it produced three hit singles, *Pet Sounds* represented the essence of what a cohesive, long-play rock 'n' roll album should, and could, be.'[98]

This conception of the album as an important genre of work is underlined by the introduction to *The Mojo Collection* ('The ULTIMATE Music Companion'), where the editors, Jim Irvin and Colin McLear, state their criteria for inclusion in the book:

> We've interpreted "popular music" in its broadest possible sense ... [But] we have been rigid about one criterion. All these records were conceived as albums. We've insisted on work that made the most of the form, in other words celebrating the best use of the format's wide possibilities rather than the tight pop nugget or the LP compiled from diverse sources. We have not rated the albums or ranked them, instead presenting them chronologically so you can see how the album has developed as both an art form and a mirror of music history.[99]

The narratives of influence and progressive evolution also suggested in this statement will be discussed in Chapter 3.

This overriding idea of the album being a work of art best appreciated as a whole is evident throughout descriptions of these albums. According to the *All Music Guide*, in the case of *Astral Weeks*, 'Listing highlights is practically pointless, as *Astral Weeks* should be taken as a whole.'[100] Describing *Nevermind*, musician Billie Joe Armstrong claims that the album should be listened to one song after the other, explaining that

---

95   Brian Wilson quoted in Charles L. Granata, *I Just Wasn't Made for These Times: Brian Wilson and the Making of Pet Sounds* (London: Unanimous, 2003), p. 235.

96   *VH1's 100 Greatest Albums*, Hoye, pp. 7–8.

97   Abbott, *The Beach Boys' Pet Sounds*, p. 142.

98   Granata, *I Just Wasn't Made for These Times*, p. 16

99   *The Mojo Collection*, Irvin and McLear, p. vii.

100 *All Music Guide*, Erlewine, Woodstra and Bogdanov, p. 222.

'it's almost like you're cheating yourself if you don't listen to one song.'[101] Similarly, Angus Batey claims in the *100 Albums That Changed Music* that: 'Strung together as an unbroken sequence of interwoven songs, *What's Going On* suffers badly if picked apart.'[102] This preference for albums that can be perceived as intentionally coherent works explains why compilation albums rarely feature in 'greatest albums' lists. As Sean Egan says, compilation albums are seen to 'mop up a series of individual statements rather than function as organic entities the way albums are intended to.'[103]

While *Never Mind the Bollocks: Here's the Sex Pistols* fails by certain traditional notions of the canonical work (it lacks compositional complexity and sophisticated recording methods, and does not have a clearly autonomous author/genius figure in the traditional sense), the success with which it presents a unified statement of punk and therefore a discrete coherent whole assures its continued importance as an album. Other, less traditionally canonical reasons for its importance in a potential canon of rock music will be addressed in Chapter 4.

The album works particularly well as a discrete work since it not only presents a single frozen performance of the music, but is also encased in deliberately memorable and individualized cover artwork. This was especially true in the 1960s and 1970s when albums would first arrive on 12-inch vinyl, and its impact has diminished somewhat with the shrinking of the record to CD. Each album cover conveys a message that contributes to the meaning of the work. One of the most famous of these is the cover art of *The Velvet Underground & Nico*, known as 'the banana album' for its design by Andy Warhol, linking the band directly with Warhol's distinctive style of pop art and recognizable art aesthetics. The cover of *The Velvet Underground & Nico* has been included along with *Nevermind* in a special edition of *Q* magazine, the *100 Best Record Covers of all Time*.[104] Such cover images are now iconic in their own right, adding a visual dimension to the album that increases its ability to become a discretely individual artefact.

Canonical Conditions of Reception

In the canons of Western literature and classical music there is, as Barbara Herrnstein Smith has noted, a 'tacit assumption of canonical audiences experiencing those works under canonical conditions.'[105] The canonical condition of reception for literature is usually that of quiet, solitary, engrossed reading. For classical music similarly attentive listening is expected, often in the rarefied yet communal environment of the concert hall. However, such conditions are unusual for rock music, which is usually associated with live performances in dingy rooms with beer and ambient

---

101 *VH1's 100 Greatest Albums*, Hoye, p. 4.

102 *100 Albums That Changed Music*, Egan, p. 184.

103 Ibid., p. 10.

104 Various Contributors, *The 100 Best Record Covers of All Time*, (London: EMAP, 2001), p. 8.

105 Herrnstein Smith, Barbara, *Contingencies of Value: Alternative Perspectives for Critical Theory* (Cambridge, MA. and London: Harvard University Press, 1988) p. 37.

noise, or large stadiums with stacks of speakers and screaming fans. Rock music is also a wallpaper feature of our lives; we are constantly exposed to it on the radio, television, through advertizements, at parties or piped into shopping complexes.

However, the expected behaviour around the 'greatest albums' is more akin to the rarefied atmosphere of the high arts than that of noisy gigs or background music. In Brian Wilson's own view, quoted in Kingsley Abbott's account of *Pet Sounds*, 'The best way to listen to the whole album is through headphones in the dark.'[106] Joe Harvard meanwhile encourages his readers to approach *The Velvet Underground & Nico* with reverence and full concentration:

> Try, when you listen to this record, to leave your preconceptions behind, and to let the music do the talking. Sit in a candlelit room, unplug the telephone, and listen to the entire album without interruption. An hour is not much time to give to a great record, considering what it will give back.[107]

Colin Larkin similarly claims that *Astral Weeks* 'cries out to be listened to without interruption'. The *All Music Guide* takes such claims even further, by averring that *Astral Weeks* is an album that 'defied passive listening. His intonation might vary too much for some ears, but if you really *listen*, his soulful vocal flights will (as Dylan said concerning the function of art) practically stop time.'[108]

Canonical works also demand re-reading, or in this case, repeated listening. This is another quality ascribed to *Pet Sounds* by Kingsley Abbott, who informs us that its 'new sonorities ... demanded a new approach' and 'repeat listening'.[109] In this way, attributes that made albums less popular initially ultimately serve to support their position of permanence. Charles L. Granata also underlines this character in the album, claiming that 'in opening his heart on record, Brian gave the world an album that bears repeated listening – a record that never becomes boring or stale.'[110] And again, this sentiment is repeated in Jim Fusilli's description of the first song on *Pet Sounds*: 'Such incredible invention, more than can be comprehended without repeated exposures, in a 2:37 pop song.'[111]

This necessity of repeated listening is also found in the descriptions of the other albums. To this effect, *Exile on Main St.* is described in *The Rough Guide to Rock* as 'one of the five or six greatest albums ever made. It's thoroughly alienating on the first several listenings, but its murky gravity exerts an undeniable force, imploding every contradictory aspect of The Stones' mythology.'[112] *What's Going On* is described by Edmonds as 'a triumph of sequencing ... Easily and endlessly listenable, it imprints its messages, problem and solution alike, a bit more each time it is played.'[113]

---

106 Abbott, *The Beach Boys' Pet Sounds*, p. 143.

107 Harvard, *The Velvet Underground & Nico*, p. 20.

108 Larkin, *All-Time Top 1,000 Albums*, 3rd edn, p. 41; Rick Clarke, quoted in *All Music Guide*, Erlewine, Woodstra and Bogdanov, p. 222.

109 Abbott, *The Beach Boys' Pet Sounds*, p. 80.

110 Granata, *I Just Wasn't Made for These Times*, p. 238.

111 Fusilli, *Pet Sounds*, pp. 41–2.

112 *Rock: The Rough Guide*, Buckley and others, p. 834.

113 Edmonds, *What's Going On?*, p. 207.

In this respect, critics are attributed with prescience, the ability to hear greatness in albums that takes others repeated listening and time to appreciate. This description of *Revolver* from the *All-Time Top 1,000 Albums* alludes not only to the necessity of repeated listening, but also the canonical notions of the wisdom of hindsight, elite wisdom, strangeness and originality:

> Music critics have always preferred Revolver to its famous successor [*Sgt. Pepper*], while fans were at first a little wary of the brilliantly bizarre 'Tomorrow Never Knows' ... Years of repeated listening unfolds quiet gems such as George Harrison's exceptional 'I Want To Tell You' and John Lennon's wondrously hazy 'I'm Only Sleeping' ... Paul McCartney was also on a creative roll with the unabashed and brave romanticism of 'Here There and Everywhere' and the classical sadness of 'Eleanor Rigby'. Subtly original and beautifully recorded.[114]

The implicit suggestion is that *Revolver* functions better than *Sgt. Pepper* as a discrete whole, disconnected from its original context and rendered timeless. Critics, it is said, prefer *Revolver* to *Sgt. Pepper* (which was more commercially successful), and this is reflected in the relative position of these albums in polls of 'greatest albums' (see Appendix).

Coupled with the tacit assumption of canonical conditions of reception is the assumption of a canonical audience. Hierarchies of audience exist in literature and classical music, ranging broadly from children at the bottom to critics at the top. This too is reflected in the reception of rock albums. The 'greatest albums' are generally considered to be appreciated more by comparatively mature audiences or rock music 'connoisseurs', as suggested by Matthew Specktor when he says, 'It's no wonder, really, that [*Astral Weeks*] confounded me as a callow twenty-one year old; nor that it was suddenly comprehensible to me as a heartbroken adult.'[115]

Alternatively these albums force young audiences to mature; *Pet Sounds* has accordingly been described as 'the most serious record this band ever did – teens confronting aging.'[116] Indeed, *Pet Sounds* was considered a risk by its record label because it appealed to a generally older, more mature (and in this context more 'canonical') audience than the earlier Beach Boys recordings, which had attracted a younger and mainly female following.[117] Jim Fusilli distances Brian Wilson from the young screaming fans of the Beach Boys, and seems instead to be suggesting that the true fans who fully understood Wilson were far more intellectual and contemplative than screaming Beatlemania-esque audiences: 'Capitol ... issued an unimpressive live album, *Beach Boys Concert*, which presented their fans in a frenzy as the group performed some of its hits and odd-ball covers [including 'Monster Mash'] that conflicted with the deeply felt songs Brian was crafting.'[118]

Such a scenario inevitably reflects that of the Beatles, whose work was taken far more seriously once they stopped touring in front of young, screaming and mainly female audiences and worked instead in the privacy of the studio; it then became

---

114 Larkin, *All-Time Top 1,000 Albums*, 3rd edn, p. 29.

115 *VH1's 100 Greatest Albums*, Hoye, p. 99.

116 *All Music Guide*, Erlewine, Woodstra and Bogdanov, p. 31.

117 Abbott, *The Beach Boys' Pet Sounds*, p. 107.

118 Fusilli, *Pet Sounds*, p. 34.

increasingly acceptable for mature adults to enjoy their music. *Exile on Main St.* is also apparently directed at a more mature audience than earlier hit singles by the Rolling Stones, as suggested by Bill Janovitz's recounted experience that 'I think I had *Sticky Fingers*, *Let It Bleed*, certainly *Hot Rocks*, and some others before I finally attained the holy grail of *Exile*. I needed those more easily digestible single-disc LPs and greatest hits collections ... before I could take on the sprawling, imposing and impenetrable *Exile*.'[119]

It is unsurprising that canonical terms and values appeal to certain writers and correspondingly mature and more contemplative audiences. Knowledge, even unconscious knowledge, of canonical terms, phrases and mechanisms are familiar through school and university, and such means of identifying greatness seem to come naturally to those educated in such a way. The negative and undemocratic aspects of canons are perhaps less noticeable outside the orbit of the academic debate over canons. With this popular use of elitist terms, the dividing line between high and low culture becomes increasingly blurred.

But it is Art?

Rock musicians are routinely referred to as 'artists', although there is little consensus over whether rock music can be considered 'art'. Yet art is the normal subject of canons. The myriad references to art in the reception of rock music, and the numerous claims for rock itself to be considered an art form are somewhat jumbled and confused. Sean O'Hagan epitomizes this grey area in his comment that *Astral Weeks* is 'as close as pop has come to the condition of art'.[120]

As many people seem to assume that this music is art as assume that it is the antithesis of art; others simply avoid the definition altogether. In the same way that the reception of rock music has been shown to be riddled with canonical terms, reference to and comparisons with the high arts punctuate accounts of rock albums in a dizzyingly intertextual manner that invites comparison or suggests parity. *The Velvet Underground & Nico* is described as being 'like the first glimpse of a Fellini movie after a lifetime of Disney'.[121] Marvin Gaye, although not long dead at the time of writing, is described by Edmonds in terms that suggest he has joined the ranks of the 'ancient masters': 'But the museums and history books are crowded with artists who couldn't live up to their art, and the sadness of [*What's Going On*] comes with the retrospective knowledge that it was ultimately of less help to its creator than to any of its listeners.'[122]

According to Alan Light, when it came to Bob Dylan, 'every press conference was an opportunity for a Dada performance piece.'[123] And the Beatles have been referred to as rock 'n' roll's 'high renaissance' and Paul McCartney as 'the musical

---

119 Janovitz, *Exile on Main St.*, p. 10.
120 O'Hagan, '*Astral Weeks*', 17.
121 *The Mojo Collection*, Irvin and McLear, p. 80.
122 Edmonds, *What's Going On?*, p. 274.
123 Light, 'Bob Dylan', p. 303.

equivalent of long-dead maestros who'd worn tights and white wigs'.[124] John Lennon himself contributed to this grey area surrounding the idea of rock in connection with art with such statements as: 'We created something, Mick [Jagger] and us [the Beatles], we didn't know what we were doing, but we were all talking, blabbing over coffee, like they must have done in Paris, talking about paintings.'[125]

Some critics regard these albums as works of art and do not question such status. For instance, Jim Fusilli says that '*Pet Sounds* opened a new world for me, one that reveals itself through art, which, in turn, illuminates the real world around me'.[126] Producer Norman Dolph similarly suggests that '90% of all the pictures that are viewed today as just awesome, the first time they were seen the reaction was "this isn't art!" ... Well, there were people who thought the VU were a waste of oxide on the back of a piece of recording tape.'[127]

Other references to art are more oblique. Greil Marcus, in his introduction to the chapter on the Sex Pistols in *The Rolling Stone Illustrated History of Rock & Roll*, quotes Manny Farber's description of 'White Elephant Art vs. Termite Art', stating that: 'The most inclusive description of the art is that, termite-like, it feels its way through walls of particularization ... eating away the boundaries of his art, and turning these boundaries into conditions of the next accomplishment.'[128] Since the quality of secondary material reflects back onto the work itself in a circle of valorization, with such sophisticated interpretations of the Sex Pistols, the reception of rock music has the potential to elevate its subject to the status of art. Alternatively it may remain non-committal on the issue of artistic status, simultaneously using and discarding terms for the high arts where it suits its purpose.

'Art rock' is sometimes regarded as a separate style in its own right, incorporating the idea of the concept album to its logical conceptual extreme. However, 'art rock' is associated most with a specific period of rock music, usually demarked as starting with the artistic ambitions of *Pet Sounds* or *Sgt. Pepper's Lonely Hearts Club Band* and ending with the nihilistic arrival of punk. On the whole, however, (due to general embarrassment) the excesses and pretensions of progressive rock or 'art rock' have excised it from the ranks of 'greatest albums'. For this reason the relative lack of ostentation displayed in *Revolver* compared to its flashy successor has made it far more valuable to many critics, as Clinton Heylin bears out in his account of *Never Mind the Bollocks: Here's the Sex Pistols*:

> It may seem a tad peculiar when viewed from an aural landscape bequeathed by the Pistols to the likes of Nirvana and Oasis, but circa 1976 music critics had a shall-we-say-tendency to consider a band's technical ability the be-all and end-all. In a sound born

---

124 *VH1's 100 Greatest Albums*, Hoye, p. 2; Various Contributors, '100 Greatest Stars of the 20th Century', *Q*, 159 (August 1999), p. 69.

125 John Lennon interviewed for *Rolling Stone*, reprinted in Jann S. Wenner, 'John Lennon: The Rolling Stone Interview', in *20 Years of Rolling Stone: What a Long, Strange Trip It's Been*, ed. by Jann S. Wenner (New York: Friendly Press, 1987), pp. 101–16 (p. 102).

126 Fusilli, *Pet Sounds*, pp. 118.

127 Producer Norman Dolph quoted in Harvard, *The Velvet Underground & Nico*, p. 6.

128 Greil Marcus, 'Anarchy in the U.K.', in *The Rolling Stone Illustrated History of Rock & Roll*, ed. by DeCurtis and Henke with George-Warren, pp. 594–607 (p. 594).

of the bastard son of the twelve-bar blues, not the glorious Ninth, playing the "right" notes had replaced rhythm and feel. *NME* had just voted *Sergeant Pepper's Lonely Hearts Club Band* the joint-greatest album in the edifice of Rock. (We can be but grateful it was alongside *Blonde On Blonde*.)[129]

According to John Rockwell, art rock inevitably 'parallels, imitates or is inspired by other forms of "higher," more "serious" music'.[130] Typically of the reception of rock music, Rockwell claims less that 'art rock' is art in itself, but rather that it reflects the qualities of art. However, there is a relatively long tradition attached to this confusion of high and low in the reception of rock music. Hierarchies of value within rock have been implied since Wilfred Mellers compared the Beatles' songs to those of Mozart, Schubert and Beethoven in *Twilight of the Gods* (1973).[131] Even earlier than this, Richard Buckle in the *Sunday Times* in 1963 described the Beatles as 'the greatest composers since Beethoven'.[132] Comparisons with classical music most often appear when there is a tangible use of classical genres or instrumentation, such as the string quartet in the Beatles' 'Eleanor Rigby' (*Revolver*) or John Cale's use of minimalist techniques and prominent viola playing on 'Venus in Furs' (*The Velvet Underground & Nico*).

However, overt classical associations actually tend to contradict the rock ideology of youth, rebellion, primitive rawness and the ephemeral, as embodied by the music and image of the Sex Pistols and the Rolling Stones, who, not unnaturally, attract far fewer direct comparisons with classical music than the other eight artists studied in this book. Classical music is viewed indirectly as a marker of status in reference to rock, rather than a blueprint for composition. Therefore albums are attributed with high art aesthetic qualities, but not in such a direct way as to overtly contradict its underlying ideology of rebellion. A sense of timelessness is often attributed to these albums (as will be explored further in Chapter 3), and this indirectly creates associations between rock music and other 'timeless music' without necessarily involving more direct comparisons in terms of composition and performance.

The Velvet Underground in particular are involved in the question of rock as art since their literary and musical (art) ambition is plain to see, as well as their refusal to recognize boundaries between high and low culture. Given that two of the most prominent members of the band were university educated in the arts (Lou Reed in English Literature and John Cale as a classical composer), reference to and use of high art sources seems inevitable. It also forms a prominent theme in accounts of the band, such as Joe Harvard's observation that 'Velvet Underground co-founder Lou Reed once said "if you're going to talk about greats, there is no one

---

129 Heylin, *Never Mind the Bollocks*, p. 6.

130 John Rockwell, 'The Emergence of Art Rock', in *The Rolling Stone Illustrated History of Rock & Roll*, ed. by DeCurtis and Henke with George-Warren, pp. 492–9 (p. 493).

131 Wilfred Mellers, *Twilight of the Gods: The Beatles in Retrospect* (London: Faber & Faber, 1976 (1973)), pp. 57 & 116 (although he notes that the music of Beethoven is inevitably more complex than that of the Beatles and that analysis of the music should take this into account: Mellers, *Twilight of the Gods*, p. 16).

132 Quoted in Peter Wicke, *Rock Music: Culture, Aesthetics and Sociology* (Cambridge and New York: Cambridge University Press, 1987), p. 3.

greater than Raymond Chandler ..." Lou had a simple plan: to "take the sensibility of Raymond Chandler or Hubert Shelley (sic) or Delmore Schwartz or Poe and put it to rock music".'[133] John Cale on the other hand has been quoted as saying, 'What we were doing (was) trying to figure ways to integrate some of LaMonte Young's or Andy Warhol's concepts into rock and roll ... We were really excited. We had this opportunity to do something revolutionary – to combine avant-garde and rock and roll, to do something symphonic.'[134]

However, although the Velvet Underground are often noted for their intellectual approach, there is ambivalence towards the idea of the rock artist as intellectual. The involvement of art school graduates in rock music is described in Simon Frith and Howard Horne's book *Art Into Pop*, in which they discuss the influence of art school ideas on the music, promotion and reception of the Beatles, the Rolling Stones, the Velvet Underground, Patti Smith and the Sex Pistols (and Malcolm McLaren), amongst others.[135] However, overt association with high art institutions tends to be cloaked, and rock music reception in general tends to be suspicious of high art ideals and intellectualism. This is one of the fundamental problems of a canon in rock, which will be discussed further in later chapters in this book.

In the case of some artists, especially Bob Dylan and Patti Smith, the line is also blurred between rock musician and poet, inviting comparisons of rock lyrics with poetry. *Horses* is described in the *All Music Guide* as 'one of the more successful matings of poetry and rock', and it is suggested that on this album Smith 'flits between tune and word without giving precedence to either'.[136] Another source suggests that the fact that the lyrics on *Highway 61 Revisited* 'were like poetry, shimmering with metaphors, similes and delightful phrases that made normal popular music lyrics sound like nursery rhyme', paved the way 'for other artists to imitate its adult concerns'.[137]

Allusion to poets, both those of popular culture (the beat poets) and high culture (Rimbaud and Baudelaire), are frequent in the reception of the work of Bob Dylan, Patti Smith and Van Morrison. *VH1's 100 Greatest Albums* locates Patti Smith in a 'boho-literary tradition' stretching from Rimbaud and Baudelaire through to 'the Rolling Stones, Bob Marley, and Bob Dylan';[138] then later on suggests that on *Astral Weeks* Van Morrison 'proves, on this album first, he is a poet'.[139] Meanwhile, *Time Out* characterizes Smith's work as 'wild, extravagant, stream-of-consciousness rock poetry'.[140]

Yet there is no escaping the fact that lyrics and poetry are fundamentally different; one conceived in the context of music, the other to be considered alone. The classical

133 Lou Reed quoted in Victor Bockris, *Transformer: The Lou Reed Story*, (New York: Simon & Schuster, 1994), quoted in Harvard, *The Velvet Underground & Nico*, p. 3.

134 John Cale quoted in Harvard, *The Velvet Underground & Nico*, pp. 57 & 67.

135 Simon Frith and Howard Horne, *Art Into Pop* (London and New York: Routledge, 1989).

136 *All Music Guide*, Erlewine, Woodstra and Bogdanov, p. 296; *100 Albums That Changed Music*, Egan, p. 243.

137 *100 Albums That Changed Music*, Egan, p. 54.

138 *VH1's 100 Greatest Albums*, Hoye, pp. 81.

139 Ibid., p. 99.

140 Various Contributors, 'The 100 Greatest Albums of All Time According to *Time Out*', p. 18.

music canon fled over time from the more pagan forms of song to the more abstract instrumental forms in a search for pure, absolute music; but the rock album is always associated with words, and its artists often both composers and lyrical authors. The ambivalence of rock towards high art pretension is epitomized by this comment made by Joe Harvard in his discussion of *The Velvet Underground & Nico*: 'Even at the height of their art rock chic, the band walked a wire between dignifying the songs via lyrical content, and rocking the fuck out.'[141] These blurred boundaries nevertheless do not affect a canon in rock if the album-as-work is taken to be the ruling logic of values. Artists can be described as poets or poetic; but what they are primarily is authors of albums. As such they have a strong identity within histories of rock. Rather than creating a debate over the 'art' status of the music, the inclusion of poetic lyrics simply becomes another marker of maturity that distances the albums now considered 'great' from the facile and disposable nature of popular music as a whole.

*

As this chapter has demonstrated, the reception of rock music is suffused with canonical terms and aesthetic criteria. Some words such as 'classic', 'masterpiece' and 'genius' tend to be used quite casually in the reception of rock music, and so their canonic implications should perhaps not be overemphasized. However it is clear that the writers of articles, books and histories recounting these ten albums and artists use such terms in order to valorize their subjects. The Chapter 3 will investigate the presence of common narrative strands of canons in the reception of rock music.

---

141 Harvard, *The Velvet Underground & Nico*, p. 73. He maintains that the closest the band came to being poetic was on 'The Black Angel's Death Song', which contains strong elements of beat poetry. See ibid., p. 130.

Chapter 3

Canonical Narratives, Structure and the Test of Time in the Reception of Rock Albums

Canons are underpinned by narratives of influence, progress and tradition, and each artist or work central to the canon has an important role in what is retrospectively conceived of as a coherent and logical story. Such narratives of influence, progress and tradition are evident in the reception of rock albums, and each album is shown to either embody a pivotal moment of revolution in rock or represent the highest achievement of a particular genre. In other words, these are the albums without which the history of rock would be very different. The roles of individual albums in these stories can usually be reduced to a few key features that are frequently recounted in their reception.

For instance, *Highway 61 Revisited* is associated with visionary revolution, a straightforwardly canonical marker of value. The album is described in the *Rolling Stone* '500 Greatest Albums of All Time' poll as being 'one of those albums that, quite simply, changed everything. "Like A Rolling Stone" … forever altered the landscape of popular music – its "vomitific" lyrics (in Dylan's memorable term), literary ambition and sheer length (6:13) shattered limitations of every kind.'[1] *The Velvet Underground & Nico* is also characterized as a revolutionary album, but this time with delayed effect. In a typical comment, *The Rough Guide to Rock* claims that 'The Velvet Underground are unique in rock history. No other band ever achieved so little success during its life span and had such a vast influence on the generation that followed.'[2] Their canonical appeal is exacerbated by their relative lack of contemporary success, and so it is through the wisdom of hindsight that the album's position of importance has evolved.

The Beatles from the beginning have been one of (if not the) most canonical bands in the reception of rock music, and this centrality means that although their work as a whole forms a constant presence in lists, the order in which their albums are ranked is often different from one poll to the next. However, *Revolver* is often afforded a position of especial importance as the mid-point of the trajectory of the remarkable evolution that the Beatles underwent with *Rubber Soul, Revolver* and *Sgt. Pepper's Lonely Hearts Club Band*, and marks the high point of their influence as revolutionary artists. The album's engineer, Geoff Emerick, maintains that he knows 'for a fact that, from the day *Revolver* came out, it changed the way everyone else

---

1   Various Contributors, 'The 500 Greatest Albums of All Time', *Rolling Stone*, 11 December 2003, 83–178 (88).

2   *Rock: The Rough Guide*, ed. by Buckley and others, 2nd edn (London: Rough Guides Ltd, 1999), p. 1057. Reproduced by permission of Penguin Books Ltd.

made records.'[3] *VH1's 100 Greatest Albums* claims that 'The Beatles with *Revolver* declared rock and roll to be a wide-open field.'[4] Conversely, *Astral Weeks* tends to be regarded as a singular achievement by Van Morrison: 'Recorded in New York over two days in 1968, *Astral Weeks* still sounds like nothing before or since … It is too intimate, too inward-looking for that.'[5] The presence of this album in lists tends to foreshadow the presence of the artist in this instance.

Pet Sounds is usually recognized for its ambition, its unprecedented achievements of studio production, and high standard of composition. In this it reflects the idea of a craft tradition that dominates the canon of classical music. The *NME* locates the album in a period of rapid evolution in rock: 'BRIAN WILSON, The Beach Boys' goofy, gifted *auteur*, decided he was going to whup Phil Spector and The Beatles – the former in the immense production stakes, the latter on the ability to craft an album of thematically linked, consistently great songs. "Pet Sounds" was all of that.'[6] Like *Astral Weeks*, *Pet Sounds* tends to be the only album by the group to feature high up in the ranks of lists of greatest albums. However, the Beach Boys (or at least Brian Wilson) are also closely associated with the Beatles in histories, and are therefore more central figures than Van Morrison to this story of progress.

The Rolling Stones are also closely associated with the Beatles in histories, and like the Beatles the presence of the band in successive polls is more predictable than the order in which their albums appear. More than the Beatles, however, the Rolling Stones represent the ideology of rock music, as this excerpt from *The Rough Guide to Rock* avers:

> More than anybody else, The Rolling Stones have defined the parameters of rock 'n' roll … Aside from forging rock's iconography and subject matter and reaffirming its blues-based foundations, The Rolling Stones have defined its basic sound: its gritty textures and overloaded highs and lows ... the history of rock 'n' roll is the history of The Rolling Stones.[7]

Exile on Main St. is often regarded as a document of their mature sound.

Patti Smith's *Horses* is hailed as a precursor to punk, and therefore a key influence on later 'great' albums. Joe S. Harrington asserts that 'if any album made the future happen faster, it was *Horses*.'[8] On the other hand, *Never Mind the Bollocks: Here's the Sex Pistols* is emblematic of punk as a whole. Punk is regarded as a pivotal turning point in histories of rock and the Sex Pistols as fundamental to the scene; Greil Marcus comments that 'as an official, aboveground group [the Sex Pistols] lasted

3   *The Mojo Collection: The Ultimate Music Companion*, ed. by Jim Irvin and Colin McLear, 3rd edn (Edinburgh and New York: Canongate, 2003), p. 66.

4   *VH1's 100 Greatest Albums*, ed. by Jacob Hoye (New York and London: MTV Books/ Pocket Books, 2003), p. 3.

5   Sean O'Hagan, 'Astral Weeks', in Various Contributors, 'The 100 Greatest British Albums', *Observer Music Monthly*, 17.

6   Various Contributors, 'Set Adrift on Memory Discs: 40 Records That Captured the Moment', *New Musical Express*, 9 May 1992, 42–5 (43).

7   *Rock: The Rough Guide*, Buckley and others, p. 831.

8   *VH1's 100 Greatest Albums*, Hoye, p. 81.

little longer than nine months ... During that time, however, the Pistols accomplished an interesting feat: They broke the story of rock & roll in half.'[9] Stephen Thomas Erlewine echoes this sentiment very closely when he declares that 'their one proper album, *Never Mind the Bollocks: Here's the Sex Pistols*, remains their most concise and effective record; without it, popular music would have been much different.'[10] However, while punk apparently demolished the course of traditional rock at the time, it has now been incorporated into the rock tradition, as can be seen in this comment from *The Rough Guide to Rock*, which states that the Sex Pistols 'only recorded one album, didn't sell phenomenal quantities of records but, in the history of rock 'n' roll, they are as important as The Rolling Stones.'[11]

What's Going On is often regarded as the pinnacle of Soul recordings in polls of 'greatest albums', due to the ease with which is fits the criteria of a unified album (rather than the more usual Motown format of singles 'with filler'). The political themes in Marvin Gaye's album also mean that it is accredited with being an album that represents its time. *Nevermind*, on the other hand, represents a generation. According to *The Rough Guide to Rock*, 'With the release of NEVERMIND (1991), it became clear that records would soon be classified as pre- or post-Nirvana ... Cobain was voicing the emptiness felt by the youth of 90s America ... "Generation X".'[12]

From this we can see that each album holds an important position in the narratives underpinning this (potential) canon. Other albums with similar (but lesser) qualities will only be peripheral to this central core; and tendrils of influence are drawn throughout histories to bind these works together.

Influence, Progressive Evolution and Transcendence

Although each canonical work is expected to be unique, as a canon they are treated as a collective group, sharing the bond of enduring excellence. Locating connections between the main figures and works adds coherence to a canon; and attempts to maintain a common identity are actually far easier for a canon of rock than the canons of literature and music, since they mostly arise from the same cultural context and the same historical point in time. Artists are thus connected through direct seams of interaction as well as perceived bonds of immediate influence.

Influence is as important to narratives of rock music as it is to the canons of literature and classical music, as has already been proven through the retrospective importance of *The Velvet Underground & Nico*. The 2003 *NME* '100 best albums' list (quoted in the introduction to this book) justifies its selections with details of subsequent 'great'

---

9   Greil Marcus, 'Anarchy in the U.K.', in *The Rolling Stone Illustrated History of Rock & Roll*, ed. by Anthony DeCurtis and James Henke with Holly George-Warren, 2nd edn (London: Straight Arrow, 1992), pp. 594–607 (p. 595). From *The Rolling Stone Illustrated History Of Rock And Roll* by Rolling Stone, edited by Jim Miller, copyright © 1976, 1980 by Rolling Stone Press. Used by permission of Random House, Inc.

10   *All Music Guide: the Best CDs, Albums & Tapes*, ed. by Michael Erlewine with Chris Woodstra and Vladimir Bogdanov (San Francisco: Miller Freeman Books, 1994) p. 287.

11   *Rock: The Rough Guide*, Buckley and others, p. 873.

12   Ibid., p. 692.

albums that were directly influenced by these early 'masterpieces'.[13] The importance of influence to the reception of albums is again made clear in the introduction to *100 Albums That Changed Music*, which somewhat bafflingly draws a distinction between 'the best' and 'the most important'. Rather than a list of the best albums ever made, Sean Egan claims that what is presented in this book is the 100 albums 'that have had a crucial influence on the development of what was originally called (and still is by many) rock 'n' roll', although he concedes that 'there is very often an overlap between aesthetic greatness [presumably 'the best'] and influence ['the most important'].'[14] Indeed, rock histories, biographies and lists in general are riddled with narratives of interaction and influence.

The strongest circles of influence involve the artists of the 1960s, and competition, interaction and influence between Bob Dylan, the Beatles, the Rolling Stones and the Beach Boys are central to histories of rock. Tales abound of how Dylan (in)famously influenced the Beatles, and, in the words of John Harris, 'goaded them towards a new maturity like a frazzled Moses'.[15] Their meeting has now become a crucial moment in rock history: 'The two key forces in 60s music met for the first time that August [1964] in New York, when Dylan turned The Beatles on to the delights of dope.'[16] Completing the circle of influence, Dylan in turn shocked his folk music audience by 'going electric' at the 1965 Newport Folk Festival, apparently as a reaction on Dylan's part to the 'electric' success of the Beatles. *The Rough Guide to Rock*, for instance, claims that 'one of the catalysts was, as ever, the Beatles. Dylan was impressed by their impact and had become envious of their success with armies of screaming girls, while he was stuck playing to the same old beards.'[17]

Another of the most prominent stories in rock is the interplay of influence between the Beach Boys and the Beatles around the time of the release of *Pet Sounds*. According to accounts of the time, Brian Wilson made *Pet Sounds* in an attempt to match the inescapable achievements of the Beatles with *Rubber Soul*: Wilson has been quoted more than once as saying that 'this album blows my mind because it's a whole album with all good stuff! ... I'm gonna try that ... *Rubber Soul* is a complete statement, damn it, and I want to make a complete statement.'[18] Both Paul McCartney and the Beatles' producer George Martin in turn are quoted in countless books and articles on *Pet Sounds*, relating the influence *Pet Sounds* had on *Sgt. Pepper's Lonely Hearts Club Band*:

---

13   Various Contributors, 'NME's 100 Best Albums of All Time!', *New Musical Express*, 8 March 2003, 35–42.

14   *100 Albums That Changed Music: and 500 Songs You Need to Hear*, ed. by Sean Egan (London: Robinson, 2006), p.8.

15   John Harris, 'Out of Their Heads', in *From Elvis to the Beatles*, *Q* Special Edition: 50 Years of Rock 'N' Roll 1954–2004, (London: EMAP, 2004), 60–65 (62).

16   *Rock: The Rough Guide*, Buckley and others, p. 66.

17   Ibid., p. 306.

18   Jim Fusilli, *Pet Sounds* (New York and London: Continuum, 2005), pp. 79–80. Excerpts from *Pet Sounds* by Jim Fusilli © 2005, reprinted by permission of the publisher, The Continuum International Publishing Group.

The Beatles got a lot from *Pet Sounds*. It blew by *Rubber Soul*, establishing a new plateau for a rock album. "Without *Pet Sounds*, *Sgt. Pepper* wouldn't have happened", said George Martin, who produced and helped arrange the Beatles' albums. "It was a spur. The way Brian handled all the elements, the vocal work and the unusual sounds he got ..."
Paul McCartney called *Pet Sounds* "the record of the time".
"If records had a director within a band, I sort of directed *Pepper*... And my influence was basically the *Pet Sounds* album."[19]

Such interplay is repeated so often that the two have become inextricably linked. Elsewhere, George Martin is quoted as saying that 'no one made a bigger impact on the Beatles than Brian [Wilson].'[20] In his book-long assessment of the making of and subsequent reception of *Pet Sounds*, Charles L. Granata asserts that 'the correlation between *Pet Sounds* and *Revolver* is key to understanding the relationship between the Beatles and the Beach Boys.'[21] Similarly, in the *Rolling Stone* '500 Greatest Albums of all Time' list of December 2003 *Pet Sounds* was placed at number two in recognition of its influence on the highest-ranked album, *Sgt. Pepper*.

Indeed, even Nirvana, seemingly stylistically and temporally divorced from the Beatles, are shown to come under their influence: 'The early influence of Lennon and McCartney served Cobain well. "Kurt loved the Beatles", recalls Vig. "He loved John Lennon. So I know that he felt self-conscious, coming from a punk background and having these kind of gorgeously crafted rock songs."'[22] The relationship between artists and works in a canon is reciprocal, and connections drawn between major figures and works strengthens the narrative of the canon, making it harder for outside works and artists to be included.

That *Spin* magazine created a list of the 'Fifteen Most Influential Albums of All Time (... not recorded by the Beatles, Bob Dylan, Elvis or the Rolling Stones)' is a strong indicator not only of the importance of influence to narratives of rock music but also the centrality of the Beatles, Bob Dylan and the Rolling Stones (Elvis Presley is something of an idiosyncratic figure here, since he is more usually associated with singles than albums).[23] Number one in this list is *The Velvet Underground & Nico*. The Velvet Underground, although contemporary with the Beatles, tend to be divorced from the circle of influence represented by Bob Dylan, the Beatles and Beach Boys in accounts of the band; but their importance has been established

---

19   Ibid., pp. 110–11.

20   George Martin quoted in Charles L. Granata, *I Just Wasn't Made for These Times: Brian Wilson and the Making of Pet Sounds* (London: Unanimous, 2003), p. 17.

21   Ibid., p. 195.

22   Jim Berkenstadt and Charles Cross, *Nevermind: Nirvana* (London and New York: Schirmer Trade Books, 1998), p. 63.

23   'Fifteen Most Influential Albums of All Time (...not recorded by the Beatles, Bob Dylan, Elvis or the Rolling Stones)', ed. by Chuck Klosterman, Greg Milner, and Alex Pappademas, *Spin*, The Ultimate List Issue, April, 2003. Quoted in Joe Harvard, *The Velvet Underground & Nico*, (New York and London: Continuum, 2004), p. 1. Excerpts from *The Velvet Underground & Nico* by Joe Harvard © 2004, reprinted by permission of the publisher, The Continuum International Publishing Group.

by later artists effectively finding their work to be an inescapable influence.[24] Joe Harvard states that the sheer number of bands influenced by the Velvet Underground 'by admission or observation' explains why, besides the music itself, 'people are still writing books about the VU'.[25] Such is the perceived subsequent influence of *The Velvet Underground & Nico* that there is now a long-standing joke that 'only a few thousand people bought that record, but all of them formed a band of their own.'[26] *Time Out* goes even further in suggesting that:

> this album exerts a weird retrospective messianic hold over the current generation of rockers. It's as if everything that anyone ever wanted to say about alienation, both sexual and social, is enshrined beneath the big banana. 'VU & Nico' is a rock reliquary.[27]

This last comment hints at the kind of reverence associated with the works of the earliest canons, and suggests that this album at least has achieved a permanent position in any potential canon of albums.

As the fate of *The Velvet Underground & Nico* suggests, the influence of these albums must be felt by the musicians of today to be considered truly influential and in effect achieve perpetual modernity. The far-reaching influences and effects of these albums are often stated at the end of books on the albums or general histories of the artists. For example, Alan Light claims that 'it is impossible to imagine the Sixties protest movement, the Seventies singer-songwriters or even the outspoken politics of rap without [Dylan].'[28] The Rolling Stones, and Mick Jagger in particular, are seen to have had a general but all-encompassing influence on the field, since according to *The Rough Guide to Rock*, 'If there had been no Mick Jagger ... hard rock, heavy metal, glam, punk and grunge would have been unthinkable ... Jagger has unquestionably developed much of rock's lyrical terrain and, more importantly, created the rock 'n' roll persona.'[29] That the influence of the Beatles appears to show no signs of diminishing is evinced by the use of the drum loop from 'Tomorrow Never Knows' in recent performances by the Chemical Brothers nearly four decades after it was written.[30] If, however, the relevance of the albums to today's musical context were to cease, then their presence would diminish over time.

The canon is most usually represented by key artists and works in a story of progressive evolution. While subsequent influence is undoubtedly important, it is

---

24   This is a list that includes 'David Bowie ... Patti Smith and the entire mid-Seventies punk-rock graduating class at CBGB ... Joy Division–New Order, U2, R.E.M. and Sonic Youth, to name a handful' according to David Fricke, 'The Velvet Underground', in *The Rolling Stone Illustrated History of Rock & Roll*, ed. by DeCurtis and Henke with George-Warren, pp. 348–69 (p. 348).

25   Harvard, *The Velvet Underground and Nico*, pp. 10–11.

26   Attributed to Brian Eno: *100 Albums That Changed Music*, Egan, p. 98.

27   Various Contributors, 'The 100 Greatest Albums of All Time According to *Time Out*', compiled by Nick Coleman and Steve Malins, *Time Out*, 21–28 June 1989, 18–23, p. 18.

28   Alan Light, 'Bob Dylan', in *The Rolling Stone Illustrated History of Rock & Roll*, ed. by DeCurtis and Henke with George-Warren, pp. 299–308, p. 299.

29   *Rock: The Rough Guide*, Buckley and others, p. 831.

30   *VH1's 100 Greatest Albums*, Hoye, p. 3.

the initial spark of originality attached to the work that makes it influential and contributes to the story of progress represented by the canon. Hence Charles L. Cross's comment that '*Nevermind* ranks as one of the few records that are important enough to stand as a time mark in the progression of rock. Just like *Sgt. Pepper's* ... *Nevermind* is a constant pop culture reference.'[31] The most valued literature, art and music in the canon is seen to have had a progressive and evolutionary impact on the field, apparently working towards some ideal state of art. While it may be a cliché, the term 'quantum leap' is often used in accounts of the albums to convey this startling sense of progress, either in the development of the artist or of rock music as a whole. For example, *Highway 61 Revisited* is described as 'a quantum leap beyond the folk and pop clichés of the time, offering new possibilities for the subject matter and vocabulary of both genres.'[32] For Stephen Thomas Erlewine, the most remarkable thing about *Nevermind* 'is the quantum leap in Kurt Cobain's songwriting'.[33] *Pet Sounds* (and its companion song 'Good Vibrations', originally intended for inclusion on the album) is also described as a 'quantum leap' in comparison to the single that preceded it, 'that fluffiest of all Beach Boys hits Barbara Ann'.[34]

At times this underlying narrative of evolution is not simply implied, it is explicitly stated. An account of Marvin Gaye's career maintains that 'unlike most soul greats, he maintained an artistic evolution (albeit sometimes erratically) over the course of three decades ... he was one of the few soul pioneers to craft lyrically ambitious, album-length singer-songwriter statements.'[35] The speed with which the Beatles progressed in artistic experimentation is often recounted with wonder, as *The Mojo Collection* notes with near disbelief that 'the progression from the zesty "yeah, yeah, yeah" of She Loves You to the mesmeric, acid-spiked Tomorrow Never Knows took four Liverpool kids just 33 months.'[36]

Another expression for such rapid evolution and originality is the idea of transcendence, yet another concept that has migrated from the canons of literature and classical music into the reception of rock music. This idea of transcendence, either personal or musical, is readily incorporated into accounts of the albums. *What's Going On* is accordingly described as 'a truly overwhelming and transcendent album, never failing to astonish'.[37] Berkenstadt and Cross identify this quality in Nirvana's music, claiming that '*Nevermind*, like all great rock 'n' roll albums, transcended the individual story of its authors and became the album of a generation.'[38] The notion of individual transcendence is one of the most celebrated aspects of the story of the Beatles; or, as John Lennon put it in a later interview, 'I came out of the fuckin'

---

31   *100 Albums That Changed Music*, Egan, p. 309.

32   *The Mojo Collection*, Irvin and McLear, p. 56.

33   *All Music Guide*, Erlewine with Woodstra and Bogdanov, p. 233.

34   Various Contributors, 'The Hundred Greatest Albums Ever Made', *Mojo*, 21 (August 1995), 50–87 (p. 87).

35   *Rock: The Rough Guide*, Buckley and others, p. 399.

36   *The Mojo Collection*, Irvin and McLear, p. 66.

37   *VH1's 100 Greatest Albums*, Hoye, p. 13.

38   Berkenstadt and Cross, *Nevermind*, p. 143.

sticks to take over the world.'[39] Even individual songs from the albums are attributed with this quality; for instance, Fusilli tells us that '"God Only Knows" is sublime. As in "transcendent" and "awe-inspiring."'[40] Although, as already discussed in Chapter 2, such canonically suggestive words seem to be used relatively casually in descriptions of these albums without too much concern for their deeper implications, their repeated use in reference to the albums has a cumulative effect, and so such concepts are increasingly associated with this music.

Structure – The Beatles as Centre

Canons do not posses a structure as such; they are instead an imaginary collocation of great works and artists, incorporeal, forever changing and nebulous. The nearest approximation to a structure displayed by the canons of literature and classical music is that of one central figure or a small number of central figures, around which other implicitly lesser figures and works orbit in a constantly shifting field. The most central figures in the canons of Western literature and classical music are almost invariably Shakespeare and Beethoven. In rock music a similar centrality and importance can be argued for the Beatles.

At the beginning of the *All-Time Top 1,000 Albums*, Colin Larkin professes that he 'can't really imagine a Top Ten without the Beatles; they really justify my belief in the greatness of pop music'.[41] Similarly, in his introduction to *100 Albums That Changed Rock Music*, Sean Egan claims that 'technically, such was their reach and brilliance ... all eleven proper UK Beatles albums are more influential than any non-Beatles album in this book', but explains the reason that they are not all included in *100 Albums That Changed Music* is that such a monopoly by a single artist (or rather small group of artists, as he also includes Bob Dylan and the Rolling Stones as having produced a disproportionate number of albums that could have been included) would be 'boring'.[42]

Many accounts of the Beatles echo the qualities that Bloom gives Shakespeare (outlined in Chapter 1) as a figure central to the canon. Among these is the idea that while other canonical artists contribute strangeness, Shakespeare's mastery was to reveal the familiar, which is reflected in Greil Marcus's assertion that 'accompanying the shock of novelty so many experienced on first exposure to the Beatles in 1963 or '64 was a shock of recognition, which bespoke the Beatles' connection to the whole history of rock & roll up to that time.'[43] The Beatles are seen to represent the universality and universal appeal associated with canons in general, and to underline this point, *The Rough Guide to Rock* declares that 'they are the ultimate pop group and one of the few bands that transcend the limitations of their art to produce music that is

---

39   John Lennon quoted in Greil Marcus, 'The Beatles', in *The Rolling Stone Illustrated History of Rock & Roll*, ed. by DeCurtis and Henke with George-Warren, pp. 209–22 (p. 220).

40   Fusilli, *Pet Sounds*, p. 99.

41   The introduction to Colin Larkin, *All-Time Top 1,000 Albums*, 3rd edn (London: Virgin, 2000), p. 8.

42   *100 Albums That Changed Music*, Egan, pp. 9–10.

43   Marcus, 'The Beatles', p. 218.

universal'.[44] Like Shakespeare, the Beatles are unique in their combined popularity and complexity. Simon Frith suggests that this complex popularity explains their continued high presence in such charts, as 'they remain too complicatedly a pop and rock group to be pigeonholed'.[45] The music of the Beatles is complex enough to sustain (if not demand) academic analysis. Their combined music and history has sustained a wealth of secondary material, and fresh interpretations of their work continue to be made.

Unlike some canonical figures, the Beatles were of course considered exceptional during their own time. As a result of this they were given a freedom (both financial and artistic) to experiment that was denied to other bands, thus exacerbating their perceived difference. Knowledge of the story of the Beatles is assumed and referred to in accounts of other bands; hence, *The Rough Guide to Rock* refers to a member of the Sex Pistols who was dropped from the band when they were on the cusp of fame as 'the Pete Best character in this story'.[46]

However, this centrality of the Beatles was not always as inevitable as it seems today. Greil Marcus recalls that nearer the time immediately after the Beatles disbanded, it was more fashionable to knock their achievements than it was to valorize their music.[47] Alex Petredis similarly remembers that 'for more than 20 years after their demise, no one saw the Beatles as a brand or appeared to consider their ongoing commercial potential – least of all the Beatles themselves'.[48] However, today the Beatles are unquestionably central to accounts of 1960s rock. They are attributed with a quality that reflects the omnisignificance Kermode suggests in relation to literary works; this is implicitly articulated in the following statement by Greil Marcus: 'The sum of the Beatles was greater than the parts, but the parts were so distinctive and attractive that the group itself could be all things to all people, more or less.'[49] Marcus even continues by suggesting that 'the form of the Beatles contained the forms of rock & roll itself', incorporating elements of

> the Fifties vocal group ... with the flash of a rockabilly band ... with the aggressive and unique personalities of the classic rock stars (Elvis, Little Richard) with the honey this-could-be-you manner of later rock stars (Everly Brothers, Holly, Eddie Cochran) with the endlessly inventive songwriting touch of the Brill Building, and delivered it all with the grace of the Miracles, the physicality of "Louie Louie", and the absurd enthusiasm of Gary "U.S" Bonds.[50]

The Beatles thus become the model rock group; after the Beatles, 'true' rock musicians had to write and perform their own material and display artistic integrity and autonomy.

---

44 *Rock: The Rough Guide*, Buckley and others, p. 65.

45 Simon Frith, 'Our Favourite Rock Records Tend to Go Round and Round', *The Observer*, 6 September 1998. Copyright Guardian News & Media Ltd 1998.

46 See *Rock: The Rough Guide*, Buckley and others, p. 870.

47 Marcus, 'The Beatles', pp. 209–37.

48 Alex Petredis, 'A Little Help From Their Friends', *The Guardian G2*, 16 January 2004, 14–15 (15).

49 Marcus, 'The Beatles', p. 215.

50 Ibid., p. 217.

As Bloom has noted in *The Western Canon*, Shakespeare is a neutral centre as well as a complex one, and he contends that 'part of the secret of Shakespeare's canonical centrality is his disinterestedness; despite all the flailings of New Historicists and other Resenters, Shakespeare is almost as free of ideology as are his heroic wits: Hamlet, Rosalind, Falstaff.'[51] However, the Beatles cannot be considered a biographical blank canvas as Shakespeare is to Bloom. Their every move during the height of their fame has been well documented and published in popular books. Instead, as Marcus suggests, what we are presented with is a remarkably complex centre due to the combination of four distinct personalities that form a whole. As a whole they are arguably neutral, their differences of personality cancelling each other out, and yet they incorporate a nexus of qualities, personalities and influences. Adding to this perceived neutrality was the insistence of their manager, Brian Epstein, that their image, especially towards the beginning of their career, be 'cleaned up'. The unified, 'clean' image of the Beatles is discussed in an interview with John Lennon conducted by *Rolling Stone* magazine editor Jann S. Wenner in 1971. As implied in this interview, the Beatles could not hold as a centre once they themselves began to unravel as a group:

> [Jann S. Wenner:] The Beatles were always talked about – and the Beatles talked about themselves – as being part of the same person.
> [John Lennon:] Well …yes.
> [Jann S. Wenner:] What's happened to those four parts?
> [John Lennon:] They remembered they were four individuals. You see, we believed the Beatles myth, too. We were a band that made it very, very big, that's all.[52]

The Beatles as a centre serve as a point of reference, of familiarity, as catalysts to change and a benchmark of canonic excellence; reference to the band in accounts of other albums is usually either as a point of reference or as a means of validation.

Canonical Periods in Rock Music

While composers and writers are considered to be at their most canonical during a certain period in their career (usually comprising their later more mature works), in rock music certain albums by artists are considered greater (or more canonical) than others. Bloom asks the question 'when is Shakespeare first Shakespeare?';[53] and similarly we see that even the Beatles appear to have a more canonical period. The Beatles' 1965 album *Rubber Soul* is often described as 'the first of their classic albums';[54] together with *Revolver*, *Sgt. Pepper's Lonely Hearts Club Band* and *The Beatles (The White Album)*, it forms the artistic (or canonic) core of the Beatles' music; these are the albums usually cited in lists of greatest albums.

---

51   Harold Bloom, *The Western Canon: The Books and School of the Ages* (London and New York: Harcourt Brace & Company, 1994), p. 56.

52   Jann S. Wenner, 'John Lennon: The Rolling Stone Interview', in *20 Years of Rolling Stone: What a Long, Strange Trip It's Been*, ed. by Jann S. Wenner (New York: Friendly Press, 1987), pp. 101–16 (p. 101).

53   Bloom, *The Western Canon*, p. 46.

54   See, for example, *Rock: The Rough Guide*, Buckley and others, p. 67.

Equally, *Pet Sounds* is indubitably the most canonical of the Beach Boys' albums. Earlier Beach Boys albums are almost perceived as non-canonical counterparts to *Pet Sounds*, which has always been treated differently to its predecessors by the band, their record company and the press.[55] The album is usually associated in histories with the work that followed immediately after, namely the single 'Good Vibrations' and the (long-delayed) album *Smile*, which was not finished at the time as Brian Wilson's drug use increased and his mental health correspondingly deteriorated. Following on from *Pet Sounds*, but apparently taking the techniques employed for the previous albums to their very limits, *Smile* was long regarded in rock history as the 'greatest album never made', with the implicit suggestion that it might have become even more central to histories of rock than *Pet Sounds*, had it been released.[56]

Bob Dylan's music is also separated in histories into distinct phases, from the early folk albums to electrification in the mid-1960s and then later his more oblique works. But it is his albums from the mid-1960s that usually feature in accounts of great albums (especially *Bringing It All Back Home*, *Highway 61 Revisited* and *Blonde on Blonde*). The Velvet Underground's earliest incarnation (when they recorded *The Velvet Underground & Nico*) is usually regarded as their most important; the subsequent changes in the band after their first album (John Cale left immediately, Lou Reed a few albums later) apparently diminished their canonic power.

While the Rolling Stones have been described as the most professional band in rock, still touring 40 years later, their image mostly depends on their young raw energy rooted in the 1960s. *Astral Weeks*, *What's Going On*, *Horses* and to an extent *Nevermind* usually represent their artist's only contribution to lists of 'greatest albums' (although Nirvana's later album *In Utero* and Gaye's *Let Get It On* are also sporadically present in lists of greatest albums). *Never Mind the Bollocks: Here's the Sex Pistols* is the Sex Pistols' only album, but their whole (short-lived) career as a band is both canonic and iconic.

Related to the idea that artists have a canonical period in their career is the idea that rock has a most canonical era, which, based on this sample of ten albums, would unquestionably be the mid to late 1960s (which includes *Highway 61 Revisited*, *Pet Sounds*, *Revolver*, *The Velvet Underground & Nico* and *Astral Weeks*). The 1970s are becoming increasingly important as well, however, as suggested by the presence of *What's Going On*, *Exile on Main St.*, *Horses*, and *Never Mind the Bollocks: Here's the Sex Pistols*. John F. Harris is even more specific in this respect in suggesting that the years 1962–74 comprise rock's 'classic period'.[57] It remains to be seen if such a centre will hold; the increasing acceptance of the 1970s may in time stretch to include the 1980s (at

---

55 See Kingsley Abbott, *The Beach Boys' Pet Sounds: The Greatest Album of the Twentieth Century* (London: Helter Skelter Publishing, 2001), p. 124.

56 In 2004, however, and to the surprise of the world, *Smile* was actually released, reconstructed from the recordings made in the 1960s and performed live by Brian Wilson and a band of young musicians. Although too little time has passed for the full implication of this release to have an impact on polls and histories, it seems likely that its belated release means that it will be regarded as a curiosity, a new relic, rather than a great album in its own right.

57 James F. Harris, *Philosophy at 33 1/3 rpm: Themes of Classic Rock Music* (Chicago and La Salle, IL: Open Court, 1993), back cover.

the expense of certain albums from the 1960s and 1990s). The drift and potential future of the canon is a subject that will be returned to in the final chapter of this book.

Canonically Excluded Identities and the Non-canonical

The ten albums chosen for study are assumed to be a reasonable representation of the favoured albums of rock. Therefore, it is significant that they replicate the same apparent biases evident in the canons of literature and classical music. As a lone female artist in this selection of albums, Patti Smith's presence may be considered one of the 'few token minorities' that Guillory suggests are included in even the most conservative of canons.[58] At Andy Warhol's instigation, German model Nico sang with The Velvet Underground but she was not involved in composition, while their female drummer (Moe Tucker) is an unusual exception to the norm of male drummers. *Pet Sounds* has one prominent female session musician (bassist Carol Kaye). But the vast majority of these albums are written, performed and produced by men. It might even be argued indeed that Smith is accepted as an honorary man, accepted on the terms of the Romantic singer-songwriter by which only men are usually exulted. Writing of *Horses*, Jeff Tamarkin claims that 'this landmark changed the role of women in rock and paved the way for rock without excess'; similarly, in its entry in *100 Albums That Changed Music*, it is suggested that '[in the] long-term, one of *Horses'* greatest contributions was to help change the image of women rock performers in general.'[59] There is some room to doubt such assertions, however, as the albums of subsequent female artists do not exert much of a presence in lists of greatest albums. Although *Horses* was ranked highly in the *Mojo* poll on which the selection of albums for this study was based, her overall position in polls and the amount of secondary material generated by her work is substantially less than for most of the other artists and albums under study.[60] This fact reinforces even more the possibility that her inclusion was as a 'token minority' whose position was replaced in other polls by other equitable minority figures. Furthermore, in defiance of her identity as a female auteur, 'greatest album' polls often recall her male record producer, John Cale, as a significant contributor, thus reducing her perceived autonomy as an artist.

Given that the unfolding suggestion of this book is that rock music has inherited many of its values and hierarchies from the old established canons, it is unsurprising that women do not feature highly, nor that the criteria for selection favour men rather than women. This suggested canon of rock replicates the patterns of identity displayed in the canons of literature and classical music that are currently being questioned in literary criticism and musicology. The tortured (male) geniuses who create 'great albums' are the most important figures in rock music; and these geniuses are all caught up in a web of influences that seldom extends to territory outside this immediate sphere of influence.

With the exception of Marvin Gaye, these canonic artists are also all white Westerners. Although rock is universally acknowledged to have its roots in black

---

58   John Guillory, *Cultural Capital: The Problem of Literary Canon Formation* (Chicago and London: University of Chicago Press), p. 8.

59   *All Music Guide*, Erlewine with Woodstra and Bogdanov, p. 296; *100 Albums that Changed Music*, Egan, p. 244.

60   Although the publication of Philip Shaw's book on *Horses* in 2008 does much to redress the balance.

music (in the blues and the rock and roll of Chuck Berry and Little Richard amongst others), any canon based on albums is inevitably dominated by white artists. Marvin Gaye's *What's Going On* is an exception, but ironically, one of the few prominent representatives of blues music in this proto-canon is the Rolling Stones. This may have more to do with genre classification than tangible racial discrimination, and yet the end result creates apparently the same biases as the established canons of Western literature and classical music; and such biases are quite alarming in what should by now be a democratic field.

If, as is being suggested, rock music is forming a canon based on the idea and ideal of the album, then it must also be forming its own conception of the non-canonical. The non-canonical incorporates those excluded not only by identity but also by genre, in this case the album-as-work (although, as is suggested above, those excluded by identity and genre are often the same people). As discussed in Chapter 2, the idea of the album as a cohesive 'work' has been traced to the mid-1960s, and so a canon based on the idea of the album already eliminates the influential singles of the 1950s.

The non-canonical is inevitably contingent to the canonical, and in the canon of classical music the non-canonical includes not only the immoral and frivolous, but also the non-published, oral or improvised traditions, and the utilitarian, such as pieces for dancing, for children or for entertainment in the salons.[61] Although popular music has long been perceived as a commercial, non-canonical counterpart to classical music, similar hierarchies of value are now found in the reception of rock albums. This ideology is reflected in the following statement made by Frank Zappa, in which the non-canonical is represented by what he describes as 'a commercial pile of shit':

> If you want to come up with a singular, most important trend in this new [rock] music, I think it has to be something like: it is original, composed by the people who perform it, created by them – even if they have to fight the record companies to do it – so that is really a creative action and not a commercial pile of shit thrown together by business people who think they know what John Doe and Mr Jones really want.[62]

Here we find the familiar canonical dislike of the commercial in favour of the autonomous singer-songwriter creating original music for purely artistic reasons.

The difference between the canonical and the non-canonical in the reception of albums is perhaps best illustrated in the contrast between the Beatles and the Monkees. Although superficially similar, the one features greatly in the proto-canon of albums, the other emphatically does not. The Beatles encapsulate the story (or ideology) of a group of friends drawn together to make music for (apparently) the purest reasons of love of writing and performing music. The Monkees by contrast were 'put together' to superficially represent the Beatles for the purposes of a television programme aimed at a young audience. The Monkees were popular, overtly manufactured, obviously

---

61   Marcia J. Citron, *Gender and the Musical Canon* (Cambridge: Cambridge University Press, 1993), p. 203.

62   Frank Zappa, originally quoted in Paul Willis, *Profane Culture* (London, Boston and Henley: Routledge & Kegan Paul, 1978), p. 154, quoted in Peter Wicke, *Rock Music: Culture, Aesthetics and Sociology* (Cambridge and New York: Cambridge University Press, 1987), p. 93.

created with the intention of making a profit, and they were appreciated most by young people who demanded music for dancing. The Monkees did not write their own music, but instead covered songs by a variety of musicians, which therefore excluded them from the possibility of being identified as artist/geniuses.

This preference for the single author/genius is part of the reason that compilation albums very rarely feature in 'Greatest Albums' lists. Compilation albums are put together more obviously for profit-orientated motives, and usually represent the vision of an industry figure with money in mind, rather than an artist with (apparent) self-expression and love of music as a motive.

Conversely, that which is radically different to the main 'canonical' album will likely not be included either. This includes the hyper-experimental, or cross-over genres that do not correspond to the criteria of album-as-work. Much of the music championed by music magazine *The Wire* is inherently non-mainstream, but also non–canonical. Although the music featured is built on the rock tradition in one sense, especially in its ambitions of progress and originality, it tends to avoid anything as obvious as a mainstream canon (evident in the long debate over whether to allow a cover feature on mainstream experimentalists Radiohead).[63] Such music is deliberately on the edges of rock music, and may only be canonized later if it proves to be an 'inescapable influence' like *The Velvet Underground & Nico*.

Once accepted into an established canon, the value of a work is assumed and shortcomings glossed over, putting a retrospectively favourable spin on history. Elements of an album or artist's career perceived as non–canonical are either ignored, explained away or mentioned only to emphasis how far the artist's career progressed. To return to the comparison of the Beatles and the Monkees, the Beatles were groomed early on in a manner similar to the Monkees by manager Brian Epstein. However, it was when they appeared to break free of this conditioning and focused instead on studio-based composition that they started to be taken seriously with *Rubber Soul* and *Revolver*.

In a similar act of glossing-over or disassociation, the Beach Boys' earlier 'miniature-golf', 'fun' and 'sun' tropes are usually ignored in accounts of their later work, or alternatively used as an example of the 'quantum leap' Brian Wilson had achieved with *Pet Sounds*. According to the album's co-lyricist, Tony Asher, 'Brian wanted [*Pet Sounds*] to be an honest album', implying that earlier, albeit successful, records were not a true representation of the artist.[64] *Pet Sounds* is further legitimized through reference to Wilson's discovery of LSD at the time of its creation, implying that it is somehow 'deeper' than previous albums because of this.[65] In a similar feat of glossing-over, Brian Wilson's appeal as the lone genius (combining semi-deafness, burgeoning drug use and incipient mental illness) forms a presence that counteracts the absence of four-fifths of the band. The fact that all the instruments are played by session musicians, rather than the band, is balanced by accounts of their superior musicianship.[66] Naïve lyrics on *Pet Sounds* are described as deliberately innocent

63   Simon Reynolds, 'Walking On Thin Ice', *The Wire,* 209 (July 2001), 26–33.

64   Abbott, *The Beach Boys' Pet Sounds*, p. 43.

65   Various Contributors, 'The Hundred Greatest Albums Ever Made', *Mojo*, 21 (August 1995), 87.

66   Abbott, *The Beach Boys' Pet Sounds*, p. 64.

and optimistic, and the fact that Brian Wilson did not write the lyrics is cloaked by cushioning accounts of the close and intense collaboration he shared with lyricist Tony Asher. According to Fusilli, 'Brian was in service of the song and the sound, and he willingly cooperated with musicians and lyricists who could help articulate his artistic vision', which is an interpretation that allows Wilson's perceived autonomy of vision to remain intact.[67]

Having been accepted into the canon, small 'non-canonical' aberrations can be explained away, almost to the point of illogicality. However, in order to achieve this protected, insulated position within the canon, a work must first survive the 'test of time' and be repeatedly valued by successive generations of critics and artists. It is this idea of enduring value that will become the focus of the rest of the chapter.

The Test of Time

No work can be considered truly canonical until it has withstood the test of time. The canon of classical music spans some four hundred years and the literary canon more than two thousand. However, if the albums of the 1960s are the earliest canonical works in rock, then the test of time has had less than fifty years to operate; yet longevity is still highly valued in the reception of these albums. The mechanisms by which the ten albums featured in this book have ascended to being regarded as 'great' albums are reflected in Colin Larkin's description of *Astral Weeks* in the *All-Time Top 1,000 Albums*: 'Quoted, recommended and worshipped by the critics for over 30 years, this underground masterpiece has now become part of the establishment.'[68] The question of the test of time and the role of canonizers in cultivating an aura of greatness around these albums will therefore now be examined in more detail.

Reproducibility and the Creation of Secondary Material

Canonical works must be able to physically survive through time, and must therefore either be physically durable or set in a form that is easily and faithfully reproducible. Any canon of albums would inherently be a canon of recordings; and although the original vinyl recordings of these albums remain, these albums have also been re-released as cassette, CD and now audio DVD and mp3 files, thus ensuring their longevity and appeal to new audiences.

However, it is not only the albums themselves that are reproduced. Works cannot withstand the test of time and become canonical unless they are culturally reproduced, and a body of secondary material is built up around them to support their position of value. These albums are now treated as special, different to other albums even by the same artist, and this is usually reflected in the way that they are marketed. Some albums have been treated and marketed as special from the time of their first release. *What's Going On* was first played on radio with a certain amount of ceremony; one DJ recalls telling his audience that he was

---

67   Fusilli, *Pet Sounds*, p. 22.
68   Larkin, *All-Time Top 1,000 Albums*, 3rd edn, p. 41.

about to play a major artist who's going his own way, and that this album was going to revolutionise black music like The Beatles had done for rock with *Sgt Pepper*. Then we played the album straight through, with only a break to change sides, and I didn't receive a single negative call ... It was unique new music ... When we found out that it was an act of rebellion against the Motown machine, that appealed to us too.[69]

Indeed, in this instance, comparisons with *Sgt. Pepper* seem to have been subliminally manufactured by the record label. According to Ben Edmonds:

The first time you picked up *What's Going On* you knew you were holding a very different kind of Motown album. For a start, the cover was gorgeous ...
    Everything about the package echoed the mature intent of the music. It was a gatefold cover that opened up like a book, unheard of for a single Motown album. If you were to take The Beatles' *Sgt Pepper* cover, open its gatefold and lie it flat front cover up, it matches the inner sleeve of Marvin's gatefold exactly.[70]

Such comparisons retrospectively help to assemble a common bond between the two albums as part of a larger canon of rock music; at the time such comparisons would still have served to mark the album out as different from other Motown albums.

More recently these albums have been treated as special through drawing attention to their position of importance in polls of 'greatest albums'. *Pet Sounds*, for instance, was re-released as a CD carrying a sticker proclaiming its position in these polls ('#3 VH-1 Top 100 Rock Albums, One of Rolling Stone's Essential 200 Albums, Top 10 in Musician Magazine's "Landmark Albums"'). *Pet Sounds* was also reproduced as a new stereo version in 1990, and then in the extravagant and comprehensive *Pet Sounds Sessions* box set in 1996 (similar to the *Anthology* series of the Beatles, but focusing on just one album), which is intended, according to the accompanying book, to be an 'exhaustive historical document ... for musicologists, musicians and just plain music lovers' and includes hours of out-takes from the studio, alternative versions and interviews with all manner of variously interested people.[71]

Similar reissues include the Beach Boys' archival box set *Good Vibrations: Thirty Years of the Beach Boys*, Bob Dylan's *The Bootleg Series Vols 1–3*, the Velvet Underground's *Peel Slowly and See: The Velvet Underground Box Set* and Marvin Gaye's *The Master* compilation.[72] Although such lavish releases will support the position of authority of the canonic albums themselves, they are arguably only of real interest to people who already believe in the value of the album. It is the reissue of the original work that is most important to canonical mechanisms, and the periodic reissue of the ten albums in question seems assured, at least for now, allowing new audiences to discover the music, and the original audience to update to high-quality CD.

---

69   Radio presenter Dan Carlisle quoted in Ben Edmonds, *What's Going On?: Marvin Gaye and the Last Days of Motown Soul* (Edinburgh: Canongate, 2002), p. 226.

70   Ibid., pp. 199–203.

71   Liner notes by David Leaf in: The Beach Boys, *The Pet Sounds Sessions*, Box Set. Capitol Records. 7243 8 37662 2 2. 1996, p. 5.

72   See *The Mojo Collection*, Irvin and McLear, p. 849.

The Beatles, as has been pointed out in Chapter 2, have been the source of an extensive number of reissues and various related paraphernalia, which, along with books and articles on their life and music, form a nexus of secondary material associated with their work. Alex Petredis suggests that the success of Beatles reissues has precipitated a 'huge "heritage rock" market of CD reissues and classic rock magazines'.[73] This has resulted in the re-release of some obscure albums, but it is unlikely that many of these re-releases will subsequently figure prominently in the lists of 'great albums'. Given that histories of rock music have focused on a few individuals more than others, it is still hard to enter a canon (or a list of 'greatest albums') retrospectively despite the relatively contemporary nature of the field. The people interested in these obscure reissued albums tend to be those well versed in the 'canonical' albums, with an interest so deep that knowledge of the obscure is necessary as a form of cultural capital. Often, however, those albums selected for reissue will support the main narrative thread, and serve to contextualize the recognized 'greatest' albums and bands.

Another form of secondary material has surfaced in the last few years in the form of reissued magazine articles and Billboard charts, most noticeably the *NME Originals* series. These include collections of reprinted original *NME* articles and reviews of a certain band or decade, and include (of 25 so far), *The Beatles: The Complete Story*; *The Beatles: The Solo Years*; *Lennon: Beatles and Beyond*; *Bob Dylan*; *Bob Dylan and the Folk Rock Boom 1964–1974*; *The Rolling Stones: The Wild Ones*; *Punk*; *Nirvana: Saviours of Rock*; *Kurt Cobain*; and *The Sixties: Swinging London*.

Mojo Limited Editions and *Q* Special Editions (both published by EMAP) follow along similar lines, with in-depth articles and glossy photographs, and thus far include a Beatles 'trilogy' (*Mojo Beatles: 1,000 Days of Revolution*; *The Beatles: Beatlemania*; and *The Beatles: Classic, Rare & Unseen*) as well as *Mojo Lennon*; *Mojo 1000 CD Buyers Guide*; *The Rolling Stones: Classic, Rare & Unseen*, *The 150 Greatest Rock Lists Ever*; *Q 50 Years of Rock 'N' Roll: 1954–2004* (in three parts); *The 100 Best Record Covers of All Time*; *Icons: The Greatest Music Stars of All Time*; *Never Mind The Jubilee, Here's the True Story of Punk!*; *Maximum Bob* [Dylan]; *Dylan: Visions, Portraits and Back Pages*; and *Nirvana & the Story of Grunge*. Such special issues create the expectation of knowledge of these central figures, as well as reinforcing their importance to the narratives underpinning the respective magazines.

Longevity, Perpetual Modernity and the State of Timelessness

It is a little absurd to suggest that these albums have survived the test of time from this vantage point of only a few decades later. However, Frank Kermode's suggestion that the test of time results in works achieving 'perpetual value' and 'perpetual modernity' (p. 9) is echoed in the reception of these albums. Joe Harvard anticipates that this perpetual relevance will apply to *The Velvet Underground & Nico*, quoting the words of the album's producer, spoken 35 years after the release of the album:

---

73   Alex Petredis, 'A Little Help From Their Friends', 14.

All great art looks like it was made this morning ... whatever it is that survives that's great was modern at the time it was made, and the modernity of it still sits there on the wall of the museum 100 or 200 years later. As you listen to the record today it still sounds modern in that sense of the word.[74]

According to Harvard, 'The Black Angel's Death Song' has 'lost none of its power to surprise over the past thirty-five years', and he ends his book on the album with the claim that *The Velvet Underground & Nico* 'is a truly great record, one that would remain vital and powerful, beautiful yet awe-inspiring long beyond the life of the band itself'.[75] Some disagreement seems to arise over whether it was ahead of its time or rather time-less; indeed David Fricke seems to confuse the issue even further by suggesting that it was both timeless and prophetic:

But the Velvets were not, as rock historians usually claim, ahead of their time. Their ambitions were, in fact, timeless: to celebrate the *art* in pop without eclipsing the *heart* of rock & roll. And the results were utterly contemporary and, even then, brutally relevant ... There is no denying the ring of dark prophecy that still resonates through these records.[76]

Similarly interchangeable claims of longevity, prescience and timelessness are often made for all of the ten albums. For instance, *Pet Sounds* has been described by Charles L. Granata as 'ageless', while David Leaf declares that 'one of the remarkable things about *Pet Sounds* is that, for the most part, the music on the album could have been composed in the 1860s as opposed to the 1960s, and it would still have a timeless feel to it.'[77]

Exile on Main St. is described as 'the kind of record that goes beyond the songs themselves to create a monolithic sense of atmosphere. It conveys a sense of time and place and spirit, yet it is timeless'.[78] *What's Going On* is described as 'an album that's forever new, a continuing message to the human family'.[79] Ben Edmonds' claims for the album grow throughout his book, until in the last chapter he declares that:

[*What's Going On*] is an album that will be listened to for as long as there is music. Some records the future will listen to and marvel at how richly they captured their moment in time. This is what they will hear first in Marvin's masterpiece, but then, like so many before them, they will hear more, and more again. They will hear the most a man – and music – can be.[80]

It almost does not matter if his claims turn out to be true. For the sake of the album in the here and now, such claims surrounding the work ensure that there will be interest

74   Harvard, *The Velvet Underground & Nico*, pp. 19–20.
75   Ibid., pp. 129 & 147.
76   Fricke, 'The Velvet Underground', p. 351.
77   Granata, *I Just Wasn't Made for These Times*, pp. 13 & 236.
78   Bill Janovitz, *Exile on Main St.* (New York and London: Continuum, 2005), pp. 8–9. Excerpts from *Exile on Main St.* by Bill Janovitz © 2005, reprinted by permission of the publisher, The Continuum International Publishing Group.
79   Comments of the Radio Broadcaster 'The Electrifying Mojo' quoted in Edmonds, *What's Going On?*, p. 227.
80   Ibid., p. 274.

in *What's Going On*. Such grand claims demand that the readers seek out the album in order to see if they can hear the greatness that Edmonds perceives in the work.

Accounts of Patti Smith's music suggest that it anticipated the future: 'Smith's splicing together of her own "*Horses*" to the standard "Land Of 1000 Dances" simultaneously declared pop history and its future.'[81] This idea of past and future encapsulated in one album is repeated in drummer Jim Keltner's description of *Nevermind* (quoted in Berkenstadt and Cross) that avows it to have been '"as good as anything ever produced in rock 'n' roll. It was talking to me. I'd finally heard a new band speaking to me from the past, present, and future." ... *Nevermind* brought music a step forward while at the same time reminding listeners of the past.'[82] Timelessness is also a quality that Colin Larkin identifies in *Never Mind the Bollocks: Here's the Sex Pistols* when he says that the album 'will stay as a classic because it will not date ... This pivotal record has not mellowed with age, thankfully.'[83]

Pet Sounds represented 1966 in an *NME* list of 'albums that captured the moment'.[84] Yet most of the songs on *Pet Sounds* are love songs and have no overt contemporary references, and it is mainly only biographic details that fix the album to the mid-1960s. Similarly, *What's Going On* is described as 'not just a remarkable, beautiful, passionate record: it represents one of those rare watershed moments where a work of art both catches the pulse of the times, and in doing so changes those times'.[85] The less a work is fixed to any particular time through lyric content or musical style, the greater its chances are of achieving permanent relevance or timelessness. Over time, canonical works have their differences and contexts erased, to be replaced by bonds of kinship with other canonic works, and their identity within the canon becomes more important than other non-canonical contexts.

Prescience and timelessness in the reception of rock music complement the (canonical) belief that it is only with hindsight that we can fully appreciate a work. Joe Harvard argues from this perspective when he says that contemporary critics are unable to judge objects of lasting value; he uses the words of Raymond Chandler to explain the fate of The Velvet Underground: '"The average critic never recognizes an achievement when it happens. He explains it after it has become respectable." ... [However] years later critics would fall over themselves to dissect and discuss it.'[86] It is through application of the wisdom of hindsight that *The Velvet Underground & Nico* has gained a position of importance in the evolution of rock, and *Revolver* has been reappraised as a superior album to *Sgt. Pepper* in numerous polls for its subsequent influence and (relatively) understated progressiveness.

Just as new meanings are discovered or read into canonical works of literature, Colin Larkin believes that some meanings in Bob Dylan's *Highway 61 Revisited* can

---

81   Larkin, *All-Time Top 1,000 Albums*, 3rd edn, p. 123.

82   Session drummer Jim Keltner quoted in Berkenstadt and Cross, *Nevermind*, p. 136.

83   Larkin, *All-Time Top 1,000 Albums*, 3rd edn, p. 48.

84   Various Contributors, 'Set Adrift on Memory Discs', 42.

85   *100 Albums That Changed Music*, Egan, p. 185.

86   Harvard, *The Velvet Underground & Nico*, p. 5, beginning with a quote taken from Raymond Chandler, *The Midnight Raymond Chandler*, (Boston, MA: Houghton Mifflin Co., 1971), p. 2.

only now be fully understood, claiming that 'there are lyrics of a generation still to
be found on this album'.[87] There is a comfort in appealing to a higher judge in this
context, in stating that contemporary audiences are in no position to properly assess
contemporary art, and demanding that history be allowed to decide the contents of
the canon, and yet this ignores the obvious fact that history is made by people who
(for the most part) replicate the judgements of previous generations.

Jim Fusilli also feel contemporary audiences are ill-qualified to judge the albums
even four decades later. Despite this, Fusilli still feels confident enough to assert that:

> *Pet Sounds* is the finest album of the rock era, and perhaps one of fewer than a dozen
> that will be valued for its depth of expression and musical sophistication long after we
> are gone. In the present, it is very difficult to have a rational conversation about rock
> music because the dialogue is rarely about music. Whether the group is popular, whether
> the genre is hip, whether the record is selling, whether the accompanying video is cool
> – all these conceits and more take precedent in a listener's mind over the quality and
> complexity of the music.[88]

In reality what we are really unable to judge is what audiences of the future will
demand of its art works. Music may change out of recognition in years to come and
all rock music could become alien to the ear; alternatively different values or genres
might usurp this nascent canon of albums. This seems for the moment unlikely,
however, and discussion of the possible future of a canon in rock music will form
the focus of the latter part of this book.

Along with a preference for the wisdom of hindsight in canons comes respect
for the ancient over the new. In the reception of rock music this is reflected in the
predominance of albums from the late 1960s and early 1970s in 'greatest albums'
lists. As a curious if distorted reflection of Charles Altieri's concept that 'canons
play the role of institutionalizing idealisation', and Bloom's assertion that the canon
is now a place nostalgia, the 1960s are often idealized as a decade of freedom, love,
experimentation, excitement, creativity and change in the West: people were 'turned
on' to new drugs, sexual freedom, liberalism and idealism.[89] In the late 1960s and
early 1970s the idea of the album was also at its most potent and fresh, before the
later excesses and embarrassments of progressive rock.

The idealization of both the 1960s and the album-as-work is evident in *Q*
magazine's justification for placing *Revolver* at the head of its '100 Greatest British
Albums Ever', (published in the year 2000): 'If Sgt Pepper was the ultimate 1967
album, then Revolver could only have been made in 1966, and by a British band.
And if the great thing about the 1960s was that they were, well, so '60s, then 1966

---

87   Larkin, *All-Time Top 1,000 Albums*, 3rd edn, p. 46.

88   Fusilli, *Pet Sounds*, p. 119. He continues by saying, 'I mean, I know a woman who
thinks Neil Young's *After the Gold Rush* is a great record because of the patches on Young's
ass in a photo on the album jacket.'

89   Charles Altieri, 'An Idea and Ideal of a Literary Canon', in *Canons*, ed. by Robert
von Hallberg (Chicago and London: Chicago University Press, 1984), pp. 41–64 (p. 52).

was the most '60s of years.'[90] The 1960s are now regarded as the 'ancient music' of rock, sufficiently in the past to be viewed with objectivity, and for individual works to become models of achievement within a history of rock. And yet many of the artists from the 1960s are still alive, and many of the albums' critics experienced them first-hand when they were first released. In such a situation the canonical figures themselves can expect to have some influence or input into their own canonization.

Canonizing

In his article 'The Making of the Modernist Canon', which was included in Robert von Hallberg's *Canons* (published in 1984), the literary critic Hugh Kenner stated that our age has been particularly canon-minded, and that current (pre-) canonical figures in the various arts have canonized themselves through reference to each other, imitation of past masters and explicit homage.[91] It is understandable, given the celebrity-led nature of the media today, that this is especially true of rock music. Sporadic references, connections, claims of influence and tributes are found everywhere in the reception of rock that link these 'canonical' artists together. The bonds are especially strong between the artists of the late 1960s, and they canonize each other through constant self-referencing and mutual praise. For instance, Alan Light states that 'John Lennon said that before hearing Dylan it never occurred to him that songs could be so personal and emotionally direct.'[92] Dylan in turn claims to have recognized the artistic importance of the Beatles long before it was acceptable to take them seriously:

> They were doing things nobody was doing. Their chords were outrageous, just outrageous, and their harmonies made it all valid ... But I kept it to myself that I really dug them. Everybody else thought they were for the teenyboppers, that they were gonna pass right away. But it was obvious to me that they had staying power. I knew they were pointing the direction where music had to go ... in my head, the Beatles were *it*.[93]

The interest of British artists in the Beach Boys helped cement their reputation in the 1960s. Mick Jagger is reported to have enthused to British DJs about the song 'I Get Around' long before it was well known and John Lennon and Paul McCartney were two of the first to be allowed to hear *Pet Sounds*: 'They wanted to hear the album and they did, several times. "They were speechless", said Bruce, who witnessed them put aside their carefree public persona to study Brian's music.'[94]

Kingsley Abbott makes a point of noting that, amongst others, Paul McCartney, George Martin, Bob Dylan, Elton John and R.E.M. have all cited the importance of

---

90   David Quantick, '*Revolver*', in Various Contributors, 'The 100 Greatest British Albums Ever' *Q*, 165 (June 2000), 59–93 (92–3).

91   Hugh Kenner, 'The Making of the Modernist Canon', in *Canons*, ed. by Robert von Hallberg (Chicago and London: University of Chicago Press, 1984), pp. 363–75 (p. 374).

92   Light, 'Bob Dylan', p. 299.

93   Bob Dylan speaking in 1971, quoted in Marcus, 'The Beatles', p. 212.

94   Fusilli, *Pet Sounds*, p. 111.

Pet Sounds to their music.[95] McCartney has been an especially important advocate of the album, given the centrality of the Beatles in the reception of rock. He recalls that '*Pet Sounds* blew me out the water ... no one is educated musically 'til they've heard that album ... a total, classic record that is unbeatable in many ways.'[96] By describing *Pet Sounds* in these terms, it could be argued that McCartney is here endorsing a canonic approach to rock albums (evinced in his reference to musical 'education' and the idea of a 'classic') and thereby bolstering his own position as an important figure in this tradition. Other respected singer-songwriters have also given tribute, including Elvis Costello's (again canonically redolent) comment that:

> *Pet Sounds* is an unbelievable record. It's like classical music. Wonderful compositions, beautiful singing. I think the compositions stand up to any kind of interpretation. I've heard "Put Your Head On My Shoulder" played on the cello and it sounds like a piece of music that's been with us for hundreds and hundreds of years. It sounds like it's always been there. And I think maybe in a hundred years' time people will be playing their songs on the piano trying to work out where they came from.[97]

Musicians can also canonize each other (or at least show a mark of respect) through cover versions. On the album *Beach Boys Party* (1965) the group sing two songs by the Beatles and one by Bob Dylan. In March 2001 there was even an 'All Star Tribute to Brian Wilson' concert, including performances of various Beach Boys songs by other artists (including Paul Simon, Elton John and Billy Joel), as well as a complete performance by of *Pet Sounds* by Brian Wilson himself that occupied the whole of the second half. This unsurprisingly sparked renewed interest not only in *Pet Sounds* but also the abandoned album *Smile*.[98]

It could be argued that Nirvana knowingly tried to canonize their album by naming it *Nevermind* (after the seminal *Never Mind the Bollocks: Here's the Sex Pistols*). Perhaps more surprising, however, are the frequent connections made in accounts of the album between Nirvana and the Beatles, as they were, on the surface at least, two very different bands. Evidently, these associations with the music of the Beatles are partly the result of Nirvana's own admiration for the band: 'Cobain was a pop lover at heart – and a Beatlemaniac: *Nevermind* co-producer Butch Vig remembers Cobain play John Lennon's "Julia" at sessions.'[99] Kurt Cobain's 'Something in the Way' appears to have been written as a twist on the words of George Harrison's 'Something' and Cobain is described as having a 'gut-wrenching roar which would later see Cobain compared with John Lennon as both a visionary and a voice'; further comparisons were inevitable once Cobain too met with an early death.[100] This frequent allusion to the Beatles carries the strong suggestion of canonizing on

95 Abbott, *The Beach Boys' Pet Sounds*, p. 124 and liner notes Leaf, *The Pet Sounds Sessions*, p. 10.

96 Leaf, *The Pet Sounds Sessions*, pp. 123–5.

97 Elvis Costello quoted in *VH1's 100 Greatest Albums*, Hoye, p. 7.

98 See Abbott, *The Beach Boys' Pet Sounds*, pp. 181–2.

99 Various Contributors, 'The 500 Greatest Albums of All Time', in *Rolling Stone*, 11 December 2003, 96.

100 *The Mojo Collection*, Irvin and McLear, p. 558.

the part of the authors, at least to the extent that they wish to situate Nirvana in the same tradition as the Beatles, albeit thirty years down the line.

The Velvet Underground & Nico is unusual in that it apparently stands outside this immediate circle of influence and canonizing relating to the Beatles, Beach Boys and Bob Dylan. Their canonizers tend to be those who followed them rather than their contemporaries. For instance, 'Bowie praised the Velvet Underground to anyone who'd listen ... freely admitting his debt to them and resuscitating Reed's flagging career, but by then it was too late for the Velvets.'[101] The more an album is praised by a respected artist (or in this context, potential canonizer), the more value is attributed to it. If in turn an album is already established as 'great', artists (or canonizers) will gain respect for having recognized its importance.

The superiority of composer over critic in the canon of classical music is acknowledged to a degree in the reception of rock. At times rock artists will make statements about their own music that seem implicitly canonical and these statements in turn are recorded and then culturally reproduced. Brian Wilson is often reported as saying of *Pet Sounds* (in a statement both far- and short-sighted), 'I wanted to make an album that would stand up in ten years.'[102] In another account, Wilson is said to have 'told [his then wife] Marilyn he was going to make the greatest rock album ever. That's a pretty good example of self-imposed pressure.'[103] Such statements of ambition are attached to the work that resulted, although the value judgements of others are needed to confirm the success of the album.

John Lennon also did not shy away from self-aggrandizement in interviews. Jann S. Wenner discussed John Lennon's self-perceived greatness with him in his (possibly tongue-in-cheek) *Rolling Stone* interview of 1971:

> [Jann S. Wenner:] When did you realise that what you were doing transcended ...
> [John Lennon:] People like me are aware of their so-called genius at ten, eight, nine. I always wondered, why has no one discovered me? ... I got fuckin' lost being in high school. I used to say to me auntie, 'You throw my fuckin' poetry out and you'll regret it when I'm famous'. And she threw the bastard stuff out.
> [Wenner:] Do you think you're a genius?
> [Lennon:] Yes, if there is such a thing, I am one.[104]

They go on to discuss his relationship with the Rolling Stones, and then move on to Bob Dylan. In answer to Wenner's question of whether Lennon saw Dylan as 'great', Lennon replied:

> [Lennon:] No, I see him as another poet, or as competition. You read my books that were written before I heard of Dylan or read Dylan or anybody, it's the same. I didn't come after Elvis and Dylan, I've been around always.

---

101 Harvard, *The Velvet Underground & Nico*, p. 14.

102 Various Contributors, 'The Hundred Greatest Albums Ever Made', *Mojo*, 21 (August 1995), 87.

103 Fusilli, *Pet Sounds*, p. 94.

104 John Lennon speaking in 1971, quoted in Wenner, 'John Lennon: The Rolling Stone Interview', p. 101. By contrast, Brian Wilson has said, 'I'm not a genius. I'm just a hard-working guy,' quoted in Fusilli, *Pet Sounds*, p. 18.

Whether or not Lennon was (at least partly) being whimsical by making such statements cannot be gleaned unless the author tells us. Given this, such statements survive as they are, and whatever their original intention (whether ironic or not), stand as testament to the artists' perceived position in rock history.

Canonizing statements are also found in unexpected places and the notes that accompany the albums often include glowing reviews, recommendations from critics or fellow rock artists. The notes for the album *The Velvet Underground & Nico* feature contemporary critics' comments on the live performances of the band, such as the comment from the *Village Voice* that 'The Velvet Underground performances at the Dom during the month of April provided the most violent, loudest and most dynamic exploration platform for this new art', or this pronouncement from the *Los Angeles Times* that 'not since the Titanic ran into that iceberg has there been such a collision as when Andy Warhol's Exploding Plastic Inevitable burst upon the audiences at The Trip Tuesday'.[105] Other sleeve notes include appraisals of the album that have been written since the album's original release to recognize its subsequent position of importance in rock history. *What's Going On*'s CD inlay now contains a short account of the album by Ben Edmonds, noting its influence on successive albums and enduring appeal.[106]

Equally, the words that Bob Dylan wrote for inclusion on the sleeve of *Highway 61 Revisited* themselves obliquely suggest that his album has a place in a future canon, referencing various figures of literature and music and creating a jumble of past, present and future: 'you are right john cohen – quazimodo was right – Mozart was right ....'[107] Patti Smith's album notes also invoke a sense of history, timelessness and death: 'only history (gentle rocking mona lisa) seals...only histoire is responsible for the ultimate canonizing...as for me I am truly totally ready to go...'[108] Such suggestions, seemingly incidental though they might be, all contribute to the sense of an album's historical identity and add to its potential to be conceived as a discrete entity in a canon of albums.

It has become increasingly evident over the course of the last two chapters that the reception of rock music uses canonical values to promote its 'greatest albums' and the artists themselves are involved in their own canonization. However, other values contingent to rock music – but considered non-canonical in the context of the canons of Western literature and classical music – are also recorded in the reception of rock music and must be considered in any potential canon of albums. The following chapter will therefore address these 'non-canonical' criteria that are central or 'canonical' to rock music.

---

105 The Velvet Underground , *The Velvet Underground & Nico*. Verve. 5312502. 1967.
106 Marvin Gaye, *What's Going On*. Tamla Motown, 5308832. 1971.
107 Bob Dylan, *Highway 61 Revisited*. CBS. 4609532. 1965. [The ellipses form part of the original text.]
108 Words by Patti Smith included in album sleeve of Patti Smith, *Horses*. Arista. 07822188272. 1975. [The ellipses form part of the original text.]

Chapter 4

The Canonical Values of Rock

At the beginning of his book on *Exile on Main St.*, Bill Janovitz describes the album as follows:

> *Exile* is not the most pristine recording … "Soupy" and "swampy" are two well-used adjectives one sees when reading about the album … It is not a collection of virtuoso performances. Though there are some continuous themes, it is not, as far as I can tell, a concept record. Aside from, or even in spite of, its length, *Exile* does not seem to reflect any extraordinary grandiose ambition to transcend rock and *take it to another level, man*. On the contrary, it seems to revel in self-imposed limitations. In fact, it sometimes sounds ancient. Other times, it sounds completely current and modern. It sounds, at various points, underground and a little experimental, and at others, classic, and even nostalgic.[1]

However, he goes on to say that:

> *Exile* is exactly what rock & roll should sound like: a bunch of musicians playing a bunch of great songs in a room together, playing off each other; musical communion, sounds bleeding into each other, snare drum rattling away even while not being hit, amps humming, bottles falling, feet shuffling, ghostly voices mumbling on- and off-mike, whoops of excitement, shouts of encouragements, performances without a net, masks off, urgency. It is the kind of record that goes beyond the songs themselves to create a monolithic sense of atmosphere. It conveys a sense of time and place and spirit, yet is timeless. Its influence is still heard today.[2]

It is quite clear from these comments that canonical values of Western literature and classical music have been absorbed into the reception of rock music, along with other, 'non-canonical', values specific to rock.

Janovitz here invokes various canonical concepts to prove the value of the album, including suspicion of virtuosity, the state of perpetual modernity, 'classics', timelessness and nostalgia, a work that is more than the sum of its component songs, and the ruling narrative of influence. However, these traditional canonical terms mingle with other values peculiar to rock in his assessment of the album. Accordingly, *Exile on Main St.* is also valued for its sound, the manner in which it was produced, the performance of the band on the album, their implied lack of professionalism, apparent lack of 'artistic' ambition (as embodied in the concept album) and the tangible urgency portrayed during its course. Janovitz's statement

---

1   Bill Janovitz, *Exile on Main St.* (New York and London: Continuum, 2005), pp. 7–8. Excerpts from *Exile on Main St.* by Bill Janovitz © 2005, reprinted by permission of the publisher, The Continuum International Publishing Group.

2   Ibid., pp. 8–9.

suggests an awareness of canonicity (even though he makes no mention of the word) since he uses 'canonical' elements to justify the value of the album; but at the same time he rejects other canonical values such as those of ambition, transcendence and overt experimentation in his description of greatness in rock.

The first three chapters of this book have explored the hallmarks of the canons of Western literature and classical music and demonstrated ways in which they are reflected in the popular reception of rock music. The second half of the book will now ask the underlying question of whether we can conclude from this that there is indeed a canon in rock, and what this reveals about the nature of canons today. This chapter will therefore deal with the possibility suggested above of other values belonging to a rock canon that are contingent to rock music and cannot be described by the terms of the canons of literature and classical music; in other words the ideology of rock. Chapter 5 will then turn to the question of authority in canonizing this music, and discuss academic approaches to the idea of a canon of rock albums. Finally, Chapter 6 will draw on all the previous material to question whether a true canon of rock music is implicated in its reception, and what wider consequences for the concept of the canon can be surmised from these findings.

The account of the albums given in Chapters 2 and 3 only seeks to locate in their reception the elements of canonicity suggested by the canons of literature and classical music (outlined in Chapter 1). On the whole, the constructs and values of the high canons are echoed quite closely in the reception of these albums. However, this creates an incomplete view of the albums. As Anita Silvers has suggested, value originates from within canonical works, rather than being a prescribed set of aesthetic criteria; therefore, some values must inherently belong to the field of rock music albums.[3] Rock music is not interchangeable with classical music any more than the presence of canonical elements in the writings on these albums proves conclusively that there is an established canon of rock albums.

There are inherent tensions involved in applying the ruling logic of a high art onto a popular field. This explains in part the ambivalence sometimes shown towards the notion of a rock canon. Therefore, the current chapter will draw attention to other qualities perceived and valued in the ten albums in question that are not central concerns to the canons of literature and classical music. These elements are intrinsic to the reception of some or all of the ten albums. As a general rule, those albums that best correspond with traditional canonical ideals (for example *Pet Sounds*) have fewer residual traits directly attributable to 'rock'. Those albums that display traits more readily associated with rock music than high art canons (for example *Never Mind the Bollocks: Here's the Sex Pistols*) reveal those qualities that may be traditionally non-canonical but are vital components of the ideology of rock music. These are the 'canonical' values of rock.

---

3   Anita Silvers, 'The Canon in Aesthetics', in *The Encyclopaedia of Aesthetics*, ed. by Michael Kelly (Oxford: Oxford University Press, 1998), I, pp. 334–8 (p. 338).

Sound and Recording

Music Production and the Record

Rock music has been, from the beginning, a recorded medium. Consequently, the role of record producer is often one of high rank, and the quality of recording is included in calculations of the value of the album. As a recorded medium, any necessity for musical notation is diminished, and so the manipulation of sound becomes more important than its presentation and preservation in written form. Peter Wicke suggests that as studio recording techniques became increasingly sophisticated, 'The focus of musical performance gradually shifted from the written parameters, pitch, dynamics and formal development, from the melodic and harmonic aspects, to the reproducible details of the expression of sound. Thus, sound became the central aesthetic category of rock music.'[4]

While the idea of a fixed and definitive recording limits the 'canonical' potential of different interpretations, it does help the album to become a discrete object that can be added to others to form a canon. As a result of this, canonical criteria of exemplary craft and originality are often transferred in rock music from compositional technique to craftsmanship and innovation in the studio. As Wicke notes, technology has become an instrument itself, which the musicians have come to manipulate with increasing sophistication.[5] This is reflected in accounts of the Rolling Stones' method of recording, such as this from *The Rough Guide to Rock*: 'By fortuitous mistakes and clever experimentation, they have pioneered the use of the studio as a musical instrument.'[6]

Sometimes in accounts of the albums the recording of each individual song is described in minute detail of production, in the kind of depth that will most probably go beyond the technological knowledge of the casual reader. Such accounts feature prominently in Bill Janovitz's account of *Exile on Main St.* For instance, he suggests that 'the ideal for many engineers is to push up a fader on a mixing console and hear only that intended instrument'; however, on this album, 'in addition to hearing Mick Jagger's intended main lead vocal … you can also almost always hear "ghost" tracks of his guide vocal underneath the mix.'[7] Similarly, in *100 Albums That Changed Music* the description of *Nevermind* gives detail of how producer Butch Vig achieved the distinctive drum sound on the album (apparently through application of a 'drum tunnel').[8]

The kind of attention to detail that might be expected in the study of the scores of Beethoven is evident in accounts of the recording of these albums. For the recording of 'Smells Like Teen Spirit' on *Nevermind*, for example, we are told that:

---

4   Peter Wicke, *Rock Music: Culture, Aesthetics and Sociology* (Cambridge and New York: Cambridge University Press, 1987), p. 13. Musicologists and non-academics are alike in finding problems notating this music for the purposes of analysis or commercial sheet music.

5   Ibid., p. 22.

6   *Rock: The Rough Guide*, ed. by Buckley and others, 2nd edn (London: Rough Guides Ltd, 1999), p. 831. Reproduced by permission of Penguin Books Ltd.

7   Janovitz, *Exile on Main St.*, p. 42.

8   *100 Albums That Changed Music: and 500 Songs You Need to Hear*, ed. by Sean Egan (London: Robinson, 2006), p. 310.

The best parts of all three takes were combined to create a composite vocal master which was then placed on to track 15. Vig then asked Kurt to isolate his vocal part, "hello, hello, hello, how low", for dropping in. This allowed Kurt to get tight on the mike and perfect the phrasing. The overdubbed "hello" bridge was placed onto tracks 21 and 22.[9]

Technical innovation and exemplary studio 'craft' are often cited with reference to *Pet Sounds*. Attention is drawn to its complex, layered arrangements, innovative use of 'primitive' recording equipment and Brian Wilson's 'mastery' of the studio resulting in original recording techniques that 'forever changed the way records would be made'.[10] The importance of recording techniques increased in parallel with crystallizing ideas of the album-as-work. This is reflected in Greil Marcus's observation that while the Beatles' first album took only 12 hours to record, successive albums took longer and longer as the band took more interest in experimenting with recording techniques and rendering more sophisticated sound.[11]

As discussed in Chapter 2, artistic autonomy and the Romantic idea of the lone artist/genius are so central to discussions of rock music that the roles of musician and producer are often blurred. Marvin Gaye is credited as the producer of *What's Going On*, as is Brian Wilson on *Pet Sounds* and Van Morrison (in later accounts at least) on *Astral Weeks*. The importance of the sound recording in rock music elevates the role of producer from the technical to the creative. In the hierarchies of music the composer is of prime importance, but a respected producer will also bring artistic acclaim. Thus Andy Warhol's role as producer of *The Velvet Underground & Nico* is frequently mentioned in the album's reception. John Cale's role as producer on *Horses* is also often noted in accounts of the album, despite its effect of fracturing the perceived artistic autonomy of Patti Smith.[12] Artistic autonomy is fragmented even further when an artist is in fact a band.

The reception of rock music supports both the lone genius such as Bob Dylan and the collective genius of the Beatles. The idea of the individual genius is beguiling, but the ruling canonical logic as dictated by the Beatles dislodges the primacy of the lone Romantic visionary. The Beatles are a group comprising more than one artist/genius, who interact and present a unified yet still plural identity. If the concept of an auteur can be extended to include a whole group of people, then the canonical idea of the sum of the parts being greater than the whole can now be applied not only to the album (being

---

9   Jim Berkenstadt and Charles Cross, *Nevermind: Nirvana* (London and New York: Schirmer Trade Books, 1998), p. 67.

10   David Leaf, 'Landmark Albums: *Pet Sounds*', in *Back to the Beach: A Brian Wilson and the Beach Boys Reader*, ed. by Kingsley Abbott (London: Helter Skelter, 1997), pp. 40–42.

11   *Sgt. Pepper's Lonely Hearts Club Band* (the album recorded after *Revolver*) took 700 hours to record, see Greil Marcus, 'The Beatles', in *The Rolling Stone Illustrated History of Rock & Roll*, ed. by Anthony DeCurtis and James Henke with Holly George-Warren, 2nd edn (London: Straight Arrow, 1992), pp. 209–22 (p. 216). From *The Rolling Stone Illustrated History Of Rock And Roll* by Rolling Stone, ed. by Jim Miller, copyright © 1976, 1980 by Rolling Stone Press. Used by permission of Random House, Inc.

12   She later claimed that she and the band had in fact ignored all of Cale's suggestions as producer, 'and that she mixed the record herself'. *100 Albums That Changed Music*, Egan, p. 243.

greater than the sum total of the individual songs), but also the band being greater than the sum total of its members. This is sometimes reflected by songwriting credits being attributed to all the members of the band, as is the case for the music of the Sex Pistols and Nirvana. Bands may be celebrated in lists of 'greatest albums' mainly for the work of one of its members, such as is the case for Brian Wilson and the Beach Boys, but equally a band may be perceived as a whole that transcends the value of its individuals as separate artists, as Janovitz argues is the case for the Rolling Stones: 'On *Exile on Main St.*, the individual musical ego is sublimated for the good of the whole. The sum of the parts is greater.'[13] Although the album *The Velvet Underground & Nico* may be thought of as mainly the work of Lou Reed and John Cale (based on writing credits, accounts of the album in popular reception and their successful solo careers after leaving the band), Joe Harvard makes a point of emphasizing that the album was in reality more of a collective creative effort:

> Rock historians habitually reduce the Velvet Underground to an entity whose brilliance came from cooperation and competition between a pair of gifted pioneers: John Cale and Lou Reed. Enormous roles were played by these mavericks, but it's a mistake to reduce the VU to the Reed–Cale Show ... the Velvets were a *band* in the truest sense.[14]

In rock, therefore, the artists/genius is still a powerful figure, but one that has the capacity to comprise more than one individual.

Recording and the Authenticity of Performance

Recording technology has created the possibility of the canonization of musical performance.[15] It follows that performance (whether live or as captured on a recording) provides a potential location of canonical value in rock music in a way dissimilar to the more segregated composition and performance sites of classical music. Visual elements of performance can also now be recorded and preserved in video footage (reproduced in documentaries), satisfying canonic requirements of preservation and perpetuation. Although this study is exploring only written secondary material on the albums, such visual documents can add to an artist's acclaim when used in television documentaries and in polls of greatest artists (such as Channel 4 television's *UK Music Hall of Fame*; the importance of image to rock will be revisited later in this chapter). Therefore bands or individuals valued for their craft of song-writing are interspersed with musicians prized mainly for their style of performance in lists of 'great' rock albums.

Since performances can be frozen and preserved on albums, the quality of the voice and the sound of the instruments, as recorded and manipulated in the studio, are often

---

13   Janovitz, *Exile on Main St.*, p. 28.

14   Joe Harvard, *The Velvet Underground & Nico* (New York and London: Continuum, 2004), p. 7. Excerpts from *The Velvet Underground & Nico* by Joe Harvard © 2004, reprinted by permission of the publisher, The Continuum International Publishing Group.

15   For an early discussion of this in the context of classical music, see Joseph Kerman, 'A Few Canonic Variations', in *Canons*, ed. by Robert von Hallberg (Chicago and London: University of Chicago Press, 1984), pp.177–95 (p. 188).

as important as the composed notes. Therefore the sound created becomes another location of perceived originality in accounts of these albums. It has already been noted in Chapter 2 that 'strange' new sounds are perceived as markers of value. Sonic originality is also a recurring theme in the reception of *The Velvet Underground & Nico*, such as this account of the experimental techniques used during the making of the album:

> When Cale initially added viola, grinding it against Reed's "Ostrich" guitar, illogically and without trepidation, a tingle of anticipation shot up his spine ... He had, he knew, found their sound ... "It wasn't until then that I thought we had discovered a really original, nasty style."[16]

The authenticity of expression demanded of the singer-songwriter (discussed in Chapter 2) is thus also applied to performance. While sophisticated and innovative production is often a valued quality, this notion of authenticity, honesty and exuberance of expression also suggests the opposite condition of technical un-sophistication as ideal. The immediate expression of the artist favours minimal (or apparently minimal) studio manipulation of their performance. Therefore, there is a perceived integrity in the low key, low budget production of the Velvet Underground's album; as Lou Reed has said of the recording process, 'No one wants it to sound professional. It's so much nicer to play into one very cheap mike. That's the way it sounds when you hear it live and that's the way it should sound on the record.'[17] In this, Paul Gambaccini suggests that 'the Velvets took Bob Dylan one step further in distancing rock from the need to have a pleasant, melodious lead vocal. With their spare production and repetitive playing, the Velvet Underground widened the providence of rock.'[18] The Sex Pistols' album is also valued for its lack of sophistication, a necessary quality in this case to reflect the do-it-yourself ethic of punk.[19]

So important is this aura of authenticity that artifice may be used in order to achieve a 'live' sound on a recording. For *Nevermind*, producer Butch Vig 'contemplated how he could change the artificial recording environment to make the recordings of Nirvana match the fury and intensity they were known for from their live shows'. After considering various options, he finally decided to put '"several sheets of plywood on the floor during tracking to make the room sound a little more live", he recalls'.[20] Such measures serve to highlight the falsity of perceiving albums as 'live' or 'real' documents, and yet layers of authenticity are read into the music based on that very notion.

---

16   Excerpt from Victor Bockris, *Transformer: The Lou Reed Story* (New York: Simon & Schuster, 1994) quoted in Harvard, *The Velvet Underground & Nico*, p. 102.

17   Lou Reed quoted in Victor Bockris, *Uptight: The Velvet Underground Story* (London: Omnibus Press, 2002), cited in Harvard, *The Velvet Underground & Nico*, p. 46.

18   Paul Gambaccini, *Paul Gambaccini Presents the Top 100 Albums* (GRR/Pavilion: London, 1987), p. 16.

19   See for example *VH1's 100 Greatest Albums*, ed. by Jacob Hoye (New York and London: MTV Books/Pocket Books, 2003), p. 47.

20   Berkenstadt and Cross, *Nevermind*, p. 31.

Other accounts of performance underpin the valuation of the albums. Describing *Astral Weeks*, one writer concludes, 'Suffice to say, no one in pop music, before or since, has sounded so consumed by what they are singing, so destabilised by desire, so "out there" in their voicing of the desperation and intensity of adolescence.'[21] In the entry on *Exile on Main St.* in *VH1's 100 Greatest Albums*, it is claimed that 'there are relatively few great songs, and yet a whole raft of spectacular performances'.[22] Janovitz is also keen to highlight the quality of vocal performance on this record, saying that 'on a record that features some of his most honest performances, [Jagger] sounds completely guileless ... without any semblance of a mask or character, as if singing a confessional lyric from a personal experience.'[23]

The perceived quality of truth in a voice is often more important than conventionally accurate or beautiful singing. Richie Unterberger claims that on *The Velvet Underground & Nico*, 'Tying it all together are the sing-speak vocals of Reed ... which project a direct, street-tough honesty unmatched by any other rock performer.'[24] John Lydon's ['Johnny Rotten'] singing lacked subtly or sophistication, but it perfectly suited the music and message of punk. Clinton Heylin, in his book on *Never Mind the Bollocks: Here's the Sex* Pistols, says 'Like all the best Pistols recordings, there is a hoarseness that gives Rotten's voice a razor edge, suggestive of a man tired of shouting the truth, locked in to an intensity that suggests this is one singer playing for keeps.'[25] Another account suggests that John Lydon was chosen to be lead singer primarily for his 'unnerving staring eyes and wheezing voice' (and that his abrasive lyrical facility turned out to be an unexpected bonus).[26] By comparison, the singing on the early albums of the Beatles is celebrated for its clarity: 'In 1964 the freshness of the Beatles' vocal assault was the sound of pure novelty; today, one hears a lovely, naked emotion in those early vocals.'[27]

In this media-driven society, the idea of artistic authenticity can also carry through, however implicitly, to the real life of the artists. Although these details will fade away over time, leaving just the album and historical memories, for a contemporary canon the contemporary behaviour of the artist has an undoubted impact. The artists and albums are written about endlessly, but the popular reception of rock music tends to focus on biography and historical context far more than typical writings on the great works of literature and classical music. This serves to bring to light the artists' extremes of experience, wisdom or seriousness about their music, and thus bolster their integrity. For instance, the dramatic biographical details of the Beach Boys, according to *The Rough Guide to Rock*, 'seem to inspire a whole industry of biographers keen to pore over every piece of minutiae about the group, in the process

21   Sean O'Hagan, 'Astral Weeks', in Various Contributors, 'The 100 Greatest British Albums', *Observer Music Monthly*, 17.

22   *VH1's 100 Greatest Albums*, Hoye, p. 35.

23   Janovitz, *Exile on Main St.*, p. 137.

24   *100 Albums That Changed Music*, Egan, p. 99.

25   Clinton Heylin, *Never Mind the Bollocks: Here's the Sex Pistols – The Sex Pistols* (New York: Schirmer Books, 1998), p. 17.

26   Sean Egan quoted in *100 Albums That Changed Music*, Egan, p. 270.

27   Marcus, 'The Beatles', p. 219.

of swamping the reality with myth-making and overanalysis'.[28] The intensity and urgency of performance, combined with knowledge of the artist's real experience, contributes to the artist's image as artist/genius/rebel.

Attitude, Rebellion and the Rock Persona

The ideology of rock is rarely explicitly defined; it is an inherently vague concept (just as the canon is intrinsically blurred), and yet certain features of this ideology are indisputable. The Rolling Stones as a band represent the attitude of rock more than any other; as Janovitz suggests, 'What the Stones did have, even back then, was an undeniable attitude and an intrinsic understanding of American blues, soul, country, and rock & roll idioms.'[29] Similarly, *Exile on Main St.* is recorded in the *Rolling Stone* '500 Greatest Albums of All Time' list as being 'the Stones' greatest album and Jagger and Richards' definitive songwriting statement of outlaw pride and dedication to grit'.[30] The appeal of the rebellious, charismatic, maverick artist is enduring in the reception of rock albums. These qualities can be expressed in various ways. For one, direct rebellion against the industry is recorded in the reception of many of the ten albums (as has already been discussed in passing in Chapter 2 in the context of aesthetic value superseding commercial value).

Artists are often described as having to overcome the demands of their own record label in order to create albums of true worth and achieve artistic greatness, as has already been demonstrated to be true of *What's Going On* and *Pet Sounds*. Bands such as the Velvet Underground are mourned for losing their apparent autonomy: 'After all this time, and with the rebellious myth dissolved by Rock 'N' Roll Incorporated, The Velvets are no more.'[31] Van Morrison himself echoed this sentiment when he stated, 'I think I'm a loner, an outsider, not because I want to be ... I found I had to be if I didn't play along with the music-business bullshit.'[32] Yet real resistance to the industry is hardly possible, since albums, once released by a label, become part of the industry itself; and the magazines that promote this ideology of resistance and artistic freedom are equally part of the global media industry. *Pet Sounds'* success in 'greatest albums' polls is today being used as a marketing tool in itself, and so it could be said that Brian Wilson's artistic rebellion has paid off dividends in the long run.

Punk appeared to provide an opportunity for true freedom from the industry by recording and releasing songs that were not intended for radio airplay, via independent and often ephemeral labels. This air of rebellion is never far from accounts of the Sex Pistols, and according to Sean Egan, 'The Pistols succeeded the Rolling Stones as Society's outlaws.'[33] Paul Gambaccini rather memorably states in *Paul Gambaccini*

28   *Rock: The Rough Guide*, Buckley and others, p. 62.

29   Janovitz, *Exile on Main St.*, p. 4.

30   Various Contributors, 'The 500 Greatest Albums of All Time', *Rolling Stone*, 11 December 2003, 90.

31   *Rock: The Rough Guide*, Buckley and others, p. 1059.

32   Ibid., pp. 660–601.

33   *100 Albums That Changed Music*, Egan, p. 269.

Presents the Top 100 Albums that 'the premier punk album stands high in our charts, gobbing on everything below'. And *Never Mind the Bollocks: Here's the Sex Pistols* is attributed with the quality of representing true 'pop-cultural insurgency ... by accepting punk and the Pistols' challenge ... one could stay faithful to every promise of eruption, defiance and transcendence that rock-and-roll had ever offered.'[34]

But as Greil Marcus explains, such independence was itself short-lived, for 'while punk's remaking of some of the means of pop production backed up the punk attack on fame, careerism and "art" that was the first premise of punk ideology', such nihilistic attempts were doomed to failure since, 'despite the punk attempt to dissociate itself from rock & roll, punk *was* rock & roll'. Again we find that there is no real escape from the industry despite the appearance of rebellion since, as Marcus notes, most of the most prominent bands in punk were in reality contracted to major labels.[35] And so this appearance of creative autonomy from the industry is partly a construction that dissociates the reality of the marketplace from the perceived authenticity of the creative act.

The Unprofessional Primitive

In line with this apparent autonomy and resistance to the industry is the ideology of purity as reflected in the image of the self-taught artist. Histories of rock suggest that it is better to have learnt from imitating records or fellow rock musicians than to learn from conventional, institutional 'teachers'. This is echoed in Wicke's statement that 'rock musicians often do not learn to play their instruments in the traditional way, but learn to control them, exhaust their tonal possibilities and to work creatively with them, often using unconventional methods.'[36] While some musicians will of course attend lessons, what is equally as important is learning by example from recordings and peers.

There are naturally exceptions to this ideal of the musically untrained, as noted earlier in the case of John Cale. However, overall, institutionalized learning is both regarded with suspicion and looked down upon as an inferior means of ultimate expression. The unschooled approach suggests a purer process, in which there is no conventional teacher–student relationship (beyond the dynamic enacted by the individual) and so musicians are able to filter music without guidance by convention. This unschooled ideal is a recurrent motif in descriptions of the Sex Pistols, whose very lack of sophistication is a marker of artistic authenticity:

> They still had little idea what (or how) they were going to play, but veered towards bands they admired, the glam rock idols (Bowie, The New York Dolls, The Stooges) and the

---

34   Gambaccini, *Paul Gambaccini Presents the Top 100 Albums*, p. 25.

35   Greil Marcus, 'Anarchy in the U.K.', in *The Rolling Stone Illustrated History of Rock & Roll*, ed. by DeCurtis and Henke with George-Warren, pp. 594–607 (p. 600).

36   Wicke, *Rock Music*, p. 22. Lucy Green describes this process in more detail in Lucy Green, *How Popular Musicians Learn: A Way Ahead For Music Education* (Aldershot: Ashgate, 2001). Although this autonomy from educational institutions is the general perception of rock, in practice there are now an increasing number of rock 'schools' and college courses.

'Lads' Bands' (The Faces, Mott The Hoople, The Who), and with a couple of mates
worked up a passable set.[37]

Such an approach became in itself influential, as 'Countless bands', according to
Stephen Thomas Erlewine, were inspired by the Sex Pistols' 'sheer sonic force,
while countless others were inspired by their independent, do-it-yourself ethics'.[38]
Echoing the quip that not many people bought *The Velvet Underground & Nico* but
those who did all started their own band, Sean Egan contends that 'though the often-
spouted cliché that few saw the Pistols live but all those who did formed a group is
obviously exaggeration, it does hold a grain of truth'.[39]

Patti Smith, as a forerunner of the punk style, is also noted for her lack of
conventional training. According to Colin Larkin, 'Her untutored voice [on *Horses*]
provides raw realism.'[40] However, being merely untutored is not in itself enough, as
some other indefinable quality is perceived in the music that is special for reasons
other than technical accomplishment. This was recognized by John Lennon in
descriptions of his own guitar playing, which, according to Lennon, was

> very poor. I can never move, but I can make a guitar speak, you know ... Most critics of
> rock & roll, and guitarists, are in the stage of the Fifties where they wanted a technically
> perfect film, finished for them, and they would feel happy. I'm a cinemaverité guitarist. I'm
> a musician and you have to break down your barriers to be able to hear what I'm playing.[41]

The ideology of rock also incorporates the idea of a raw, primitive state of being.
When John Lennon was asked, 'Why do you think [rock & roll] means so much to
people?', he responded, 'Because it is primitive enough and has no bullshit, really,
the best stuff, and its beat gets through to you ... it goes through the world – it's as
simple as that ... And the thing about rock & roll, good rock & roll, whatever good
means – is that it's real.'[42]

This primitivism is an essential component of the ethos of punk; according to
the *100 Albums That Changed Music*, the Sex Pistols' manager, Malcolm McLaren,
'believed in the virtue of incompetence' and so tended to promote the idea of the Sex
Pistols' instrumental shortcomings in the face of the fact that they could (with the
exception of Sid Vicious) all play their instruments reasonably well.[43] By contrast,
the Rolling Stones are now derided for their perceived 'professionalism', and their
current distance from their earlier embodiment of rebellion and the urgency and raw
power of youth:

37 *Rock: The Rough Guide*, Buckley and others, p. 870.
38 *All Music Guide: the Best CDs, Albums & Tapes*, ed. by Michael Erlewine with Chris
Woodstra and Vladimir Bogdanov (San Francisco: Miller Freeman Books, 1994), p. 287.
39 *100 Albums That Changed Music*, Egan, p. 270.
40 Colin Larkin, *All-Time Top 1,000 Albums*, 3rd edn (London: Virgin, 2000), p. 123.
41 Jann S. Wenner, 'John Lennon: The Rolling Stone Interview', in *20 Years of Rolling
Stone: What a Long, Strange Trip It's Been*, ed. by Jann S. Wenner (New York: Friendly Press,
1987), pp. 101–16 (p. 107).
42 John Lennon quoted in ibid., p. 116.
43 *100 Albums That Changed Music*, Egan, p. 271.

On their world tours, the faithful continue to turn out en masse to see the self-titled 'world's greatest rock and roll band' go through its paces. But perhaps 'the world's most professional rock and roll band' would be a more appropriate monicker as they shamelessly plumb the depths of corporate sponsorship.[44]

It is for their more 'rough' recordings and performances that the Rolling Stones are celebrated, as seen in the quotation at the beginning of this chapter that describes the sound of *Exile on Main St.* as 'soupy' and 'swampy', '… sounds bleeding into each other' and so on. When this urgency was lost in later years, they also jettisoned their integrity according to the underlying ideology of rock and are now perceived as pandering to a more commercially-driven form of mass nostalgia.

Nihilism and Hedonism

One function of popular music is to provide a means of expression that the young can embrace and claim for themselves, as part of the rebellion against parental control that becomes a stage of growing up. Following this, a (surface) rejection of a tradition that includes the music of the previous generation is only to be expected. This rejection of tradition is clearest (at least on the surface) in punk. According to Greil Marcus, the Sex Pistols were 'clear inheritors of Chuck Berry, Phil Spector, the early Who, the Velvet Underground', but they 'nevertheless denounced their forbears as farts and fools, dismissing the claims of the past as they denied the worth of the future'.[45] The importance of this perceived rebellion and rejection of the 'rock establishment' led to bassist Glen Matlock being 'kicked out of the band for exhibiting revisionist tendencies. ("He wanted to make us *fun*", Rotten explained in horror. "Like the Beatles!")'.[46]

As well as incorporating narratives of enduring value (as has been demonstrated in the previous chapter), rock ideology also values the ephemeral; or, as Lester Bangs phrases it, 'As mindless Fifties American groups had proved before and punk rockers have proved since … rock & roll at its core is merely a bunch of raving shit, its utterly hysterical transience and intrinsic worthlessness the not-quite-paradoxical source of its vitality.'[47] The nihilism of the Sex Pistols was a powerful expression of the disposability of pop and the simultaneous celebration and destruction of the moment, yet the vitality generated by this music of the late 1970s has left an enduring mark on rock histories for all its reported transience. This nihilism displayed by the Sex Pistols is less evident yet still present to varying degrees in the reception of the other artists featured in this book. Nirvana in particular are depicted as a destructive force as reported in accounts of the behaviour of their singer-songwriter: 'Cobain developed a taste for trashing equipment in true nihilistic style.'[48]

---

44 *Rock: The Rough Guide*, Buckley and others, p. 834.

45 Marcus, 'Anarchy in the U.K.', pp. 596.

46 Ibid., p. 598.

47 Lester Bangs, 'The British Invasion', in *The Rolling Stone Illustrated History of Rock & Roll*, ed. by DeCurtis and Henke with George-Warren, pp. 199–200 (p. 201).

48 *Rock: The Rough Guide*, Buckley and others, p. 692.

This nihilism becomes one way of avoiding hypocrisy in the face of the increasingly conflicting values in the ideology of rock. The ephemeral and the disposable cannot support a canon; it presents a contradiction, a paradox of sorts. If you value nihilism, you cannot honour your forbears or claim to be working for posterity. If you represent youth, you cannot be seen to age; 'better', as the old rock adage goes, 'to burn out than to fade away'.[49] Accordingly, the Sex Pistols were only officially together as a band for nine months; however, their legacy as a band has lasted far, far longer. Moreover, their location within the tradition of rock is now virtually complete, for all their apparent rejection of the forebears at the time. The Sex Pistols may have appeared on the surface to reject and demolish rock tradition, but ultimately this tradition subsumed the band and incorporated punk into its firmament.

Patti Smith, whose music is often cited as a forerunner of punk, is also credited with an apparent break with tradition; and yet in Smith's case, her rebellion against tradition seems more a perception of her audience than an accurate reflection of her intentions. Smith has released versions of Van Morrison's 'Gloria' and the Who's 'My Generation', 'her respect' according the *The Rough Guide to Rock*, 'for 60s idols contrasting with the deep loathing affected by punks – or at least the British punks – towards rock "tradition". Some found this a strange contradiction – the high priestess of the alternative scene praising the rock deities others thought she had come to bury.'[50] Histories seldom have room for grey areas and so artists tend to be categorized as either fully embracing or rejecting the rock 'tradition'.

As stated at the beginning of this chapter, the more artists or albums fit the values of the canons of literature and classical music, the less they tend to be associated with these other values more specific to rock. The Beatles and the Rolling Stones are often contrasted in this respect, with the Beatles regarded as the mainstream and the Stones a comparatively underground act. Greil Marcus notes that the while the Beatles' image was deliberately 'cleaned up', the image of the Rolling Stones was deliberately sullied; for the Beatles, 'Rebellion was fine as long as tactics were restricted to wit.'[51] However, such a relatively inoffensive or un-extreme centre is incidentally desirable for a canon.

A related idea to that of nihilism is the celebration of hedonism, excess and immorality in the ideology of rock, again most often associated with the Rolling Stones. Describing *Exile on Main St.*, Colin Larkin says that 'hedonism and bacchanalia ooze from every pore, emphasizing an air of sexual degeneracy encapsulating the Rolling Stones' appeal. This expansive and important LP is now rightly recognised as one of the pinnacles of their incredible career.'[52]

The association of rock music with drugs is arguably a cultural inevitability of the 1960s, but it also exacerbates this central tenet of hedonistic nihilism. Even

---

49   So powerful is the influence of this motto that Kurt Cobain quoted it in his suicide note. See Dan Silver, 'Love Will Tear Us Apart', in *From U2 to the White Stripes*, *Q* Special Edition: 50 Years of Rock 'N' Roll 1954–2004, (London: EMAP, 2004), 84–7 (87).

50   *Rock: The Rough Guide*, Buckley and others, p. 910.

51   Marcus, 'The Beatles', p. 217.

52   Larkin, *All-Time Top 1,000 Albums*, 3rd edn, p. 51.

the bands not immediately associated with this overtly rebellious side of rock are, retrospectively, viewed in these terms. Despite the 'nice' quality of *Pet Sounds*, it is remembered in histories as a drug-influenced record. The Beatles' image as clean-living musicians in contrast to the Rolling Stones was partially undone in subsequent interviews, such as Jann Wenner's interview with John Lennon, which alluded to their experiences with Amsterdam prostitutes and compared their tours to Fellini's *Satyricon*: 'When we hit town, we hit it, we were not pissing about.'[53]

The influence of drugs is plain in the musical innovations of *Revolver*, and this is reaffirmed in accounts such as John Harris's article 'Out of Their Heads', in which he states that 'Lennon had become an evangelical LSD zealot', leading to the mesmeric, highly experimental sound loops of 'Tomorrow Never Knows'.[54] Similarly, Harvard suggests that while Lou Reed's literary influence was the poet Delmore Schwartz, his songwriting influence was 'every drug conceivable'.[55]

Extreme states of being and, by extension, early death are central to the ideology of rock. John Lennon and Marvin Gaye, Sid Vicious and Kurt Cobain are all regarded as martyrs either to their art or to the spirit of rock through their respective murders, fatal drug overdose and suicide. While not a direct feature of the albums themselves, the extreme of emotions these events represent is transferred to the albums by association. Similarly, Brian Wilson's mental breakdown after *Pet Sounds*, attributed in equal measure to his drug use and self-imposed pressure to compete with the Beatles, has only consolidated his position as one of the most celebrated figures in rock history.

Image and Youth

Although image does play a role in our perception of classical music, it is valued less than intangible aesthetic achievement. Image, however, is integral to certain styles of rock music, especially punk. As Greil Marcus remembers:

> Punk came together within a few short months as a whole set of visual and verbal signs: signs that were at once opaque and revelatory, depending on who was looking.
>
> With cruelly dyed and slashed hair, mutilated faces, bondage gear (from McLaren's shelves of course, which was only fair), wrecked clothes – a lumpen, day-for-night-of-the-living-dead style – punk drew lines, divided the young from the old and the young from the young, forced new loyalties, forged new identities and, as it announced that all possibilities were closed, opened up possibilities of negation and affirmation that a year before had not existed even *as* fantasies. This was revolt into style; it was also style into revolt.[56]

Clinton Heylin even suggests that John Lydon was initially brought into the Sex Pistols purely on the grounds of his arresting image: 'Rotten's compact lyrical flair was a most unexpected bonus from the green-haired youth with the ripped T-shirt

---

53   Wenner, 'John Lennon', p. 104.

54   John Harris, 'Out of Their Heads', in *From Elvis to the Beatles*, *Q* Special Edition: 50 Years of Rock 'N' Roll 1954–2004, (London: EMAP, 2004), 60–65 (62).

55   Harvard, *The Velvet Underground & Nico*, p. 22.

56   Marcus, 'Anarchy in the U.K.', pp. 596–7.

whom McLaren had recruited as a frontman solely because of his belligerent stare.'[57] In rock music originality can evidently be located and valued in the visual, which, combined with performance on the record (and accounts of live gigs), presents an enduring statement.

The importance of image in rock destabilizes hierarchies associated with classical music without eradicating them completely; although the ear is still usually believed to be superior to the eye, it is more of a reciprocal arrangement. Corresponding with the loosening of restrictions on image and the emphasis on performance created by the record, the superiority of composer over performer is shaken to a degree. In terms of a rock canon as epitomized by the ten albums under study, image and performance both contribute to the aura of the work. Producer Paul Kolderie suggests that the appeal of the Rolling Stones 'had to do more with the way they *looked*: the shaggy hair ... And that picture on *Exile* with Mick and Keith singing backup vocals ... they made it seem like the coolest thing you could do was just get as wasted as possible'.[58] However, image alone is not enough to sustain an artist in a canon of albums, and so it becomes valuable only in as much as it contributes to the overall perception of the music.

This preoccupation with image is associated with another facet of the ideology of rock, the idealization of youth. Bob Dylan's lyrics from the song 'Forever Young' are used as the frontispiece to *20 Years of Rolling Stone: What a Long Strange Trip It's Been*, thus equating the manifesto of rock music with a privileging of youth.[59] Being young, charismatic, and, ideally, tragically beautiful, is an essential state of popular music. Nirvana were described in *Melody Maker* as 'one of the most visceral, intense and beautiful bands on the face of the planet'. According to Berkenstadt and Cross, '"Smells Like Teen Spirit" [the most anthemic song on *Nevermind*] at once mocks the concept of youth rebellion and musically embraces it. Cobain's rebel ambivalence mirrors a young John Lennon, who could not decide whether the listener should count him "in/out" on the Beatles song "Revolution".'[60]

Different artists have matured at different times in their lives, but in rock, youth plays such an important part of the ethos that composers are expected to, and usually do seem to, create their most vibrant, acclaimed and original work in their teens or twenties. The long-running band who continues to progress and compose with a popular following is the exception rather than the rule, and traditionally careers in rock music are short. Once more the sentiment of 'better to burn out than to fade away' underpins the ideology of rock in assertions such as this, which appears in what is an otherwise glowing assessment of *Pet Sounds* by Jim Fusilli:

---

57 Heylin, *Never Mind the Bollocks*, pp. 11–12.
58 Producer Paul Kolderie quoted in Janovitz, *Exile on Main St.*, p. 23.
59 'Forever Young' originally appeared on the album *Planet Waves*, 1971. The subject of youth and rock culture is discussed in numerous academic texts, including Simon Frith, *Sound Effects: Youth, Leisure, and the Politics of Rock 'n' Roll* (New York: Pantheon, 1981); and the chapter 'Rock and Youth' in Lawrence Grossberg, *We Gotta Get Out of this Place: Popular Conservatism and Postmodern Culture* (New York and London: Routledge, 1992), pp. 171–200.
60 Berkenstadt and Cross, *Nevermind*, pp. 68 & 117.

The Beach Boys beat it into the ground. They didn't know when to quit. The Beatles made a clean break: up on the roof, January 30, 1969; "I hope we passed the audition." Everything they've done since then has sought to reinforce the legend. Almost everything the Beach Boys have done since … has torn the legend down.[61]

According to *NME's* special commemorative issue on Kurt Cobain, 27 is 'the "supposed death age" at which musicians including Jimi Hendrix, Janis Joplin and Brian Jones had all exited this mortal coil,' a fact apparently known to Cobain at the time of his suicide at this age.[62] However, by now, some rock figures are dying of old age or at least the ailments of the old. The ideology of rock is embodied in the swagger of youth, danger, living without care, life on the edge, and fearlessness. But the fact that the musicians and the original audience of rock have now grown up creates a conflict of ideology, a yearning for a more stable canon, while new generations emerge, necessitating both a rejection and an embrace of the rock of their parents' generation. On the albums, however, the artists will remain 'forever young', and so the ideology of youth can become permanent through the albums' crystallization into a canon.

The Contemporary Relevance of Rock

The subjects of the 'greatest' albums represent the common tropes of rock music, and while much of popular music in general is devoted to fun and escapism, the most privileged rock albums tend to represent more serious issues. These subjects have been explored by James F. Harris in his book *Philosophy at 33 1/3 rpm: Themes of Classic Rock Music*, where he claims that the ideological motifs of the 1960s are especially important to what he terms 'classic rock'. According to Harris, 'True friendship, true community, social and sexual alienation, the death of God, the importance of the present moment, individual autonomy, the corruption of the state, revolution, the end of the present age – such are the intellectual themes of classic rock.'[63]

Because of the immediacy and contemporary nature of rock music, albums are often valued if they serve as commentaries or reflections of their time; it is only later that timelessness and longevity become an issue. Since rock is meant to both define and represent a moment, its references and its politics are often specific to a certain time. This idea underscores the ruling logic of *NME*'s list of '40 Records that Captured the Moment'.[64] This list consists of one album or song nominated for each year from 1952–92; the records selected include Bob Dylan's 'Like A Rolling Stone' (from *Highway 61 Revisited*), *Pet Sounds*, *The Velvet Underground & Nico*, *Astral Weeks*, 'Anarchy in the U.K.' (from *Never Mind the Bollocks: Here's the Sex*

---

61   Jim Fusilli, *Pet Sounds* (New York and London: Continuum, 2005), p. 38. Excerpts from *Pet Sounds* by Jim Fusilli © 2005, reprinted by permission of the publisher, The Continuum International Publishing Group.

62   Paul Moody, 'Kurt: the Final Weeks', *New Musical Express*, 10 April 2004, 24–6 (24).

63   James F. Harris, *Philosophy at 33 1/3 rpm: Themes of Classic Rock Music* (Chicago and La Salle, IL: Open Court, 1993), back cover.

64   Various Contributors, 'Set Adrift on Memory Discs: 40 Records That Captured the Moment', *New Musical Express*, 9 May 1992, 42–5.

Pistols), and *Nevermind*. Simon Frith offers a further explanation for the presence
of contemporary issues and political questions in rock, suggesting that 'the truth of
youth culture is that the young displace to their free time the problems of work and
family and future. It is because they *lack* power that the young account for their lives
in terms of play, focus their politics on leisure.'[65] The social awareness of rock is
therefore a natural extension of the political awareness of youth since the 1960s.

Dylan is a quintessential but problematic figure in the politics of rock music.
His music was used in protests and civil rights events, and his early, folk 'phase'
(characterized by the albums preceding *Highway 61 Revisited*) contains references
to politically charged issues.[66] However, his own evasiveness on political issues in
interviews makes him hard to pin down and his legendary 'electrification' draws
a line between earlier folk/political work and his more enigmatic music of 1965
(*Bringin' It All Back Home*) and later. *Highway 61 Revisited* is regarded as a turning
point: 'His former protest style was transmuted into a surreal stream of imagery; the
protests were still there, but had become more a matter of implication and inference
than direct address, as Dylan responded to the literary influence of French Symbolist
poet Arthur Rimbaud and beat novelist William Burroughs.'[67]

Accounts of *What's Going On* deliberately separate the album from Marvin
Gaye's previous work; this new, more political approach was emphasized by Gaye
in interviews with comments such as: 'I wanted to write songs that would reach the
souls of people. I wanted them to take a look at what was happening in the world.'[68]
Punk, as chiefly embodied by the Sex Pistols, is recorded in histories as a political
statement, underscored by the idea of class struggle. The song 'Anarchy in the U.K.'
is described as: 'Searingly relevant in the political doldrums of the 70s, the song had
a snotty-nosed arrogance of the finest rock 'n' roll kind.'[69] Another critic suggests
that the band created a very real threat to society, claiming that 'while the band
played simple rock & roll loudly and abrasively, Rotten arrogantly sang of anarchy,
abortion, violence, fascism, and apathy; without Rotten, the band wouldn't have
been a threat to England's government ...'[70] Ultimately, however, punk's nihilistic
attitude ensured its own demise; as Greil Marcus states, 'Punk rock was an aesthetic
and political revolt based in a mass of contradictions that sustained it aesthetically
and doomed it politically.'[71]

Ignoring contemporary political issues, on the other hand, can be costly in terms
of the esteem of rock critics and *The Rough Guide to Rock* observes that the Beach
Boys' image was 'dented by their unwillingness to embrace music as a political
tool'.[72] Conversely the Rolling Stones were derided for an unsuccessful attempt at

---

65   Frith, *Sound Effects*, p. 201.

66   See for example *Rock: The Rough Guide*, Buckley and others, p. 305.

67   *The Mojo Collection: The Ultimate Music Companion*, ed. by Jim Irvin and Colin
McLear, 3rd edn (Edinburgh and New York: Canongate, 2003), p. 56.

68   Marvin Gaye quoted in Various Contributors, 'The 500 Greatest Albums of All Time',
in *Rolling Stone*, 11 December 2003, 90.

69   *Rock: The Rough Guide*, Buckley and others, p. 871.

70   *All Music Guide*, Erlewine with Woodstra and Bogdanov, p. 287.

71   Marcus, 'Anarchy in the U.K.', p. 595.

72   *Rock: The Rough Guide*, Buckley and others, p. 61.

politics: 'With its unspeakably lame political theme, 1984's UNDERCOVER was a career low.'[73] Therefore engagement with politics in rock music is a risky but apparently valuable exercise; political engagement appears to be a necessary strategy that the artists undertake for their music to be taken seriously.

Given the cliché of 'sex, drugs and rock 'n' roll', it might be expected that these would also form central tropes of the 'greatest' rock albums. However, while drugs may underpin the accounts of the creation of these albums, they are less often made the central subject (one obvious exception being the Velvet Underground's 'Heroin'). The sex of 'sex, drugs and rock 'n' roll' is also a less prominent subject than might be expected in these albums (with the Velvet Underground again providing an exception). On the contrary, the songs on *Pet Sounds* are for the most part love songs. Jim Fusilli sees 'God Only Knows' as a 'distillation of what much of *Pet Sounds* is about: the sense that if we surrender to an all-consuming love, we will never be able to live without it.'[74]

As Wicke observes, sexual references and ambiguity have been present in rock from its roots in rock 'n' roll, but 'obvious sexual meaning has in the meantime been neutralised'.[75] Marvin's Gaye's overtly sexual *Let's Get it On* is passed over in critics' lists in favour of his political *What's Going On*. When love is the subject of the 'greatest albums', it tends to be a more mature, complex conception, as evinced in Van Morrison's *Astral Weeks*, than the naïve, unambiguous and light-hearted incarnation represented by the early singles of the Beatles and the Beach Boys. The subjects of an album are intertwined with our knowledge of the singer-songwriter: *Astral Weeks* is inextricable from Van Morrison; likewise Patti Smith from *Horses*. The album's themes are therefore just one component that contributes to the perceived unity of the album as a discrete statement or work.

Secondary Material in Rock

Lists

Canons are inevitably simplified views of the history of a particular field, presenting only its most valued works and artists. However, canons cannot be reduced to the bare simplicity of a list. As Hugh Kenner states, 'A canon is not a list, but a narrative of some intricacy, depending on places and times and opportunities. Any list – a mere curriculum – is shorthand for that.'[76] Lists present a subject in black and white, sometimes in explicit rank order, and leave little of the blurred edges integral to canons. Even Bloom's *Western Canon* caused some controversy, due in part to the very specificity of its contents. The canon is highbrow; a list is lowbrow. The canon is indefinable; a list is not.

---

73   Ibid., p. 834.
74   Fusilli, *Pet Sounds*, p. 101.
75   Wicke, *Rock Music*, p. xii.
76   Hugh Kenner, 'The Making of the Modernist Canon', in *Canons*, von Hallberg, pp. 363–75 (p. 373).

However, lists have been associated with rock from the beginning, initially in the form of the commercial Billboard chart. Soon after the 'great' albums of the late 1960s were created, lists of greatest albums began to appear.[77] Indeed, lists are so integral to the reception of rock music that *Q* magazine has even published a special edition of 'The 150 Greatest Rock Lists Ever'. Although it may be argued that these lists (especially in the case of magazine polls as opposed to lists in book format) are somewhat disposable and transient, they are today routinely collected and presented on the Internet on websites such as Henrik Franzon's http://www.acclaimedmusic.net, and others including http://www.timepices.nl, and http://www.rocklist.net, making these lists highly accessible to anyone interested in such things via the World Wide Web, and effectively disseminating these lists to a much larger audience while making them permanently on display.

These lists are in many ways crude and can appear somewhat illogical, and yet they have the power to underpin the values of rock music. The magazines that compile and publish many of these lists are bought more regularly and in greater numbers than general histories of rock music. And the authors of these critics' lists are in many cases the same authors who write books on individual albums and general histories of rock, and are therefore able to reinforce their values in other secondary material.

These lists are inevitably more susceptible to change than general histories, as new albums are constantly added to bring them up to date. [See the Appendix for a selection of lists discussed in this study.] Adam Sweeting's comments in *The Guardian* summarize the power of lists to provoke debate and engage interest. According to Sweeting, 'People never tire of reading subjective lists of favourite records. Doubtless that's because of the provocatively flawed nature of the exercise. No two individuals will ever agree on the list of choices, and besides, who is capable of deciding whether Iron Butterfly are better than Alisha's Attic?'[78]

These lists are generally created by polling professional critics and/or musicians or alternatively a magazine's readership, and some difference is perceptible between the two kinds. Readers' polls on the whole will generally include more recent and more popular albums. However, the resultant lists still tend to include a high representation of 'canonical' albums (including the ten studied in this book), suggesting that the public is steered by the views of critics when it come to these polls of greatest albums (this subject will be revisited in the discussion of the role of the public in the reception of rock music in Chapter 5).

Although lists cannot be viewed as synonymous with canons, the albums that appear with increasing regularity have some claim to canonicity. Paul Morley's comments in the introduction to *The Observer Music Monthly* magazine's '100 Greatest British Albums' of 2004 describe the enduring appeal of lists:

---

77   The first *NME* list of 'Greatest Albums of All Time', for instance, appeared in 1974.

78   Adam Sweeting, 'Ton of Joy', *The Guardian*, 19 September 1997, 2. This article was based on a recently published 'music professionals' top 100'. The question of authority in the reception of rock implied in Sweeting's statement will be addressed in Chapter 5.

You shouldn't read anything into lists but you can't help yourself. They end up as a combination of great music that gets you worked up because they come in an order that makes a kind of sense, but which lacks statistical, historical and aesthetic integrity. It's just a snapshot developed out of tastes of the people asked, but somehow it contains a grain of truth about the shape of things. The Beatles and the Stones remain, however much these lists get revamped and assaulted by new generations of fans and critics.

Morley goes on to suggest that these lists have a deeper function than as disposable aids-to-argument, and concludes by intimating that lists may be able to sustain a permanence that is usually attributed to canons, albeit a permanence that is continually characterized by change:

> We list not just for comfort and because it's a nice new parlour game. We list to remember albums such as *Astral Weeks*, and *Five Leaves Left*, *This Nation's Saving Grace* and *Basket of Light*, to remember that such albums might have disappeared without lists like this. We list to remember that for every album like those four, there are others as worthy of our attention just out of hearing. Albums and songs waiting to be listed because, like it or not, the list goes on forever.[79]

Following these comments, Morley goes on to implore readers to buy *Astral Weeks* (placed at number 4), as a demonstration of why such lists are valuable, saying, '*Astral Weeks* is the real thing people are looking for when they buy their Norah Jones, their Corrs, their Joss Stone.'[80] Although lists may go on forever, their susceptibility to change makes them a dubious repository for enduring values.

Introductions to these lists are often very telling for the perceived ruling logic that underpins them (whether deliberate or apparently incidental). For instance, Jacob Hoye's introduction to *VH1's 100 Greatest Albums* claims that the list only includes albums that 'stand the test of time ... albums that tackle the human experience'.[81] A similar guiding logic is spelled out by Adam Sweeting in his description of a *Guardian* critics' poll of 'greatest' albums:

> Our rigorously-compiled list of the all-time 100 best albums ... enshrines the vanishing ideals of artistic integrity and musical merit. These aren't merely albums, but watermarks of the zeitgeist. To put it another way, this is a list of discs you can keep listening to for years and not get bored with, at least not until you have to decide whether to buy them all again on Digital Versatile Disc.[82]

Although the canonical undertones of this statement are clear, the somewhat evident sarcasm employed hints at the ambivalence towards canonicity in the field that will be discussed more fully in Chapter 5.

---

79 Paul Morley's introduction to Various Contributors, 'The 100 Greatest British Albums', *Observer Music Monthly*, 10 (June 2004), 4.

80 Ibid. The implicit gender bias in this statement poses an interesting (or inflammatory) point which rather corroborates the idea that the gender biases of canons have been replicated in the reception of rock music (see Chapter 3).

81 *VH1's 100 Greatest Albums*, Hoye, pp. xiv–xv.

82 Sweeting, 'Ton of Joy', 2.

Much, or nothing, could be made of the positions of albums in these lists from decade to decade. Patti Smith's *Horses*, while always featured, tends to move up and down the ranks a tremendous amount, supporting the notion that one reason for its presence in these lists is as a representative of (what might be perceived as) 'token' minority figures. *Revolver* is gradually gaining near universal favour over other Beatles records. However, while there is obvious and continual change on the surface, a core of works and values remains constant.

Fundamental changes in the values represented by canons only occur over a long time, whereas each new 'greatest albums' list appears to be a (largely rebellious) reaction to the last whilst maintaining the overall status quo. The lists generated every ten years or so by the *NME* are a case in point (see Appendix): the top ten of the 1974 list features three albums by the Beatles, but the list from 1985 is notable for its lack of Beatles albums (the first being *Revolver*, atypically placed at a lowly number 11). However the balance is rectified in the next *NME* writers' poll in 1993 in which the Beatles once more have a high representation (*Revolver* is second and *The White Album* eighth).

These lists make fascinating if inconclusive reading from the perspective of canon formation. For instance, the 1989 album *The Stone Roses* by the Stone Roses emerges fifth in the *NME* poll of 1993. By the time of the *NME* list of 2003, its perceived importance has grown even more, ranked as it is at number one, while most of the other albums from the 1993 poll have been scattered down the ranks. But the values supporting the position of *The Stone Roses* at the top of the 2003 poll are precisely the same as the values outlined previously in this study of canons; the ideas of the discretely different work, individual style, influence, attitude, nihilistic/ hedonistic drug use, strangeness, invention and originality, and ambition are all apparent in this account of the album that accompanied the poll:

> The Stone Roses stood apart ... the embodiment of their age. They were sucking up the expansive melodies of the '60s ... [and] attacking the status quo with the moral arrogance of the Sex Pistols ... They had a style of their own that soon became a style for everyone ... They were given £10 each a day to live on, but much of this was spent on non-prescription pharmaceuticals to help them through their night-work. It all contributes to the shimmering, goggle-eyed other-worldliness of the album...you can hear echoes of their '60s forefathers at times, but never as pastiche, only as a guiding light ... there's joyful invention too ... the band knew when they'd finished mixing the album that what they'd made was a benchmark.[83]

The new importance of *The Stone Roses* is confirmed by the *Observer Music Monthly* '100 Greatest British Albums' poll of 2004, which placed the album first, despite a complete absence of overlap in the panellists of these two polls. The accompanying article is similarly suffused with canonical suggestion, touching on virtually all the points of the last three chapters, and suggesting, more perhaps than any other quotation, that these canonic values are now fully integrated in the reception of rock albums:

---

83   Various Contributors, 'NME's 100 Best Albums of All Time!', *New Musical Express*, 8 March 2003, 35–42 (36).

The Stone Roses were four lads from Manchester who believed they could be better than the Beatles. They had influences, sure, but they wanted to be individual. Because only then could they last. Only then would they mean something to future generations. The Stone Roses survives and shines because the band wanted their debut album to be a timeless record. Listening to it may take you back to baggy, to Madchester, to ecstasy and dancing in fields in floppy hats and flares. But it also exists in its own space.

They didn't worry about the influences of Jimi Hendrix or Johnny Marr, they just wrote what was in their hearts. You can't create genius; it just is.

When *The Stone Roses* was released in May 1989, it almost instantly became a classic ...

John Leckie's clever production allows the band to explore their ideas, leaving the songs with raw edges and making them feel real rather than synthetic ...

In some ways this is not the sound of Manchester in the ecstasy-fuelled late Eighties, but a universal sound born of the Sixties ...

Fifteen years on, what we are left with is the art, the music.[84]

Equally there can be no doubting the growing centrality of Radiohead, who feature increasingly and consistently in such lists of greatest albums for very similar reasons. In this way a new generation of artists are being incorporated into the lists and yet the underlying (canonical) values remain intact, thereby reaffirming the importance of the earlier, influential albums.

Most notably of all, the aforementioned *NME* writers' '100 Best Albums of All Time' list of 2003 (which is quoted in brief at the beginning of this book) starts with an introduction that shows both a definite awareness and an absolute dislike and mistrust of the concept of the canon:

It's around ten years since the combined NME staff decided that the best album ever made was 'Pet Sounds' by The Beach Boys. In that time, we've been hit by everything from the death of Kurt Cobain to the birth of The Strokes. Musical movements like nu-metal, new grave, electroclash and NAM have swept the nation – or not. A whole host of brilliant new acts have appeared on our cover, from Suede to the Yeah Yeah Yeahs. The world, in short, has changed – would we still rate Brian Wilson's '60s masterpiece above everything else?

More importantly, we're living through a musical golden age, a time where it's a pleasure to introduce potentially life-altering new artists every week in these pages. But what about the records that influenced *them*? Hopefully, you'll get an idea of that too in this new list of NME writers' favourite albums – as well as a pointer to which of those back catalogues selling for a fiver in your local megastore you might want to add to your collection. This isn't a boring attempt to create some kind of canon of 'classics' – just an honest account of what continues to rock our world as we speed through the 21st century.[85]

This statement shows a certain lack of awareness as to the nature of canons; although apparently unchanging, they do tend to reflect the values of the time. However, the *NME* has every reason for wanting to change their selection of 'canonical' albums at periodic intervals. Their weekly magazine relies on public interest in current bands, in believing that we are indeed in a 'musical golden age', and that there exists today

84 Amy Raphael, 'The Stone Roses: *The Stone Roses*', in Various Contributors, 'The 100 Greatest British Albums', *Observer Music Monthly*, 10 (June 2004), 8.

85 Various Contributors, 'NME's 100 Best Albums of All Time!', *New Musical Express*, 8 March 2003, 35–42 (35).

an exciting music scene to rival that of the 1960s, which requires weekly updates from the *NME* in order for the reader to keep abreast of contemporary artists. Aside from this, 'greatest album' polls are popular and boost sales. In reality, despite the protestations of this list's introduction, the previous polls of the *NME* are some of the most canonically suggestive ever created. Although relatively few people will have bought, still own and still refer to the original copies of the *NME* from 1974, 1985 and 1993 that hold the previous incarnations of '100 Greatest Albums', these particular lists are readily available on the Internet on sites such as www.acclaimedmusic.net. The earlier lists in the series show quite clearly the bias towards the Beatles, the Rolling Stones and Bob Dylan that the later poll of 2003 apparently tries to suppress. The question of whether these lists really represent change in values or are more indicators of stasis will be revisited in the final chapter of this book.

A more solid indicator of enduring interest in artists and albums is when they are made the subjects of books. However, magazine lists are likely to be regarded as indicators of popularity and importance by commissioning editors of book series and will also be a deciding factor in the selection of subjects for *Q*, *NME* and *Mojo* special editions. Therefore the importance of these lists to a potential canon of rock music albums cannot be underestimated.

Other Secondary Material in Rock

While Bob Dylan is comparatively underrepresented in the *NME* 2003 writers' poll (which surprisingly omits both *Highway 61 Revisited* and *Blonde on Blonde*), the *NME* still runs features on Dylan periodically, and in 2005 produced an *NME Originals* special edition on 'Bob Dylan and the Folk Rock Boom 1964–1974'. The introduction to this special issue notes a revived interest in Dylan in 2005 and attributes it to the three-hour Martin Scorsese documentary on Dylan released in that year, as well as the *Bootleg Series* CDs.[86] Evidently, secondary material other than lists are also responsible for perpetuating the value of albums and artists.

Another form of secondary material in rock is the cover version.[87] Each new articulation of a song adds another layer of intertextual meaning and increases the album's chance of survival. Covers demonstrate a way in which albums are open to multiple readings and reinterpretation, vital to the generation of secondary material. The 'canonic' artists are more often covered than coverers, creators not imitators or interpreters. Songs by the Beatles have yielded the most cover versions of any band ('Yesterday' in particular having been covered countless times) and, as previously mentioned, a tribute concert for Brian Wilson consisted of one half of Beach Boys covers and one half a performance of *Pet Sounds*. Those bands more readily associated with the canonical notions of craft and more traditional song construction are more

---

86   'Bob Dylan and the Folk Rock Boom', ed. by Steve Sutherland, *NME Originals*, 2/5 (2005), 4.

87   For further discussion of cover versions, see Dai Griffiths, 'Cover Versions and the Sound of Identity in Motion', in *Popular Music Studies*, ed. by David Hesmondhalgh and Keith Negus (London: Arnold, 2002), pp. 51–64.

likely to be covered, since songs that rely on the performance of the original artist for their value offer less scope for successful reinterpretation.

Other forms of secondary material surrounding these albums are perhaps peculiar to rock in their highly modern and often populist nature. The profusion of books, clothes, commemorative models, tribute bands, CDs, DVDs, television and radio programmes devoted to the work of the Beatles has already been noted, and all the artists featured in this book have their own array of related paraphernalia. Bob Dylan has inspired an American radio station dedicated to his music, described as a 'Dylan scholarly collective and pirate radio station known as WBOB'.[88] There is also an interactive CD ROM of *Highway 61 Revisited* (*Highway 61 Interactive*) which includes out-takes of the album in progress, and the back cover of the CD version of *Highway 61 Revisited* includes a global hyperlink reference to bobdylan.com.

The Internet is not a universally respected source of information due to the uncontrolled (or uninstitutionalized) nature of its contents. Yet the Internet bears witness to a substantial ongoing debate about the various virtues of different albums in the history of rock music, and provides access to a wealth of music in the form of (legal and illegal) downloads. The *Rolling Stone* list of '500 Greatest Albums of All Time' was sponsored by an online CD retailer whose Web address was included in the feature for the convenience of the reader, so that they could instantly purchase all 500 albums from their online store.[89]

The Internet also plays host to websites devoted to both discussions of lists and lists of lists compiled by people with an amateur interest in 'canonical' rock albums or particular figures in rock (including www.acclaimedmusic.net on which the selection of albums for this book was partially based). There is a community (of sorts) of secondary canonizers active on the web, who compile lists and make value judgements on these albums as a form of absorbing hobby. Individuals no longer need to have their opinions published in the conventional sense for them to be heard. These forms of secondary material are largely peculiar to popular culture, and by traditional measures are not highbrow enough to be considered the actions of legitimate canonizers. However, any field of popular culture should perhaps allow for canonizing by the populace, and the question of who has the ultimate authority to dictate any canon in rock music will now be addressed in the next chapter.

---

88 See *VH1's 100 Greatest Albums*, Hoye, p. 61.

89 Various Contributors, 'The 500 Greatest Albums of All Time', *Rolling Stone*, 11 December 2003, 83–178.

Chapter 5

Canonical Discourse and the Question of Authority in Rock

The reception of popular music is both located and disseminated primarily outside academia, in popular magazines and books, on the radio and television, and on the most modern and lowbrow source of all, the Internet; and so there is a crisis of authority underlying the validation of an apparent canon of albums. The issue is further complicated by direct resistance to canonization in the popular reception of rock. This chapter will therefore look at forces in rock that make the presence of a canon problematic, and will mainly address the issue of canonic authority.

Following this, the issue of a canon in rock music will be addressed from the perspective of popular musicology. In doing so , both canonizing and critical approaches will be explored, together with the problems currently being faced in the academic study of popular music, which is torn between the need for a unifying collocation of works or theories and the determination to structure its object of study in a way that avoids the pitfalls of traditional canons that are currently being debated in other disciplines.

Resistance to the Canon and Problems of Authority

Criticism

As popular music is perceived to be a subversive counterpart to classical music, there is naturally some resistance, or at least ambivalence, in the reception of rock music towards its apparent canonization. This is most evident in the introduction to the *NME's* '100 Best Albums of All Time!' feature of 2003 (quoted at the beginning of this book) that states quite clearly that 'this is not a boring attempt to create a canon of "classics" – just an honest account of what continues to rock our world as we speed through the 21st century'.[1]

The criticism of this nascent canon of rock albums often, unsurprisingly, follows in a similar vein to criticism of the older canons. An article by Tim Footman (a professional rock music writer), written in response to the *Rolling Stone* '500 Greatest Albums of All Time' feature of 2003, mentions many of the objections to canons that have arisen in musicology and literary studies. Having acknowledged *Rolling Stone*'s central role in the development of rock music writing, Footman is aghast that

---

1   Various Contributors, 'NME's 100 Best Albums of All Time!', *New Musical Express*, 8 March 2003, 35–42 (35).

the *Rolling Stone* could today produce a list that is '*so* anodyne, *so* conservative, *so* desperate not to bruise the sanctity of the Rock Canon, that it becomes outrageous in its very lack of outrageousness

He notes the predictability of the albums listed highest in the list, suggesting that 'if *Pepper* is the *Citizen Kane* or *War and Peace* of such lists, then *Pet Sounds*, *Blonde on Blonde* and *Astral Weeks* are the equivalent of *The Seven Samurai* or *Moby Dick ...*'

The *Rolling Stone* list is admittedly more conservative than the lists of the *NME*: as Footman makes a point of noting, '10 percent of the Greatest Albums Ever Made are essentially the work of just five acts,' namely the Beatles, the Rolling Stones, Bob Dylan, Bruce Springsteen and the Who. Equally shocking to Footman, however, is the lack of recent albums included in the *Rolling Stone* list. Indeed, this particular poll does seem to value 'the test of time' more than most, and the top 20 is dominated by music from the 1960s and 1970s (an archaic move in comparison with the *NME*'s poll of the same year, which placed *The Stone Roses* (1989) at the top of its list). As Footman says, 'Sure, you can argue that we're talking long-term significance here, and no music hack wants to be the butt of hindsight's jokes', but the fact that Nirvana's *Nevermind* is the only album featured in the top 50 of this poll to have been released after 1990 leads Footman to the question, 'What's *wrong* guys? Not bought a CD player yet?'[2]

The article goes on to bemoan biases of race and nationality and wearily notes the low representation of women in the list. Footman also questions the album as the defining parameter of greatness in popular music and highlights the issue of musical style, recognizing that the *Rolling Stone* selection does at least include some 'soul, country, hip-hop ... blues, and ... jazz albums', but none by any classical composers; 'Surely John Cage and Stockhausen and Stravinsky have done more to change the sound of popular music than the Eurythmics (scraping in at 500) ever managed?' This reaction of Footman's is written with lively humour, but it has an undercurrent of anger to it that suggests future resistance to a conservative canon in rock music. He concludes by saying, 'Happy in their Mark Knopfler headbands, jacket sleeves rolled to the elbow, the compilers of this list have done what Pat Boone, Ed Sullivan and Tipper Gore never managed. They've made rock 'n' roll safe for your dad.'

Footman's primary objection to this list seems to be its strong reflection of canonical values and the possibility that these values may become entrenched in the reception of rock music. His awareness of canons is evident from his sardonic use of the term 'Rock Canon', and his objections to conservatism, male, white Western dominance, bias towards certain genres and the preference for old works over new mirror closely those objections to the traditional canons discussed in Chapter 1. It is the relative lack of rock 'values' of nihilism, rebellion, the ephemeral and youth (at least today's youth rather than that of 40 years previous) that apparently aggrieves him the most. However this quasi-canonical type of criticism could in itself be

---

2   This (and the following) paragraph quotes from 'Gathering Moss: The Fossilization of *Rolling Stone*' by Tim Footman, published by *Rock's Backpages*, at www.rocksbackpages. com, November 2003. Used by permission.

regarded as a truly positive indicator of a canon of albums, since any canon must come with its own defenders and critics.

Footman's most interesting point from the perspective of this study is a suggestion of a broader canon, through reference both to a nascent canon in another field (*Citizen Kane* and *Seven Samurai*) and the potential expansion of the present canon of albums to include composers of classical music (which is perhaps a more likely scenario than the canon of classical music embracing, for instance, the Sex Pistols, but still an unlikely prospect). Footman's casual mention of *Citizen Kane* in a discussion of albums echoes a comment made by Simon Frith in reaction to the *All-Time Top 1,000 Albums* in 1998: 'What's going on here is the same as in the lists of 100 best books or films. Such lists can be divided into two categories: classics and recent cult hits, *Blonde on Blonde* and the *The Bends*, F. Scott Fitzgerald and Irvine Welsh.'[3] Through casual allusion to canons in other fields in the discussion of albums, there is the implicit suggestion of an overarching canon that would encapsulate all the greatest works of all the arts in history. Harold Bloom has already suggested a potential world canon, in which Shakespeare would of course take the central role. Such a world canon does exist after a fashion, when people are asked to think of the 'greatest works of art' in our culture – a jumbled confusion of Beethoven's Fifth Symphony, the *Mona Lisa*, and *War and Peace*. However, this imagined 'universal' canon is still, for now at least, predominantly Western in its scope.

Such criticism does, however, raise the issue of authority in connection with a potentially enduring canon of rock albums. While the canon of classical music has been taught and perpetuated from within academia, no such claim is made for rock music. Although schools occasionally place popular music on the GCSE curriculum, there is no pretence that they are the main arbiters of value in the subject, and the lessons taught tend to focus on the potential of popular music (especially the Beatles) to be studied in a similar way to classical music (but with the added incentive of being apparently more appealing to the young). While academia is increasingly regarding popular music as an absorbing object of study, there is little indication that academics feel that it is their role to govern this music; rather, they observe from a distance and comment on its cultural complexity. Academia has taken such varied approaches that little sense of communal enquiry has formed thus far, as will be discussed later in this chapter. Popular musicologists and sociologists are determined not to fall into the politically dangerous trap of canon formation, perceived as regressive in academia, but then the question remains of how to approach this music, given its cultural richness and importance.

Problems of Authority and Institution

As discussed in Chapter 1, the boundaries and basis of repertory and canon in classical music are defined by a multiplicity of musical disciplines, including academia and

---

3   Simon Frith, 'Our Favourite Rock Records Tend to Go Round and Round', *The Observer*, 6 September 1998. Copyright Guardian News & Media Ltd 1998. This article is also discussed briefly at the beginning of Chapter 2 in connection with its comments on a solidifying canon in rock music.

the concert hall, but also 'the recording industry, the music-publishing industry, the music-book publishing industry, and performing-groups organizations'.[4] However, the opinions of academia and highly respected institutions of performance (such as the leading orchestras) will ultimately be considered of greater authority than the popular reception of the art.

An even greater divergence of interests and authorities exists in the reception of rock music today. Since, as also noted previously, the study of any canon should be conducted with full awareness of the institution that created and supports it, this has to be determined in relation to a canon of albums in rock music. The question of authority is a problematic one in popular culture, and various groups claim a degree of authority in the field, including popular music critics, academics and the general public.

It seems, however, that the institution most responsible for the generation of values (and a potential canon) in rock music is the popular media. Here we have the irony that canons are traditionally a construct of academia and yet the clearest indications of a canon in popular music come from non-academics. The most powerful canonizers in rock music include those who decide the content of music magazines and commission books on particular albums, the people who decide which artists to promote in television documentaries and polls, and those within the music industry who select the music that will be released and re-released and promoted as 'classics' in their field.

Music awards also have the power to dictate values in the field and their judgements feed into the values of rock lists of 'greatest' albums and general histories.[5] In America the Grammy Awards and in Britain the Mercury Music Prize and Brit Awards hold annual ceremonies to award prizes in various different categories of music that also contribute to perceived boundaries of classification in the field. The 'Mercury Music Prize' is a one-off prize awarded annually for the greatest album of the year and is therefore particularly interesting from the perspective of values associated with albums, given that the panellists represent industry 'specialists' and rock music critics (including Simon Frith). However, the albums selected for the Mercury prize have not thus far featured highly in lists of 'greatest' albums.[6]

As has been demonstrated, value judgements that implicitly suggest a canon in rock music are present in music magazines, popular histories, compiled lists, television and radio programmes, the Internet, the choice of albums for commercial re-release, and the choice of music for industry support and financial backing. Rock

---

4   Marcia J. Citron, *Gender and the Musical Canon* (Cambridge: Cambridge University Press, 1993), pp. 22–3.

5   The role of award ceremonies in rock music reception is discussed in more detail in David Sanjek, 'Institutions', in *Key Terms in Popular Music and Culture*, ed. by Bruce Horner and Thomas Swiss, (Massachusetts and Oxford: Blackwell, 1999), pp. 46–56; and its role in boosting sales of particular artists discussed in Mary R. Watson and N. Anand, 'Award Ceremony as an Arbiter of Commerce and Canon in the Popular Music Industry', *Popular Music*, 25/1 (January 2006), 41–56.

6   Some winners of the Mercury Prize, such as Pulp's *Different Class* and Portishead's *Dummy*, often feature in such lists but not in the upper reaches; whereas Radiohead's *The Bends*, an album often featured highly in lists of 'greatest albums', was not nominated.

journals serve precisely the same function Marcia Citron has ascribed to the early music journals of classical music (such as *Allgemeine Musikalische Zeitung*):

> Reporting on concerts, reviewing and publishing new music, and presenting articles on miscellaneous topics of interest. Features on earlier composers, theorists, and musical practices were especially significant in creating a respect for the past. This historicizing slant acted as a means of instilling "correct" aesthetic values in the readership – values that could influence taste in the consumption of music. It can be argued, in fact, that historicism in general was motivated by a "concern for the taste of the present".[7]

Different music magazines have different priorities and are generally aimed at slightly different audiences. For instance, *Q* magazine tends to focus more on contemporary artists with broad appeal, but still has special features and lists that are quite canonical (such as the *Q* '100 Greatest Stars of the 20th Century' feature which is discussed in Chapter 2). Its sister magazine, *Mojo*, is aimed an older and more 'canonically' aware audience (in the sense of an assumed knowledge of rock history). The *NME* is usually more concerned with weekly reports of the latest news, live performances, short interviews and more openly subjective opinions, but still carries features such as the '100 Best Albums of All Time' polls (discussed in Chapter 4). However, the different values represented by these magazines are drawn together in the popular consciousness, especially when greatest albums lists are based on the opinions of the general public (such as the *All-Time Top 1,000 Albums* which claims to have polled 200,000 non-specified people, and *Q*'s '100 Greatest Albums Ever! * As Voted By You' list of 2006 – see Appendix).

The language employed in popular writing on rock is varied, which presents a problem of claiming authority through secondary material that could in effect have been written by most fans of the music. As noted in Chapter 2, quasi-scientific academic rigour is the exception rather than the rule in rock's secondary literature, and so the intellectual authority of this secondary material is questionable, and is compounded by the wayward nature of the Internet and its role in perpetuating the lists of greatest albums. The difference between opinion and fact, which is eroded in writings on the canons of literature and classical music, is more prominent in rapturous writings about albums. The language (quite often extreme and personal) used in reviews reveals its judgements to be quite clearly that of an individual, and therefore open to dispute. Few rock critics correspond to the 'ideal critic' as described by Barbara Herrnstein Smith as 'one who ... has, through exacting feats of self-liberation, freed himself of all forms of particularity and individuality, all special interests ... and thus of all bias'.[8]

Rock critics more usually take the stance of being 'one of us' who happens to have a job reviewing records. Their authority lies in the very fact of their normality, combined with a keen interest in music, resulting in the kind of broad knowledge, it is implied, that other people would have if they had the time. This non-professional/professional figure of the rock critic reflects its subject, and the preference (as noted

---

7   Citron, *Gender and the Musical Canon*, p. 34.

8   Barbara Herrnstein Smith, *Contingencies of Value: Alternative Perspectives for Critical Theory* (Cambridge, MA. and London: Harvard University Press, 1988), p. 42.

in Chapter 4) for self-schooling and primitivism celebrated in the artists. Knowledge is accordingly displayed through a broad knowledge of the field (demonstrated through reference to obscure music or perceived influences on the music of today).

Rock critics, or, as Frith terms them, 'professional rock fans', guide their readers' tastes; Frith also refers to these figures as 'ideological gatekeepers' in his book *Sound Effects: Youth, Leisure, and the Politics of Rock 'n' Roll*, in which he describes the gradual move towards more serious and critical journalism in the reception of popular music that occurred over the course of the 1960s.[9] Rock music began to be conceived of in terms of a serious cultural form from the time of William Mann's reviews of the Beatles in *The Times* in 1963, and later in the decade magazines such as *Rolling Stone, Crawdaddy* and *Creem* took their readers and the music itself seriously to an unprecedented degree, and engaged in in-depth criticism of the music. The readership of these magazines (as characterized by the readers of *Rolling Stone* magazine around 1973) were 'twenty to thirty-five years old, mostly male, white, affluent, interested in rock even as they settled down and lost their youthful fanaticism ...' These magazines aimed to be 'an artistic response to rock: music is valued for its complexity, musicians for their intensity of feeling'. *Rolling Stone* magazine especially tended to promote the figures of the past, and reaffirm their importance; Frith suggests that 'rock is defined by a particularly nostalgic use of leisure – it is old people's youth music'. Even older music magazines that had formerly perceived their role as primarily promoting the stars of popular music responded to this changing perception of the music. The *NME* underwent such a transformation during the 1970s, successfully switching 'from its old pop audience – single-buying, chart-concerned, star-struck – to the new rock audience – album buying, hip'.[10]

However, although *Rolling Stone* magazine may have been founded on ideologies of artistic integrity, it was still governed by commercial logic, which has become more apparent today as it features fewer in-depth, thought-provoking articles and more coverage of popular rock, more reviews, celebrity interviews, and such 'safe' 'greatest albums' lists as affronted Tim Footman in the excerpt above. But the ideology of rock rose through the early days of *Rolling Stone, Crawdaddy* and *Creem* in the late 1960s and the embryo of a canon started with the serious reception of these albums.

Publishers of secondary material and industry figures who decide whether or not to commission re-releases and box sets also hold power in the tentative future of a canon in rock. However, unlike the traditional role of canonizers in canons of the high arts, their interest is not in preserving 'great' works, but instead is necessarily dictated primarily by commerce. Albums will only be reissued if a market exists in which they will sell; books will (mostly) only be published if the album has generated enough interest for ensured sales. However, canonization will only truly emerge through the decision to continue reissuing albums, and in the decision to

---

9   Simon Frith, *Sound Effects: Youth, Leisure, and the Politics of Rock 'n' Roll* (New York: Pantheon, 1981), p 165. The following paragraph is based on the chapter on 'The Music Press' in Frith, *Sound Effects*, pp. 165–77.

10   Ibid., pp. 171–2.

reprint some of the books on albums that still hold contemporary interest. These are likely to be chosen on grounds of their perceived influence on later works and their status of importance through other secondary material (as discussed in Chapter 4).

The backgrounds (and thus presumably the interests) of the authors of books on the albums vary greatly, even within a series of books. The Continuum series *33 1/3* which addresses one 'great' album per book, employs a variety of authors: the book on *Pet Sounds* is written by a music journalist and mystery writer, Jim Fusilli; the author of the book *The Velvet Underground & Nico* is music producer/musician Joe Harvard; the volume on *Exile on Main St.* is written by (rock group) Buffalo Tom's singer, guitarist and songwriter, Bill Janovitz; and the volume on *Highway 61 Revisited* is written by poet, translator and director of publications at the Museum of Fine Arts in Boston, Mark Polizzotti; and the book on *Horses* is written by a Reader in English, Philip Shaw. Looking beyond the ten albums under study, the book on *OK Computer* was written by popular musicologist Dai Griffiths. All such commentaries claim an authority on their subject matter. However, in the field of popular culture others also claim an interest in the valuation of music.

Canonical Audience

A canon of rock albums is not an impersonal issue that concerns only a small number of experts with suitable credentials. Instead, such a canon in popular culture would appear to, and arguably does, potentially involve everyone (a legion of armchair experts). Everyone's experience of culture counts and polls such as the Channel 4 television *UK Music Hall of Fame* may be an indicator of a possible future canon in popular music, a public poll heavily steered by critics, which focuses on artists rather than albums.

The public currently has an ambiguous role in the canons of literature and classical music. In the case of classical music during the eighteenth century, the general public were seen to have the greatest ultimate authority, despite being divorced from the central theory and learning of classical music.[11] However, today classical music is primarily organized by institutions of high culture, whereas, as Citron suggests, the authority of the literary canon does not rest with the general public; the literary canon consists mainly of 'classics' from the past, while the public tends to concentrate on current literature, especially the 'best-sellers':

> Eventually some may become canonic and be immortalised in educational circles. But in general it is the institutional population and the relatively few independent "highbrows" that support literary classics. The public's fascination with the new, and with what becomes popular, resembles the situation in popular music. In both, currency and what is "hot" count for a lot. These will change relatively quickly – certainly much more quickly than the membership of traditional canons.[12]

---

11 See William Weber, 'Canon and the Traditions of Musical Culture', in *Canon vs Culture: Reflections on the Current Debate*, ed. by Jan Gorak (New York and London: Garland, 2001), pp. 135–50, (p. 142).

12 Citron, *Gender and the Musical Canon*, p. 21.

However, there is a compelling case to support the notion that the public also plays a strong role in the canonization of rock albums, while simultaneously being interested in what, as Citron says, is 'hot'. Rock music is part of popular culture, and is something that directly affects and is consumed by a far larger number of people than the consciously elitist canons of high art. The Beatles *Anthology* series in the mid-1990s found a wide audience, and music fans are the primary consumers of books on their favourite bands (which explains why these books tend to be so valedictory).

Magazine readers' polls now appear with the same regularity as critics' polls; this may be explained by commercial imperatives (readers will buy the magazine that contains the poll to which they contributed), but it also gives the readers a feeling of empowerment and authority. While Henrik Franzon has noted that readers' polls tend to focus on more recent music, echoing Citron's observations above, they are still shaped by similar values, albeit tempered by the increased prominence of more recent and more popular albums.[13] Polls such as *Q*'s 'The 100 Greatest Albums Ever! * As Voted By You' of 2006 suggests that the values and tastes of the readers are guided by those of the critics (*Nevermind* is at number four and *Revolver* is at number five), but that strong preference is also shown for more recent albums such as those of Radiohead, Oasis and R.E.M. (see Appendix).[14]

In his introduction to the *All-Time Top 1,000 Albums*, Colin Larkin suggests that a canon is being formed through the audience as they pass their favourite albums down to their children, thus preserving the values attached to albums. Larkin claims that 'a household brought up hearing the Beach Boys or Miles Davis will naturally form a familiarity and affection with that music', and in this way music will be passed down the generations

> not in a forceful way, but by way of sharing something that is great. I hope my own tin lids will appreciate their exposure to the Beatles and Bob Dylan. If the music is great then it will surely endure. Today's young parents will do their own part in passing on the music of Radiohead or Nirvana.[15]

However, even assuming a preference for Radiohead and Nirvana among today's future parents, this kind of canonization will only be effective against a background of canonizing activity that will affirm the value of these albums. Larkin's statement also echoes the views of conservative defenders of the canon that great works are inherently great and will survive purely on grounds of aesthetic merit alone; the attitude that 'if the music is great, then it will surely endure' is a position that tends to ignore the canonical mechanisms of selection that exclude certain genres and identities from the canon (mechanisms that critics of the canons attempt to expose).

Yet further problems of authority arise even if it is accepted that the public have a legitimate role in the canonization of rock music, since the importance of youth to the ideology of rock music implies that the intended audience of this music is the adolescent. The sense of urgency and vitality and the raw power of emotion associated

---

13   See Franzon's website http://www.acclaimedmusic.net, accessed 05/08/07.

14   Various Contributors, 'The 100 Greatest Albums Ever! * As Voted By You', *Q*, 235 (February 2006), 47–79.

15   Colin Larkin, *All-Time Top 1,000 Albums*, 3rd edn (London: Virgin, 2000), p. 5.

with adolescence are criteria of greatness in these lists. However, the albums chosen tend to be more adult, restrained, and contemplative (with the arguable exceptions of the albums by the Rolling Stones, Sex Pistols and Nirvana out of the ten in this study). What the lists of 'greatest albums' represent is in effect, as Frith pithily says, 'old people's youth music'.[16] The adolescents of the 1960s and 1970s (the 'classic period' according to James F. Harris) are now in the position to spend money on a canon of albums, as they now have a steady income and the leisure time in which to be nostalgic for their lost youth, as encapsulated on record.

Contrary to Larkin's suggestion that 'great albums' are neatly passed down from one generation to the next by parents exposing their offspring to their album collections, the taste of the young is more likely to be dictated by outside influences, through peers, television, radio or magazines. Ideologically, rock is meant to represent the raw vulnerability of growing up, which usually entails the (partial) rejection of parents and authority figures and by extension their music preferences. This music *mattered* to their parents' generation, but cannot mean the same thing to them. Adolescence traditionally involves extreme emotional experiences, brought out by, enriched by, described by and possibly exacerbated by the music.

To some people, recognizing this music as a communal possession is painful since they feel deeply that it belongs to them. This emotion explains why people argue so heatedly over lists of greatest albums, but it is also a reason why such lists generate sales. To have your youth-as-epitomized-by-an-album validated by some higher authority confirms that what you experienced was true, it was real, it was good. But adolescents, by definition, are not fully mature, nor in a position to make fully rounded, reasoned judgements. As such they make problematic canonizers.

Perhaps having a canon is a consolation prize for the more mature audience of rock, for whom the first great spark of emotional engagement has ceased and so they react more intellectually to the music. If this is true, it might be anticipated that rock's canonical albums will bring comfort to the same audience in their old age as the canonical works of classical music and literature do; therefore, increasing conservatism is to be expected. However, this is an entirely different proposition from a canon truly contingent to contemporary rock music, an idea which contains so many inherent contradictions that its future stability is the subject of great doubt.

Critics, the media, the music, magazine and book publishing industries, and the public (young and old) all appear to have a claim of authority in canonizing this music. Although academics have generally taken an observational rather than a participatory position in these processes, some academic approaches towards canonizing rock have emerged, and will now be discussed for the remainder of this chapter.

Academic Debate

Although creating canons and buttressing them may be the traditional role of musicologists, academics have so far been somewhat ambivalent towards a canon in the field of popular music. If, as Barbara Herrnstein Smith has suggested, it is

---

16   Frith, *Sound Effects*, pp. 171–2.

the 'normative activities of ... the literary and aesthetic academy' that are largely responsible for the stabilizing of labels and expectations of classified objects in a community, this may explain why the lack of consensus in the discipline of popular musicology as to what its goals are, and in its attitude to a canon, is reflected in the situation outside academia.[17]

Part of the reason for ambivalence is the question of authority. It is not clear that academia has any authority over popular culture beyond criticism from a distance. Critics or commentators will often assume that their audience has similar tastes to their own, or at least that the audience *should* have similar tastes. However, academic theorizing of popular music is often (not unnaturally) more sophisticated than its everyday practice and popular reception, and academic interpretation of issues such as authenticity can seem far removed from general everyday practice. For instance, Lawrence Grossberg's transformation of authenticity into authentic inauthenticity ('The only authenticity is to know and even admit that you are not being authentic, to fake it without faking the fact that you are faking it'), touches on the complexity of engagement that is possible with popular music, but is likely to be a somewhat alien concept to the majority of this music's audience.[18]

Schools and universities do not (as yet) see it as their responsibility to expose each new generation to the great works of rock music, nor are the activities of popular musicologists comparable to the past scholarship of classical music or literature that seeks to support, expand on and maintain esteem for the works of the canon. Academic syllabi vary from school to school at GCSE level; in universities value judgements happen implicitly through the selection of works and subjects that are taught, but these are generally determined by the individual lecturers concerned, as they do not have to conform to a countrywide academic syllabus.[19]

A few of the individual issues and values of canons discussed in this book so far have formed the subject of studies entirely separate from the issue of canon formation. Some academic books on popular music that discuss subjects with canonic implications are mentioned elsewhere in this book (relating to rock and Romantic ideology, art school values and authenticity in particular). Further examples include Sheila Whiteley's discussion of gender roles in *Women and Popular Music: Sexuality, Identity and Subjectivity*, and the discussion of race and the canon in Christopher Wilkinson's 'Deforming/Reforming the Canon: Challenges of a Multicultural Music

---

17   Herrnstein Smith, *Contingencies of Value*, p. 43.

18   Lawrence Grossberg, 'The Media Economy of Rock Culture: Cinema, Post-Modernity and Authenticity', in *Sound and Vision: The Music Video Reader*, ed. by Simon Frith, Andrew Goodwin and Lawrence Grossberg (London: Routledge, 1993), pp. 185–209 (p. 203).

19   While outside the scope of this study, a survey of academic syllabi and university modules, reading lists and library holdings would indubitably meet with interesting results. The lack of common understanding in the field is discussed in Lawrence Grossberg, 'Reflections of a Disappointed Popular Music Scholar', in *Rock Over the Edge: Transformations in Popular Music Culture*, ed. by Roger Beebe, Denise Fulbrook and Ben Saunders (Durham and London: Duke University Press, 2002), pp. 25–59; and the field of popular musicology is discussed in Martin Cloonan, 'What is Popular Music Studies? Some Observations', *British Journal of Music Education*, 22/1, 1–17.

History Course' published in the *Black Music Research Journal*.[20] Two books that summarize key issues in popular music studies, Roy Shuker's *Key Concepts in Popular Music*, and *Key Terms in Popular Music and Culture* edited by Bruce Horner and Thomas Swiss, contain articles about and references to albums, auteurship, authenticity, authorship, aesthetics, cultural capital, ethnicity/race, gender, high culture, institutions, taste cultures, text, and youth.[21] However, neither of these directly discusses canon in relation to popular music.

Various academic articles have been written directly on the ten albums featured in this book; and closely reflecting the situation in the popular reception of rock music, it is the Beatles and Bob Dylan who have attracted the most individual attention in academic literature on the subject.[22] However, while there is resolutely no clear canon of works presented in the academic study of popular music, some broadly canonizing activity is present in the field.

Canonizing Rock in Academia

It would be wrong to believe that since popular musicologists have generally avoided the idea of a canon in popular music, that this indicates a lack of awareness of the possibilities and indeed its presence in the reception of rock music. For instance, the subject arose in the general context of discussing canons in music in John Davies' article, 'Baroque and Roll' published in the *Times Higher* in December 1995.[23] Those interviewed include lecturers and professors of classical music, composers, ethnomusicologists, popular music academics, performers, a conductor and the then controller of BBC Radio 3. Each person interviewed was asked the (deliberately 'crude and journalistic') question: 'Is there, or should there be, a canon of great works or great composers that any serious student of music should be familiar with? And could you nominate a list of ten such works or composers – preferably, though not necessarily, in order of significance?' Of the 12 people who responded in depth,

20   Sheila Whiteley, *Women and Popular Music: Sexuality, Identity and Subjectivity* (London and New York: Routledge, 2000); Christopher Wilkinson, 'Deforming/Reforming the Canon: Challenges of a Multicultural Music History Course', *Black Music Research Journal*, 16/2 (Fall 1996), 259–77.

21   Roy Shuker, *Key Concepts in Popular Music Studies* (London: Routledge, 1998); *Key Terms in Popular Music and Culture*, ed. by Bruce Horner and Thomas Swiss (Massachusetts and Oxford: Blackwell, 1999). In the chapter 'Institutions' in *Key Terms in Popular Music and Culture*, David Sanjek suggests in passing that the Grammy awards present one idea of a canon in popular music, not '*the* notion of an acceptable canon': Sanjek, 'Institutions', pp. 53–5; however, the subject of canonicity is not addressed directly.

22   These articles address various issues, such as cover art, lyrics and poetry, problems of text, intertextuality, and authenticity, including Michael Brocken, 'Some Other Guys! Some Theories About Signification: Beatles Cover Versions', *Popular Music & Society*, 20/4 (1996), 5–36; Mark Mazullo, 'The Man Whom the World Sold: Kurt Cobain, Rock's Progressive Aesthetic, and the Challenges of Authenticity', *The Musical Quarterly*, 84/4 (Winter 2000), 713–49; and Wilfred Mellers, 'God, Modality and Meaning in Some Recent Songs of Bob Dylan', *Popular Music*, (1981), 143–57.

23   John Davies, 'Baroque and Roll', *Times Higher*, 15 December 1995, 13–14.

only five actually supplied the requested list and then with qualification, reflecting the general reluctance by the majority of respondents to be considered canonizers. Dai Griffiths was one of the respondents (his comments have already been discussed at the beginning of Chapter 2); however, he declined to provide a list. Simon Frith was one of the few who supplied a list, with the clarification that his was a list of

> 'obviously canonical artists' in rock music. Not, he emphasises, a critics' canon, but a canon of performers with whom 'it would be very odd for someone who systematically wanted to be a rock musician not to be familiar' ... Again in no particular order – and excluding genres such as reggae and country music – they are as follows: The Beatles, Rolling Stones, Bob Dylan, Jimi Hendrix, James Brown, Beach Boys, Motown ('defined generically'), Fairport Convention ('in its various guises'), Led Zeppelin, and Paul Simon.[24]

Frith makes a distinction here between the idea of a critics' canon, and what is effectively a canon of influence. Given the importance of influence to lists of 'greatest albums', however, it is hard to see how such a difference can be sustained. Such overt statements of canonization in popular musicology are extremely rare, and given that Frith made these comments in the context of a one-off interview for a newspaper article on canons, it would be misleading to take his provided list as an overt attempt to 'canonize' the field on his part.

Although popular music studies have so far avoided a uniformity of direction and subject matter, some arguably canonizing work exists within academia. The most obvious expression of this is the *Beatlestudies* series of conferences and books. This excerpt from the introduction to the first volume of conference proceedings (published in 1998) amply clarifies the manifesto of the original *Beatlestudies* conference:

> This book is intended to be the first volume in a continuing series of article collections and monographs concentrating on the music of the Beatles. Hence the name *Beatlestudies 1*. If the reader recognized a similarity between these opening words and those of Alan Tyson's preface to *Beethoven Studies*, written a quarter of a century ago, it was not a mere coincidence – it was intended to be so. Actually, *Beethoven Studies* was not merely the first volume in a series of further studies on Beethoven but began what would seem to be a continuing series of books devoted to individual composers, with an emphasis on the compositional process as examined from the source critical point of view ... The authors of this essay believe that there is a need for similar publications in the field of popular music. And if Beethoven was the first composer of classical music to have "his own studies", it seems natural enough to start the popular music "individual studies" series with the Beatles ...
>
> The Beatles are, without doubt, one of the most significant and enduring musical and cultural phenomena of the 20th century. During its relatively short existence the group changed the rules of the entire production process of popular music as well as the popular music itself. The Beatles also changed the fashion and way of living of a whole generation. It is simply impossible to imagine what contemporary popular music and culture would be like today had the Beatles never existed ...
>
> Traditional musicology has not been all that interested in the study of popular music. However, it has developed perhaps the most efficient tools for music analysis, some of which are considered to be as valid in the analysis of popular music as that of classical music ...

---

24   Davies, 'Baroque and Roll', 13.

The history of musicology has shown that concentrating comprehensively on a single case – for example, on a single composer – may prove fruitful as to the subsequent studies on different representatives of the same musical genre ... And the editors of *Beatlestudies 1* hope that this book as well as the subsequent issues of the *Beatlestudies* series might promote Beatles research and popular music research in general in much the same way as the *Beethoven Studies* publications promoted Beethoven research and research on other classical composers.[25]

This is an unusual but explicit attempt to bring popular musicology in line with traditional musicology. The implication here is plain: popular musicology needs a canon founded on historiographical research and composed of major figures, and the most significant figures are reckoned to be the Beatles. Privileging the Beatles in this way immediately puts at a disadvantage any popular music that does not reflect the models provided by the Beatles, a situation already familiar to traditional musicology where genres associated with Beethoven have long been valued above others. However, the centrality of the *Beatlestudies* project to popular musicology as a whole must not be overestimated, as these conference proceedings are not widely available even in academic libraries (in the UK at least), and their brief does not reflect the direction of the academic study of popular music in general. So far there have been two further *Beatlestudies*, but none on other popular music artists, although it is easy to imagine that *Dylan Studies* might be regarded as the next desirable step.

As the *Beatlestudies* suggest, it seems inevitable that in the academic study of popular music there has been some overlap of methodology with more traditional, canonical subjects. Many popular musicologists have a background in classical music or literary studies, and rock music shares a common basis in tonality with classical music. Where popular music shows striking similarities to the canons of literature, such as the marginalization of female and black or non-Western perspectives, this is addressed in a way similar to the criticism of traditional canons. Where popular music has been influenced by the high arts, this too is discussed, such as the influences of Baudelaire and Rimbaud on the music of Patti Smith and others.[26] There is also some overlap of figures and works between academic approaches and the popular reception of popular music. The Beatles and Bob Dylan are central to both accounts and the intellectualism of the Velvet Underground makes them an interesting subject of study from both perspectives. However, some artists have been of more interest to academic writers than their non-academic counterparts. While the Beatles have been of obvious interest to the academic writers of the *Beatlestudies*, so far most of the writing on the Beach Boys is non-academic in origination.

In the third volume of *Beatlestudies*, Walter Everett's paper on 'The future of Beatles research' is also very canonically suggestive. In it he proposes six areas of

---

25   Yrjö Heinonen and others, '(Being a Short Diversion to) Current Perspectives in Beatles Research', in *Beatlestudies 1: Songwriting, Recording, and Style Change*, ed. by Yrjö Heinonen and others (Jyväskylä: University of Jyväskylä Press, 1998), pp. i–iv.

26   See for example Michael Dunne, '"Tore Down A La Rimbaud": Van Morrison's References and Allusions', *Popular Music and Society*, 24/4 (2000), 15–30; Carrie Jaurès Noland, 'Rimbaud and Patti Smith: Style as Social Deviance', *Critical Inquiry*, 21/3 (1995), 581–610.

study that should be undertaken on the Beatles. First, a thorough history of the Beatles' performance practices; second, a more complete study of the Beatles' compositional style; third, a closer study of the stylistic forbears of the Beatles; fourth, a need for a definitive urtext of the Beatles canon; fifth, to start a series of Beatles sketch studies; and finally, the need for a widely available and comprehensive system of indexing, repositioning and distributing both source materials and scholarly work on the Beatles.[27] Clearly it is in Everett's best interests to promote the writing of secondary literature that would create a canon of popular music in which the Beatles are the centre, since much of his published research is based on the Beatles. This includes two volumes on the Beatles as musicians, in which their composition, performance and recording practices are analysed, for which he 'pick[s] up and put[s] aside various methodological tools as the material demands'.[28]

However, Everett is not the only notable academic to have written on the Beatles in depth. In 1997 Cambridge University Press published a Cambridge Music Handbook on the Beatles' *Sgt. Pepper*, written by Allan Moore.[29] The Cambridge Music Handbook series comprises over fifty books on different works, and all the others in the series (with the exception of one on George Gershwin's *Rhapsody in Blue*) are studies of canonical classical works, including three works by Bach, four by Mozart and six by Beethoven. Therefore the decision to include one handbook on a popular music album and for that album to be the Beatles' *Sgt. Pepper* is highly suggestive of the perceived importance of the Beatles to academic studies.

Allan Moore's Cambridge Handbook includes chapters on the historical and musical context of the album, a chapter on the album's reception and another on the legacy of *Sgt. Pepper*. In the chapter titled 'commentary', Moore uses quasi-Schenkerian notation to illustrate the harmonies and structure of the songs, but stresses that these are not intended to be functioning Schenker graphs, and he underlines his unease with the idea of popular music being regarded and studied as an extension of classical tonality. However, while such an apparently strong example of canonizing secondary material would suggest that Moore is also keen to construct a canon with the Beatles as the centre, his other writings suggest otherwise.

Academic Criticism of Canons in Rock

Since elsewhere in academia the attempts to 'open up the canon' are seen as an effort to undo the 'damage' of entrenched canons in their respective fields, it is unsurprising that few academics have seen it as their role to create an academic canon of popular music. Despite having written the Cambridge Handbook on *Sgt. Pepper's Lonely*

27 Walter Everett, 'The Future of Beatles Research', in *Beatlestudies 3: Proceedings of the BEATLES 2000 Conference*, ed. by Yrjö Heinonen and others (Jyväskylä: University of Jyväskylä Press, 2001), pp. 25–44.

28 Walter Everett, *The Beatles as Musicians: Revolver Through the Anthology* (New York and Oxford: Oxford University Press, 1999), p. viii; See also Walter Everett, *The Beatles as Musicians: The Quarry Men Through Rubber Soul* (New York and Oxford: Oxford University Press, 2001).

29 Allan F. Moore, *The Beatles: Sgt. Pepper's Lonely Heart's Club Band* (Cambridge: Cambridge University Press, 1997).

Hearts Club Band, in his other writings Allan Moore has actively sought to avoid contributing to a growing consensus about who the 'greats' of popular music are and what constitutes its masterpieces. Moore's *Rock: The Primary Text* is a study of popular music theory, analysis, styles and semiotics, rather than an account of the great figures of popular music such as Grout presents for classical music.[30] Moore states in his introduction to this book that:

> My examples are many and varied. One important reason for this comes from my attempt to subvert the growth of an accepted 'canon' of popular music (which already accepts the Beatles, 'punk' and Bob Dylan at the very least). The study of European 'classical' music has been greatly hampered by an over-profusion of studies of 'the great composers' at the expense of those whose music is considered self-evidently to be of lesser value. Popular music studies must not be allowed to fall into the same trap.[31]

Moore's statement is even more explicitly anti-canonical than the *Beatlestudies* introduction is canonical; and yet this is in itself a tacit acknowledgement and thus confirmation of a canon in rock (the Beatles, Bob Dylan and punk). Moore's comments suggest that subversion of a growing canon is now originating from within academia, ironically making popular music writers and publishers the more conservative force of the two. From the perspective of academic study, it seems that there is an onus on the part of academics (who would in the more usual course of events be responsible for constructing and maintaining a canon) to resist its formation, having witnessed the perceived negative effects of canons on what would otherwise be a highly pluralistic culture. This assumes that canon formation is a very definite choice, as opposed to a structure that our thinking gravitates towards, or an inevitable result of historicizing culture.

An indirect commentary on canons in popular music has also emerged in the collected essays that comprise *The Musical Work: Reality or Invention* edited by Michael Talbot.[32] Richard Middleton's article 'Work-in-(g) Practice: Configuration of the Popular Music Intertext' recognizes that the critics' 'classic album' articles and lists of greatest albums are broadly canonizing activities that exist alongside the pluralities of intertextuality in popular music. However, Middleton disagrees with the idea that albums are the only definitive version of a work, viewing records as being both frozen musical artefacts and also simply one record of music in time that exists among many alternatives, complicating the idea of a canon based purely on albums.[33] Philip Tagg, in 'The Work: An Evaluative Charge', concurs with Middleton's opinion that albums (as 'works') form uneasy canonical objects, but for somewhat different reasons. His objection to a canon of albums (particularly in academia) is that the concept of the work is 'too pretentious for application in the

---

30   Allan F. Moore, *Rock: The Primary Text, Developing a Musicology of Rock*, 2nd edn (Aldershot: Ashgate, 2001).

31   Ibid., p. 7.

32   *The Musical Work: Reality or Invention?*, ed. by Michael Talbot (Liverpool: Liverpool University Press, 2000).

33   Richard Middleton, 'Work-in-(g) Practice: Configuration of the Popular Music Intertext', in *The Musical Work: Reality or Invention?*, ed. by Michael Talbot, pp. 59–87 (p. 77).

field of popular music scholarship', especially if it is embedded in a discourse of social hierarchies of taste.[34] Tagg concludes his article with a warning about emerging canons in popular music, by referring back to the nineteenth-century canonizers of Western classical music:

> Just as their attempts ... to systematise specific aspects of (then) contemporary trends in music were later institutionalised, petrified, falsified, preserved and repeated like litanies for over a hundred years, we need to be acutely aware of our own processes of institutionalisation; of our own canons (however 'subcultural', 'emergent' or 'alternative' they may currently appear to be) ... Without such self-reflection and historical awareness, popular music scholars could end up like the rearguard of the old aesthetic canon, ethnocentrically claiming universal, absolute and other supra-socially transcendent values for one set of musical practices and ignoring the real conditions, functions, contexts and structural complexities of others.[35]

One such awareness of canonicity in the reception of rock music, and its dependence on the values of classical music and literature is presented in this book; Tagg's statement, however, is also warning against unconscious canonizing in popular music studies. Perhaps surprisingly in the context of such ambivalence towards the notion of a canon in popular music in general, the articles in the 'Special Issue on Canonisation' of *Popular Music* that appeared in January 2006 all take the presence of canon/s in popular music for granted, without always defining their understanding of the concept. This has resulted in a fascinating collection of essays that presents no single, clear outcome on the idea of a canon in popular music; as Motti Regev says in the introduction to the issue, 'The articles presented here are hopefully only an appetiser for future research on this subject.'[36] Other academic approaches that touch on the idea of a canon in popular music have been generally more dismissive of the idea of creating a canon, but recognize its potential to exist in popular culture. Interest in this subject is growing, however, and the debate is likely to be treated increasingly more directly in the future.

Even so, academic attempts to subvert the growth of a canon through academia cannot prevent popular histories of rock music emerging using traditional or canonically based models of greatness. The question of whether or not rock can be considered an art is an ongoing debate; indeed the borderlines between art and popular music, and indeed classical music and popular music, are more fluid than binary oppositions allow for. There is a sleight of hand involved in praising rock music through using classical music or canonical values on the one hand, and on the other hand asserting its difference. This question is a concern of academics and popular music writers alike, especially considering that some figures, notably Simon Frith, are difficult to classify as one or the other.

---

34   Philip Tagg, '"The Work": An Evaluative Charge', in *The Musical Work: Reality or Invention?*, ed. by Talbot, pp. 153–67 (p. 165).

35   Ibid., pp. 166–7.

36   Motti Regev, 'Introduction to Special Issue on Canonisation', *Popular Music*, 25/1 (January 2006), 1–2 (p. 2).

In *The Rolling Stone Illustrated History of Rock & Roll*, John Rockwell suggests a future for the definition of art and value in rock that is quite different from the canonic values of complexity and high unpleasure. Instead, Rockwell suggests that:

> Maybe real art is that which most clearly and directly answers the needs of its audiences. Which, in turn, means we can prize pure rock and pure pop, from Chuck Berry on, as "art" in no way inferior to that which may entail a more highly formalised technique for its execution ... Roll over Beethoven, indeed, and make room for us.[37]

Rockwell's suggestion hints at a way of potentially creating a canon based on values other than those of Western classical music and literature that may satisfy the viewpoints of critics like Tim Footman and Allan Moore, who seem deeply dissatisfied with the valuing of rock music through traditionally canonical terms. This canon is based on the success with which popular music satisfies given needs of its audience (including dance, escapism and exuberance), but can still allow room for the value of albums that satisfy a different audience through more traditional canonical values. The values of canons are, to an extent, external forces that have been applied to popular music; inherited ideals rather than inevitable conclusions. Following this, the final chapter of this book will return to the question set in the introduction of whether there is a 'canon of classics' emerging in rock music, and asks if the reception of rock reflects the future of canons in other fields.

---

37   John Rockwell, 'The Emergence of Art Rock', in *The Rolling Stone Illustrated History of Rock & Roll*, ed. by Anthony DeCurtis and James Henke with Holly George-Warren 2nd edn (London: Straight Arrow, 1992), pp. 492–9 (p. 498). From *The Rolling Stone Illustrated History Of Rock And Roll* by Rolling Stone, edited by Jim Miller, copyright © 1976, 1980 by Rolling Stone Press. Used by permission of Random House, Inc.

Chapter 6

The Rock Canon and the Future of Canons in our Culture

In the reception of rock albums a canon is often implied, but rarely spoken of. It is an assumed presence in some cases and yet rarely clarified. The actual word itself is seldom used in the reception of rock, and yet the values, terms and mechanisms of the canons of high art are demonstrably present in accounts of the ten albums studied. In this chapter two alternative perspectives will therefore be considered, the one assuming that there is a canon in rock, the other assuming that there is not, in order to explore the presence, usefulness, limitations and implications of a canon in rock music, as suggested by this study. Finally the discussion will turn to the pluralized nature of canons in today's culture and its implications for the future.

The Case For a Canon in Rock (Benefits and Crystallization)

Given reasonable qualification, there is clearly a growing canon of albums in rock music. As Chapters 2 and 3 of this book demonstrate, the qualities prized in canonical works are evident in the reception of these 'greatest albums', alongside the qualities described in Chapter 4 that are more contingent to rock. These albums are judged on similar terms and treated in similar ways to the masterworks of literature and classical music, they form a powerful presence in their field, and the greatness of some of these albums is becoming assumed, as indicated by their repeated positions of prominence in books and magazine polls of 'greatest albums'.

A canon comprises the works and artists generally considered to be the greatest in their field, and in the reception of rock music, albums can be considered as works with canonic potential and enduring appeal. To a certain extent, the fluidity of the concept of the work (as demonstrated by the varying approaches taken by the different authors of *The Musical Work: Reality or Invention?*) allows rock to define its own works.[1] However, albums also meet general requirements of the work in that they can be perceived as discretely individual, are reproducible and attributable, and are ascribed with status, originality and 'aura'. As suggested in Chapter 4, the identity of the artist, the particular music and subject matter, and the conditions under which the album was made (in the context of rock music as a whole and also the artist's personal story) all combine to present a discrete, identifiable whole, greater than the sum of its parts. As this study has also shown, the reception of these albums also reflects the

---

1   Michael Talbot, 'Introduction', in *The Musical Work: Reality or Invention?*, ed. by Michael Talbot (Liverpool: Liverpool University Press, 2000), pp. 1–13 (pp. 3–5).

qualities of wholeness, coherence, organicism, unity and genius associated with the concept of the work in music.[2] Through narratives of influence and repeated citation these albums are drawn together as a collocation of works.

There is a significant (and growing) number of books, including biography, analysis and social commentary, focusing on the ten albums and artists studied (this is especially true of the Beatles, but also Bob Dylan, the Beach Boys, the Rolling Stones, punk and Nirvana in particular). These form a constellation of secondary material supporting the value of the original works. Although the position of the academic study of popular music regarding the canonization of this music has thus far been somewhat ambivalent, aside from the *Beatlestudies* there is also an increasing number of critical essay collections focusing on central albums and artists, including *'Every Sound There Is': the Beatles' Revolver and the Transformation of Rock and Roll*, and *The Music and Art of Radiohead* (both published by Ashgate).[3]

The selection of the ten albums in Chapter 2 was deliberately objective, taken as they were from the *Mojo* critics' list of 1995, and they represent some of the albums and artists that have been most culturally reproduced. However, a cursory glance at the lists reproduced in the Appendix reveal that a host of other albums could easily have been chosen for analysis without markedly changing the argument or outcome, including *Dark Side of the Moon* (Pink Floyd), *Electric Ladyland* (the Jimi Hendrix Experience), *London Calling* (the Clash), *The Queen is Dead* (the Smiths), *Blonde on Blonde* (Bob Dylan) and *Sgt. Pepper's Lonely Hearts Club Band* (the Beatles). This strongly suggests a wider, or deeper, canon than just the ten albums featured in this book.

The most canonical album of all, and therefore the strongest indicator of canonicity in the reception of rock music, is arguably *Revolver*.[4] Assuming the Beatles to be the centre of the canon (comparable to Shakespeare at the centre of Bloom's canon), then *Revolver* is the most canonical album by the most canonical group. It is famously innovative but less fixed to a specific time than the psychedelic *Sgt. Pepper's Lonely Hearts Club Band*; influential (especially for the experimental production of 'Tomorrow Never Knows') but less ostentatious and flamboyant than *Sgt. Pepper*. It marks the midpoint of the Beatles' canonically experimental phase of rapid evolution as represented by the albums *Rubber Soul*, *Revolver* and *Sgt. Pepper*, and an increasing move away from simple, direct love songs and towards more challenging and opaque ideas (a direction already in evidence with *Rubber Soul*). *Revolver* presents the band as a far more autonomous, integrated unit compared to

---

2   See 'Work' in David Beard and Kenneth Gloag, *Musicology: The Key Concepts* (London and New York: Routledge, 2005), pp. 189–92.

3   *'Every Sound There Is': The Beatles' Revolver and the Transformation of Rock and Roll*, ed. by Russell Reising (Aldershot: Ashgate, 2002); *The Music and Art of Radiohead*, ed. by Joseph Tate (Aldershot: Ashgate, 2005).

4   This is corroborated at least in terms of 'greatest lists' by Ralf von Appen and André Doehring, 'Nevermind The Beatles, Here's Exile 61 and Nico: "The Top 100 Records of All Time" – A Canon of Pop and Rock Albums From a Sociological and an Aesthetic Perspective', *Popular Music*, Special Issue on Canonisation, 25/1 (January 2006), 21–39 (23). *Revolver* is second in Henrik Franzon's amalgamated list of 'greatest albums' on www.acclaimedmusic. net (*Pet Sounds* is first). However, given the centrality of the Beatles, overall *Revolver* may be considered the more canonical of the two.

the increasingly individual artistic identities they showed in later albums (apparent in the distinctly separate songwriting and vocal performances on *The Beatles/The White Album* of 1968). It marks, according to John Harris, the point at which the Beatles started to lose their young female (non-canonical) audience in favour of a more serious, more mature and more masculine following.[5] This album is also one of the earliest to feature prominently in polls of greatest albums, and therefore it has thus far survived the greatest 'test of time' and appears to be maintaining permanent relevance to new generations of critics and audiences.

The qualities of seriousness, ambition and artistic challenge that canons promote and represent may not form a central role in the ideology of popular music as a whole, but are notably present in the work of the ten artists selected, especially Bob Dylan, the Beatles and the Velvet Underground & Nico. As Simon Frith and Howard Horne observe in *Art into Pop*, artistic ambition and artistic sensibility have long since transferred into rock music, often directly through art schools and university institutions.[6] Therefore a canon in rock music satisfies Charles Altieri's idea that canons present a 'set of challenges and models'.[7]

Any definition of the canonical creates a non-canonical, and the canon has in the past been a means of differentiating between high and low culture. Seriousness is one of the qualities that mark the difference between rock and pop, and the disposable single and manufactured band (simple, repetitive, dance-driven, 'childish' pop) forms the non-canonical to this emergent canon of albums. Patti Smith, the only female representative in the albums featured in this book, is a singer-songwriter in the tradition of idiosyncratic artists, and therefore not a non-canonical identity in any aspect except gender. Even so, *Horses* is far less central to discussions of greatest albums than most of the other ten albums. Stylistically, this canon shows a bias towards singer-songwriters working in the traditional medium of rock (vocal, guitars and drums); and although the defining genre of album-as-work does not preclude the inclusion of other styles (such as rap, R&B, hip-hop and soul), on the whole these other styles have yet to be assimilated. The general biases of gender, race, genre and style displayed in the lists of 'greatest albums' reflect the internal categories of the canons of Western literature and classical music, and therefore draw comparisons and increase the suggestion of a canon in rock.

It is unsurprising that the reception of rock music has found qualities to admire in the albums that accord with the values of the literary and classical music canons, since rock music contains both words and music that have points of connection with these traditions. Even the attributes described in Chapter 4 as being non-canonical in the context of the canons of Western literature and classical music are in their own way modern reincarnations of older canonical qualities. Although the emphasis may be on production and performance rather than traditional notions of composition

---

5   John Harris, 'Out of Their Heads', in *From Elvis to the Beatles*, *Q* Special Edition: 50 Years of Rock 'N' Roll 1954–2004 (London: EMAP, 2004), 60–65 (62).

6   See Simon Frith and Howard Horne, *Art Into Pop* (London and New York: Routledge, 1989).

7   Charles Altieri, 'An Idea and Ideal of a Literary Canon', in *Canons*, ed. by Robert von Hallberg (Chicago and London: Chicago University Press, 1984), pp. 41–64 (p. 44).

(as defined by classical music), the albums are still valued for their originality and innovation in these areas. And it could be argued that the rock persona of the rebellious individual is simply a modern incarnation of the artist/genius.

The respect afforded to *The Velvet Underground & Nico* for its apparent influence on later albums suggests a strong narrative of influence in the reception of rock music, and also the retrospective creation of a tradition. That this respect is somewhat more notable than the album's general popularity is suggestive of the canonical mechanisms of privileging the difficult and the complex. The value attributed to these albums is displayed more through written reverence than airplay on the radio. And so the division between canon and repertory ('a canon is an idea, a repertory a plan of action') suggested by Joseph Kerman in 'A Few Canonic Variations' seems complete.[8] They may be voted as 'greatest albums', and agreed to be such by general consensus, but as Frith has noted in a light-hearted article for the *Observer*, many people will not own them, much less listen to them regularly.[9]

Yet these are also the albums that, it is assumed, are more likely to be revisited at different points in people's lives, rediscovered, and rethought, albums that appeal to a more mature audience. In other words, these albums appear to meet Bloom's canonical criterion that 'one ancient test for the canonical remains fiercely valid: unless it demands rereading, the work does not qualify'.[10]

There is an (almost) unspoken agreement of the importance of these albums, but this apparently unspoken agreement is actually created by magazine polls and the values displayed in the general reception of rock music. They are becoming the naturalized standards to be met, and their greatness increasingly assumed. As Citron has noted, 'As canonic values become entrenched over time, the prescriptive and normative powers of canons become even greater.'[11] The longer the Beatles, Bob Dylan and *Pet Sounds* remain central to narratives of greatness in rock music, the more subsequent music will be valued relative to these models.

If the lists of 'greatest albums' in music magazines are to be taken as a strong indicator of canonicity, then the age and interests of the critics and readers needs to be considered. The readership of the *NME* and *Mojo* tend to be adolescents or young males in their twenties and thirties and the writers of the magazine, adopting the attitude of being 'one of us', tend to reflect this age group. It is critics who traditionally form canons, either directly or indirectly through steering the opinions and values of the readers. The public do, however, have a greater say (than they would with traditional canons) in what lasts, since they form a direct audience for books on bands and albums. The prevalence of older albums in a canon largely created, or at least partially perpetuated by, the current generation of youth (such as

8   Joseph Kerman, 'A Few Canonic Variations', in *Canons*, ed. by Robert von Hallberg (Chicago and London: University of Chicago Press, 1984), pp.177–95 (p. 177).

9   Simon Frith, 'Our Favourite Rock Records Tend to Go Round and Round', The *Observer*, 6 September 1998. Copyright Guardian News & Media Ltd 1998.

10   Harold Bloom, *The Western Canon: The Books and School of the Ages* (London and New York: Harcourt Brace & Company, 1994), p. 30.

11   Marcia J. Citron, *Gender and the Musical Canon* (Cambridge: Cambridge University Press, 1993), p. 15.

the *Q* poll of 2006) can be taken as a strong indicator of canonicity since they were not the original audience for these albums, and so this music is being valued by successive generations.

A canon of albums in rock music, contingent to its institutions and its field, would have to recognize the importance of lists, rapid change and relatively large audience participation, at least for the moment. Lists especially are an inherent phenomenon of rock music reception, and one integral to the canon that is implied in music magazine polls and special features. Although the *NME* revolutionized their 1985 and 2003 lists of greatest albums to diminish the hegemony of artists such as the Beatles and Bob Dylan, these artists and albums have by now enough secondary material to no longer require the validation of high positions in these lists; indeed the lists are (deliberately) controversial *because* of their occasionally low ranking of these artists and albums. In effect they are simply expanding the canon with new works to complement the older, more established albums. The obscure albums that feature in these polls are often the most interesting in this context, as their presence justifies the guiding narrative of the heart of the list – they are generally perceived either as being influences on or having been influenced by the main albums concerned. Truly entrenched assumptions, stasis and a reduced number of experts commenting on the canon can only occur after more time has elapsed and more distance created from this music; however, the basic mechanisms of canon formation are already in place.

The Benefits of a Canon of Albums in Rock Music

The reasons we need canons in our culture (as outlined in Chapter 1) are still present, arguably more so since we now have almost limitless access to music through the record store, radio, television and Internet. The canon is inextricably bound to the practice of evaluating and valuing music; and canonization is a logical outcome of the process of trying to privilege any particular album (or music) over others. Individual albums are judged, and when these judgements are brought together, there is a semblance of order imposed in order to create an imagined but unified collocation of works. This imagined canon of albums in rock is intended to suggest music that is worthy of our time and money. These are the albums, it is implied, you should experience before you die. As more and more music is released and some albums also 'rediscovered', the choice facing music fans is bewildering, and so a canon is now, more than ever, useful in steering our choices.

There are sound commercial benefits to canons, since a canon of albums can be marketed as such. This is evident in the case of *Pet Sounds*, which has been sold with a sticker on its cover announcing its achievements in album polls; the authority of the music magazines is used to directly increase the value of the product. It has already been noted that commercialization was a strong reason in itself for generating a canon in classical music for the income to be made from 'publishing older music, promoting their performance, and writing about them', and this is reflected in the growing body of literature on the albums.[12] The canonical lists in rock music magazines are also a marketing opportunity: the 2003 *Rolling Stone* poll 'The 500 Greatest Albums of All

---

12   Ibid., p. 36.

Time' was littered with advertisements for the CD retailer Rhino.com;[13] while the full heading of the *NME*'s poll of 2003 reads '*NME*'s 100 Best Albums of All Time!: How many have you got?'[14] Thus the creation of a canon of rock albums is both a statement of aesthetic value and a shrewd business calculation.

Record labels that own these albums have strong reasons for wishing to crystallize a canon in which their product plays a central role. Artists will naturally enjoy greater royalties if their albums continue to be reissued due to their position in such a canon. The authors of books on the albums also have a vested interest in the longevity of the albums themselves for financial and often personal reasons, since the authors of such books tend to be far more overtly 'fans' of their subjects than authors who write from a more academic perspective. Ensuring the longevity of these albums and their high regard is therefore an ongoing concern for the artists, their critics and the music industry in general.

The values imbued by canons are the institutionalized models of good and bad; therefore, it is unsurprising that they be called upon for the purposes of legitimizing popular music. They are naturalized assumptions and criteria, and pass, consciously and unconsciously, into other realms of thought. Some, if not all, criteria of value in canons do seem 'natural' and universal in music of this type. Influence, for instance, is quite reasonably a mechanism recognized in the narratives of evolution that describe rock music. Noting that it is a quality shared with the high arts is not to necessarily say that it has pretensions of high status, and yet it draws comparisons through identified similarities.

Another benefit associated with the canon is that it brings prestige and stability to a field. This prestige may be bestowed directly onto the canonical artists who created these albums, onto the music, or onto the writers of secondary material for their role as experts on the albums. Rock music critics need a canon to define a field in which to display a deeper understanding, while musicologists have the authority of academia to support their position, and they influence the reception of rock only indirectly. Critics of popular music have constructed an ideology of rock; academics at least give the impression of observing at one step removed, able to criticize this ideology and question its integrity.[15] Therefore, the prestige bestowed on a field through a canon is arguably more desirable to the popular reception of rock music than academic reception, which may be one reason that this canon seems to be developing outside the institution of academia (the traditional propagator of canons). Canonical prestige and respect can make rock music more acceptable to a more conservative, sophisticated or mature audience, crossing, potentially, into an audience shared with the canons of classical music and literature. It also has the potential to broaden the appeal of rock music so that it is no longer considered purely the contemporary music of the young but also accommodates older classics for more general appreciation.

---

13   Various Contributors, 'The 500 Greatest Albums of All Time', *Rolling Stone*, 11 December 2003, 83–178.

14   Various Contributors, 'NME's 100 Best Albums of All Time!', *New Musical Express*, 8 March 2003, 35–42 (35).

15   This has happened since the earliest days of academic writing on popular music, for example Simon Frith, '"The Magic That Can Set You Free": The Ideology of Folk and the Myth of the Rock Community', in *Popular Music*, 1 (1981), 159–68.

The canon defines the boundaries of the field that both rock music writers and collectors work within, and deep knowledge of this field bestows a form of cultural capital. *High Fidelity* (both the book by Nick Hornby[16] and film starring John Cusack) is a well-known demonstration of the cultural capital present in rock music, and it reveals the largely 'canonical' values being employed in the rarefied environment of the vinyl record store populated by serious record collectors. Their knowledge is demonstrated through their constant compilation of lists and the breadth of their record collections. In the film of *High Fidelity* it is the naïve customer who is chastised for not owning Bob Dylan's *Blonde on Blonde*, and the customer who insults the shop by enquiring after non-canonical pop music who is forcibly ejected. These self-appointed experts who care deeply about a subject have devoted time to its study and believe themselves to have superior knowledge over the non-expert. As this authority of the 'expert' is difficult to claim in an inherently popular field, it is only in rarefied environments like specialist record stores that such cultural capital and assumed knowledge of the canon becomes highly pronounced.

The canon also represents permanence. While temporary fame is relatively easy to achieve in today's media environment, immortality comparable to that presented in the older canons is unlikely to result without a canon in rock that promotes and privileges longevity and perpetual modernity. Canons present a complex yet coherent account of the greatest achievements in a field, and this becomes a tradition that is affirmed by the valorizing actions of later critics and audiences. It remains to be seen if these albums require the formation of a canon in order to maintain a continued cultural presence.

While the canon of albums suggested in this study does not appear to function as a didactic model in academic institutions (similar to that of the literary canon in the ancient school), it does serve as a set of models for new artists. According to the ideology of rock suggested in Chapter 4, rock musicians tend to be self-taught; however, this still allows them to learn directly from canonical texts. This is what Frith implied when he named a canon of "'obviously canonical artists" in rock music … not … a critics' canon, but a canon of performers with whom "it would be very odd for someone who systematically wanted to be a rock musician not to be familiar"', for John Davies' article on canons in 1995.[17] These artists effectively represent the tradition of rock music, and their works serve as models to later generations.

The canon is also useful for drawing attention to the potential of the medium; it represents idealism and by extension maintains high standards. The ability of canons to 'implant the desire to struggle under the weight of the past to achieve comparable greatness' is not only applicable to the high arts.[18] New bands are seen to emulate the achievements of artists from the 1960s (implied in the *NME* list of 2003 that used subsequent influence as a criterion of greatness). Alternatively, the recognition of a fully cemented canon of works in rock music may encourage a new phase of radical departure and experimentation, such as has been seen in the modernist phase of classical music which split away from the established canon even as it was influenced by it, but in doing so, confirming the value of the original canon.

---

16   Nick Hornby, *High Fidelity* (London: Gollancz, 1995).

17   John Davies, 'Baroque and Roll', *Times Higher*, 15 December 1995, 13–14 (13).

18   Altieri, 'An Idea and Ideal of a Literary Canon', p. 52.

The canon also presents a common set of questions and a common object of study for readers of rock music magazines. Chapter 1 suggests that the sense of unity and shared culture created through canons promotes nationalism or a sense of community in an otherwise disparate culture. This unity created by the canon of rock albums manifests itself less through nationalism and more through a common community or audience for a particular magazine's views. As we are constantly immersed in the media, a canon in rock serves the very real purpose of delineating one type of music from the cultural swarm. Knowledge of the canon of albums is assumed in the readership of *Mojo* and, where there are gaps, it instructs by publishing special editions on certain artists and styles. It creates a readership with a common interest in the canon as well as new music that can be valued for similar reasons.

The canon is also a discursive tool, not a definite object and certainly not an unchanging object. It maintains standards, both in the sense of levels of achievement and also standard works that embody that achievement. Discussions of the great artists and works in the arts have continued for centuries and the canon supposedly represents the common consensus arrived at by authorities in the area. The lists of greatest albums are especially effective at prompting discourse about values in rock music, and the frequency with which they are published is a vivid expression of this ongoing debate.

A Crystallizing Canon of Increasing Conservatism

Insufficient time has elapsed to forecast how much of the change in lists of 'greatest albums' is an indicator of changing tastes, and how much is really deceptive movement hiding stasis. What remains constant for now are the values underpinning these lists, the importance of influence and progression, the album as a work, the genius singer-songwriter or band, and the perceived test of time. The importance and centrality of the Beatles in critics' polls and secondary literature is currently assured, reinforced periodically with anniversaries commemorating the albums and the band members. There is little to indicate that a canon will not continue to crystallize in a form recognizable to that of its present state.

While a celebration of the ephemeral (also implied in the nihilism) is important to the ideology of rock, longevity is an active concern for the canon. The longer the Beatles remain important and central to the reception of rock music, the more canonical they must be considered, in that they possess the quality of enduring value. Indeed, the members of the Beatles have come full circle from trying to distance themselves from their work in the Beatles to accepting their own canonical status. As Paul Trynka states:

> It's very different to be overshadowed by your work from five or 10 years ago than to be asked about your work from 30 years ago as if it's an evergreen classic of the genre. One is saying 'You were better in the old days' and the other is saying 'You will continue to influence popular culture 50 years from now.'[19]

---

19 Paul Trynka, discussing Paul McCartney's changing attitude towards the Beatles, quoted in Alex Petredis, 'A Little Help From Their Friends', The *Guardian G2*, 16 January 2004, 14–15 (15).

Production often meets the demands of reception, especially in rock where a high turnaround of new albums is expected. If the narrative dominated by the Beatles continues to persist, then more musicians will follow this path with an eye to posterity. To give coherence to the narratives of rock music histories, these bands will be promoted as natural successors to the great artists of the past. The same criteria of greatness have been applied to the new albums that are currently being added to the ranks of 'greatest albums'. This is especially, as noted in Chapter 4, the case for the album *The Stone Roses*; this particular album reinforces the canon as it becomes prominent within it, since it represents a more recent album that shows the 1960s to be an inescapable influence. Radiohead's increasing prominence in polls for the albums *OK Computer* and *The Bends* follows similar 'canonical' methods of justification.[20] These albums suggest the values and standards by which future albums will be judged. This situation, if it continues as it is, will lead to an ever more frozen canon which is only added to rather than usurped over the years.

The more the albums are identified as discrete works rather than intertextual facets of the cultural landscape, the more they are able to be crystallized into a canon. And the album, both in terms of being a unified musical work, and in terms of being a physical object that is durable, reusable, reproducible, and provides fully realized sound, makes an enduring canonical object. The album also creates none of the problems of interpretation faced by performers of score or text-based classical music, and so presents a complete object for canonical discussion.

In any 50-year time period neither the canon of Western literature nor classical music upholds as many as 100 works as truly 'great' as do the lists of greatest albums, much less the 500 that *Rolling Stone* magazine presented in 2003 or the (periodically updated) 1,000 offered by the *All-Time Top 1,000 Albums*. For any five decades of history, only a handful of artists will be recognized as artistic giants. Over time the current canon will most likely be reduced to a far smaller number of great artists and works; assuming that current trends will continue, then rock may come to effectively confirm a canonical trinity of the Beatles, Bob Dylan and the Rolling Stones who represent the values and achievements of the canon (just as the trinity of Haydn, Mozart and Beethoven have represented classical music in the past).

The lists of 'greatest albums' increasingly include albums of the 1970s, and new albums follow a pattern of inclusion and later exclusion (with the possibility of reappearance later on). As already noted in the case of *Revolver*, those albums that remain from the 1960s are in a sense the most canonical as they are the longest survivors of the test of time, but are still central to rock music narratives. Simon Frith also identifies this pattern in the *All-Time Top 1,000 Albums*, saying 'In the 1,000 Albums Chart, the late Sixties/early Seventies and the Nineties are the creative years, nothing much happened in the Eighties, it seems.' For the future, however, he predicts that 'in 10 years' time Eighties albums will have become classics: Nineties albums

---

20   See for example the successive editions of the *All-Time Top 1,000 Albums*, quoted in the Appendix; in the second edition of 1998, Radiohead have one album, *The Bends*, in the top ten. By the time of the third edition, Radiohead have two albums in the top ten, but the Beatles still have four and Bob Dylan one.

disappeared from memory.'[21] This was naturally, however, only conjecture, and in the ten years since that article was written, the music of the 1980s has failed to rise in prominence at the expense of that of the 1990s in lists of 'greatest albums'. The Stone Roses and Radiohead, both generally considered 'Nineties' artists, are rapidly gaining dominance in critics' polls without the re-emergence of the 1980s.[22] 'Canonical' values and lines of influence back to the 1960s are easier to trace in the albums of the 1990s compared to the synthesized pop and metal of the 1980s, and album polls may eventually, with a few notable exceptions (such as *Hounds of Love* by Kate Bush or *The Queen is Dead* by the Smiths), bypass the decade in its entirety.

Unless popular music makes a very definite shift away from the rock album tradition as epitomized by the ten albums studied here, contemporary works will continue to interfere with the order of greatest albums lists. Only when everything is sufficiently in the past, all the artists concerned are dead and the reception of this music is based on secondary sources rather than primary experience, is this likely to change; then there is a strong possibility the Beatles, the Rolling Stones, Bob Dylan, the Beach Boys, the Velvet Underground and others will be fully acknowledged as canonical artists and thence the canon will change far less. It will be in a state of suspended animation, detached, reflecting the frozen canon of classical music. According to this theory, there will be less need for the canon to keep changing as it will have a less direct influence on current, new, contemporary music. Currently the field is more claustrophobically *present* than the great works of literature and the great artists of classical music. This is another reason for selecting albums (mainly) from the late 1960s and early 1970s. They represent canonical values but are also safely stowed in the past, allowing for far more (apparently) objective assessment.

Works must have the potential to be reconfigured many times to satisfy successive audiences, and they will not survive if they directly oppose the values of those who select them. This indicates that it is not only the complex, but also the broadly inoffensive, in other words the most conservative, that will survive in a canon. The albums that are integral to the ruling narratives of rock, that do not contradict the values embodied in the canon, and that are easy to defend in terms of value (calling on structures of value from the high arts for justification) are the most likely to survive. However, as popular music is omnipresent and still very recent, there is less need to suppress undesirable aspects in canonical works as we can simply choose albums that concur with the values of the day. Time, again, is needed to test these albums against changing values.

There is, in addition to (or perhaps one reason for) this increasing conservatism, a growing interest and audience (or market) for nostalgia in rock, and the celebration of the 'old'. This is unsurprising as the audience of rock music now comprises the young and the formerly young. In the reception of rock music such celebration of the past includes the retrospective articles and special editions of *Mojo* magazine,

---

21   Simon Frith, 'Our Favourite Rock Records Tend to Go Round and Round'.

22   Although *The Stone Roses* was released in 1989, it is perceived as being one of the first albums in the Britpop phase of the 1990s, and although Radiohead are still together at the time of writing, two of their most 'canonical albums' with which they are often most associated, *The Bends* and *OK Computer*, were released in 1995 and 1997 respectively.

the anthologizing of the Beatles' work in the mid-1990s, and 'greatest hits' tours of older artists (including the Beach Boys, and more recently, Paul McCartney) or nostalgic cover bands (notably the Bootleg Beatles). Indeed, Andrew Goodwin suggests that a stasis in rock music (comparable to the situation in classical music) has already arrived, since the ubiquity of CDs has resulted in the reissue of 'oldies' and contemporary rock appeals to all ages.[23]

Returning to the question posed in the introduction to this book: is rock music in the process of creating a canon of classics? If a canon can be reduced to the idea of a collocation of works, that supports and preserves the values of a society or community, and which is riddled with the values of artist/genius, progressive evolution, influence and indefinable greatness, then a canon of albums is indisputable. But this canon is less stable than the 'ancient' canons of literature and classical music, and appears dependent on the logic and authority of the canons of literature and classical music. As Citron notes, the canon in classical music is based on:

> An exaltation of the persona of the composer; and emphasis on originality and innovation; a preference for the large over the small – in length, performing forces, and performing location; and recognition of the signs of participation in the public arena – professionalism, publication, reviews.[24]

While most of these elements have been shown to underscore the reception of rock albums, the same cannot be said for popular music as a whole. Citron goes on to suggest that these values are socially contingent paradigms, 'not natural and universal' ideas;[25] and if these ideals are not natural and universal, they are therefore not inevitable. This position opens up the possibility of alternative canons, or alternatives to canons altogether, which will now be explored through the alternative position that there is not, and possibly never will be, a canon in rock music.

The Case Against a Canon in Rock (Limitations and Fragmentation)

It is easy to see how the elitist standards of the old canons have been applied to the high arts; it is more contestable that these elitist values should now be deemed appropriate for the reception of rock music. While rock music writers undoubtedly use canonical values in their reception of the music, the ideology of rock (including rebellion, youth, urgency, hedonism and nihilism, and its hoary connections with everyday culture) repels the idea of a fixed canon. Any attempt to represent this music as a collection of works with deep lasting meaning independent of contemporary culture is therefore inherently problematic.

The rebellious ideology of rock also makes the idea of an institutionalized canon anathema. Popular music deliberately sets itself against the high culture of literature and classical music; as has been said more than once, 'Roll Over Beethoven'. But in

---

23 *On Record: Rock, Pop and the Written Word*, ed. by Simon Frith and Andrew Goodwin (London: Routledge, 1990), p. 258.

24 Citron, *Gender and the Musical Canon*, p. 202.

25 Ibid., p. 202.

doing so, it is setting itself against the possibility of gaining similar status in the arts, to which the canon is an integral concept. Given that the state of rebellion is inherent to the ideology of rock music, it seems unnatural that if rock were to develop a canon it should do so on the terms of established high culture; this explains the objections of Tim Footman to the conservative selection of albums made by *Rolling Stone* in its 2003 list of 'greatest albums'. It also explains *Time Out*'s claim back in 1989 that *Let's Get It On* is 'a better record than "What's Going On", which is merely "important"'.[26]

Aside from this, no canon can include nihilism, as epitomized by the Sex Pistols, without a certain sense of irony. And yet that in itself is not a problem to the formation of a canon, since *Never Mind the Bollocks: Here's the Sex Pistols* can be regarded as 'great' for the enduring reasons of sonic originality and as an aural representation of nihilism in itself. However, such internal struggles destabilize the internal logic, and thus authority, of a potential canon.

Another element of the ideology of rock, that of youth, reacts against the formation of a canon of old classics; tradition (as embodied by the tastes of their parents) is there to be rebelled against. Canonization suggests extended, detached study and publications by mature individuals, while much popular music is appreciated for its ebullience; whether such a quality endures is another matter.

Aside from this, rock music cannot gain the same respect as literature and classical music purely through demonstrating the presence of high-art qualities or values in the reception of its albums, and it is both under- and overestimated by these canonical terms. Much of the power of popular music, which is seen to rest in its immediacy of emotion, mass appeal and connection with contemporary culture, is ignored in this process of canonization. The reception of these albums has noted these canonical qualities, and it is true that the albums are relatively more complex, more mature, more serious, more original, more intellectual, larger scale, and more associated with 'genius' than most popular music. And yet, relative to the works of the canons of Western literature and classical music, they are generally simpler, more youthful, more fun, less intellectual and less serious, smaller scale and associated with not one but many authors (if all band members and producers are to be accounted for). Even though these albums represent the more serious, complex and difficult end of the popular music spectrum, they barely meet Bloom's contention that the purpose of canonical works is not to give immediate pleasure, but rather a 'more difficult pleasure' or even a 'high unpleasure'.[27] The immediacy of popular music presents no such sombre subject, and leads more usually to instant pleasure. Since rock music cannot compete with the works of the canons of literature and classical music on the terms by which they were selected, such comparison invites scorn and derision, and suggests a weakness in this music in that it appears to be seeking borrowed glory.

Rock music could instead be considered an inherently intertextual, kleptomaniac culture that uses high cultural values where it suits it, to give the impression of longevity and complexity, while simultaneously discarding and refuting such values. If this is the case, then rock music has only fragmented reflections of a canon, not a

---

26 Various Contributors, 'The 100 Greatest Albums of All Time According to *Time Out*', compiled by Nick Coleman and Steve Malins, *Time Out*, 21–28 June 1989, 18–23, p. 18.

27 Bloom, *The Western Canon*, p. 30.

collocation of works that are privileged by logic internal to the discipline. However, this situation contains a sleight of hand that defies definition: on the one hand the reception of the ten albums featured in this book clearly shows that the writers wish to privilege this music for 'canonical' reasons (true even of the *NME* poll that defiantly declared it not to be a canon of 'classics'), while on the other hand they very rarely claim similarity with or a desire to be compared with classical music. Instead a new definition of art is employed, one that defines works of art as revelatory, groundbreaking, but also contemporary. The model of the canon derived from those of literature and classical music (as described in Chapter 1) can be employed to explain the value of certain albums; and in certain cases like *Pet Sounds* it works reasonably well. At the same time, when an album contradicts the apparent underlying values shared by canonical works, it can be celebrated for being a canonical anti-canonical gesture (as is particularly the case for the Sex Pistols). The terms 'canonical' and 'non-canonical' are therefore redrawn in the reception of rock music.

The reception of rock music is less often critical than it is an attempt to bring the experiences of live music and the character of the singer-songwriter to the reader. This does not reflect the 'quasi-scientific', 'empirical' reception of canonical works of art (as discussed in Chapter 1), but can on the other hand be said to reflect the subject matter it is describing. Often, canonical terms such as 'sublime', 'transcendent' and 'timeless' seem to be used simply as buzzwords or to emphasize a point, without any real evidence that they are intended in the same way as they are employed in the reception of high art. The attempt to describe music in words has always been problematic; curiously the recommendations included on the inside cover of the Continuum series on rock albums draws attention to this fact by admitting that 'reading about rock isn't quite the same as listening to it, but this series comes pretty damn close'.[28] However, the relatively low status afforded to this reception (in music magazines and populist books) does not easily lend authority to any canon.

In academia there is obvious ambivalence towards the idea of a canon in rock music, as was demonstrated in Chapter 5 through contrasting Allan Moore's anti-canonical position with the overtly canonizing *Beatlestudies* project. And given Philip Bohlman's assertion that 'creating canons and buttressing them is indeed a normative task for musicologists', then this gives reason to doubt any possible future for a canon in the field.[29] Popular musicologists are in a sense already considered non–canonical academics compared to more traditional musicologists studying Beethoven and Bach. And for many musicologists, the qualities of popular music that are most redolent of classical music (and to a degree literature) are of less interest because these qualities have already been debated elsewhere. Other figures than the Beatles and other styles and genres of popular music than the rock album have proven fascinating to academics in the last 20 years. Often it is qualities that have little to do with canonicity that attract the attention of popular musicologists.

---

28   A quote from *Neon NYC* in Jim Fusilli, *Pet Sounds*, 33 1/3 Series (New York and London: Continuum, 2005), inside front cover.

29   Philip V. Bohlman, 'Epilogue: Musics and Canons', in *Disciplining Music: Musicology and Its Canons*, ed. by Katherine Bergeron and Philip V. Bohlman (Chicago and London: University of Chicago Press, 1992), pp. 197–210 (p. 199).

A similar ambivalence is witnessed in popular reception, as seen in the *NME* quote that heads the introduction to this book. Given the number of rock music critics and potential figures of authority in the field, a consensus will be hard to achieve. Perhaps we are waiting for a book comparable to Bloom's *The Western Canon* to elucidate the canon in rock music; and yet such a book is more likely to trigger more intensified debate on the subject rather than bring about a consensus. Artists have also reacted differently to the idea of their music being taken seriously and analysed as potential canonical works. Things designed for play are rarely taken seriously, and yet popular music can sustain serious academic investigation. However, this idea is undermined by the perception voiced by Bloom that 'cultural criticism is another dismal social science, but literary criticism, as an art, always was and always will be an elitist phenomenon.'[30] Popular music is, by its most obvious definition, deliberately popular and so an elitist criticism (and canon) would seem to warp its fundamental basis. When the *NME* introduction to the 2003 critics' poll of '100 Best Albums' stated that 'this isn't a boring attempt to create some kind of canon of "classics" – just an honest account of what continues to rock our world', they were reacting against the idea of their magazine promoting a staid and conservative doctrine, while retaining the canonic notion that the music that survives is that which attains perpetual modernity (or permanent relevance).[31]

Another problem with the idea of a canon as a collocation of works (albums) is that both canons and works have somewhat fluid and interdependent definitions as concepts, variously applied over time and by different people. The majority of the writers on popular music in the collection of essays on 'the work' edited by Michael Talbot, *The Musical Work*, argue for a conception of popular music that is based on practice rather than texts (or works). While the ten albums have been treated as discrete aural texts in 'greatest album' polls and individual books about the albums, when they are considered in the context of the field of popular music as a whole, it is harder to maintain this separation. Even if we accept albums as works, the obvious differences between the different albums in these polls (even the ten featured in this book) threaten their common identity as a collocation of works. Marvin Gaye's *What's Going On* belongs to a distinctly separate musical tradition from the Beatles' albums, and *The Velvet Underground & Nico* occupies a niche of its own, whereas accounts of *Never Mind the Bollocks: Here's the Sex Pistols* represent the album as a nihilistic challenge to the rock music tradition that the canon represents. Only with time and the erosion of difference can these albums become a unified tradition.

Canons embody ideologies of timelessness and distilled wisdom; however, the canon of rock albums, such as it is, is in a constant state of flux, which is all the more noticeable due to the compressed time span it encapsulates, the need for change from the perspective of magazine polls, and the need to prove its vitality and progressive momentum. The focus of the reception of rock music is still predominantly on contemporary artists and albums (although, as noted above, there is a growing tendency towards privileging the music of the past), and so the identification of a confirmed canon would appear, at the very least, to be premature.

---

30 Bloom, *The Western Canon*, p. 17.
31 Various Contributors, 'NME's 100 Best Albums of All Time!', *New Musical Express*, 35.

Usually canons deal with works created numerous decades or even centuries ago and secondary material supporting their value represents the ensuing debates over many generations. In rock music, however, there seems little room for such a debate as the past, present and future (as represented by the audience of rock) are all present at the same time. Canons cannot shift on a weekly basis, but this is the reality for music magazines. Lists are inherently disposable unless presented in books such as Grout's *A History of Western Music* or Bloom's *Western Canon*, or used as the basis of a didactic textbook. Were it not for the great number of lists of 'greatest albums' that surround us, these might actually hold some weight, but even by considering only the lists generated by the *NME* every ten years, we soon weary of the inevitable juggling of old and new, fully aware that a similar shuffling of albums is scheduled to happen in ten years' time. The canon is only ever a partially defined collocation of works, apparently (if not actually) unchanging over centuries, whereas the selection and rejection of these albums is constantly in view, and therefore highly questionable.

Another problem that needs to be resolved before a canon can be formed is the lack of consensus between canonizers over the field and criteria of value that the canon should include. While Chapters 2 and 3 of this book quite reasonably present the ten albums as being central to narratives of rock, the field of reception is not as clear cut as this (necessarily) suggests. The Continuum series of books on albums does include one each on *Pet Sounds*, *Exile on Main St.*, *The Velvet Underground & Nico*, *Highway 61 Revisited* and *Horses*, but not the other five. The rest of the series (which is still growing rapidly) includes at least two emphatically non-canonical albums in the form of Abba's *Abba Gold* and Celine Dion's *Let's Talk About Love*, and several far more obscure albums than those discussed in this book. While these books on albums are available to the public, they are unlikely to be bought and read by anyone who is not already an ardent fan of the artist, and so their long-term canonizing potential is debatable.

An enduring consensus is needed between the various institutions of rock, and also a large body of secondary material that supports this consensus of the core values and prized works of the discipline, before a canon can be consolidated. A canon supported entirely by lists is insubstantial and far too prone to change to generate an enduring canon. The reception of rock music in magazines has the potential to diversify or to unify the field, and given that a canon of albums is by no means representative of popular music as a whole, these tensions may continue to fight against the formation of a permanent canon.

There are other reasons why a canon of rock music is problematic. Canons are arbiters of cultural value and cultural capital, yet without a recognized institution of authority such values and capital will always be open to debate. Music magazines may appear to be the most authoritative institutions in this field, and yet they are also likely to deny their position as propagators of a canon, due to the attendant conservatism that such a construct implies. Moreover, popular music has always been intended to be understood by the masses, and if it does contain additional layers of meaning for future generations to dissect, it is unlikely to have been wholly deliberate given the generally contemporary nature of the field. Having a canon (in its oldest sense) suggests that works have value for centuries, not just decades. And so far those who might be considered the main canonizers in the field have yet to reach a consensus of whether rock should have a canon at all, let alone the terms on which to base such a structure. This does not necessarily mean that a canon cannot form, but rather that it has a weaker presence and authority over the field than the canons of literature and classical music.

Since canons represent stasis, the presence of a canon may suggest that we have come to the end of rock's creative period and rock music can now be left to rest. If indeed the dominance of the Beatles were to become (even more) overarching, it might just as easily precipitate a revolution of values in the field as lead to a confirmed canon. In a field where rapid changes of opinions are hardly remarkable, and fashions and styles last mere weeks or months rather than decades or centuries, such a static concept as a canon is unlikely to take root amid the continual flow of material, unless it is to become detached from this flow and marooned in history (as is the usual fate of canons to some extent).

Other objections include the limiting nature of a canon in the choice of music it presents to us. One of the main problems with a canon of rock albums as understood in Chapters 2 and 3 is that it revisits and reinforces the perceived negativity of the established canons of literature and classical music. Many of Tim Footman's objections to the *Rolling Stone* '500 Greatest Albums of All Time' (discussed in Chapter 5) are based on such limitations, including the repetitive nature of these lists, the small number of artists that represent a large proportion of the list, the marked preference for older music over new, the bias towards the album-as-work, the bias towards rock over soul, folk, hip-hop or jazz, the conservatism displayed in the selection, the dominance of men and the 'sheer monoculturalism' presented in such lists.[32]

In such a contemporary, popular medium, democracy of representation seems a more realistic goal than for the old established canons. However, as this study has shown, the reception and practice of rock music is notable for its replication of the same (art) values that support a canon of Western, white (increasingly dead) men, created, by and large, by white male critics. A canon in any field represents what is important, and what endures. But a canon cannot hope to represent what is important to everyone, and so the canon's anti-democratic nature must be understood if it is to be accepted.

A Canon With No Future?

The future of any canon in rock music seems unstable; this is, however, true to an extent of all canons. As noted in Chapter 1, canons in their very nature are not stable as they constitute the binary opposites of unity and difference, progress and stasis. However, stability needs to exert itself for these values to become entrenched and therefore resistant to large-scale change and usurpation.

As long as rock music magazines keep visibly reshuffling and augmenting their lists of greatest albums, and as long as academics continue to resist a dominant canon, a nascent canon may not become entrenched. Perhaps this embryonic canon is simply the music that fits the criteria of the canons of high art, no more or less. Not a canon that has grown on its own, but rather the representation of a jumble of

---

32 Taken from 'Gathering Moss: The Fossilisation of *Rolling Stone*' by Tim Footman, published by *Rock's Backpages*, at www.rocksbackpages.com, November 2003. Used by permission.

canonic values mapped onto popular music: a parasite canon, dependent on other canons for its survival but with roots in the low or the popular; or, alternatively, the shadows that the canons of the high arts cast onto popular music. While the Stone Roses have been noted to have canonized the music of the 1960s by finding it to be an inescapable influence, it remains to be seen if this heralds the end of progress into ever decreasing circles or if new directions will be sought to continue a forward-moving tradition, departing increasingly from the values of the canons of Western literature and classical music.

This potential canon of rock albums seems to be going through stages of canonization at an accelerated rate, as other, established canons have already done much of its thinking for it. Objections to its formation take the same form as the anti-canonic protests that the literary and classical music canons are facing. And since it uses the values of canons from other fields to value its own music, it may transpire that the canon of rock is built on illusory foundations that render it far more vulnerable than the established canons.

Frank Kermode has described canonical works as possessing 'something like omnisignificance'.[33] The question remains whether there is enough inherent complexity and the potential for further reading into these albums to satisfy the needs of successive generations in the way that Shakespeare is endlessly re-read and reconfigured. The impressive amount of information we possess on the biographies of the artists involved limits our powers of imagination in reinterpreting works. If a work no longer satisfies our curiosity, then it may be discarded.

Perhaps a canon of rock can only form if it resists the usual mechanisms of canons by maintaining the cultural context of the album as part of the work itself. Popular music is highly dependent on and is woven into the fabric of contemporary culture and the value of the artists is calculated partly through their cultural impact. Greil Marcus describes the 'pop explosion' that occurred with the Beatles' arrival in America:

> A pop explosion is an irresistible cultural upheaval that cuts across lines of class and race (in terms of sources if not allegiance), and, most crucially, divides society itself by age. The surface of daily life (walk, talk, dress, symbolism, heroes, family affairs) is affected with such force that deep and substantive changes in the way large numbers of people think and act take place.[34]

This is, for some, the true power of the Beatles, and yet such an impact is lost when the cultural context is eradicated. These composers and bands are part of the cultural fabric, famous across the world. For instance, Dan Silver claims that 'by April 1994 Nirvana were, if not the biggest, then certainly the most significant band in the

---

33   Frank Kermode, *Forms of Attention* (Chicago and London: University of Chicago Press, 1985), p. 62.

34   Greil Marcus, 'The Beatles', in *The Rolling Stone Illustrated History of Rock & Roll*, ed. by Anthony DeCurtis and James Henke with Holly George-Warren, 2nd edn (London: Straight Arrow, 1992), pp. 209–22 (p. 214). From *The Rolling Stone Illustrated History Of Rock And Roll* by Rolling Stone, edited by Jim Miller, copyright © 1976, 1980 by Rolling Stone Press. Used by permission of Random House, Inc.

world, and Cobain's death was headline material.'[35] Removing the albums from their cultural context and original effect on audience, culture and society strips them of much of their value. Canonic works are deemed to be autonomous, but the process of recontextualizing the allegedly decontextualized canonic works has been a growing concern of literary criticism and musicology in recent years.

If this canon of albums is declared to be universal, especially if the field it represents is popular music by its broadest definition, then it needs to represent a large number of different perspectives – too large a number to be governed by the internal logic of one canon. Too many people are apparently concerned, given the status of rock music as belonging to the masses, to have such a clear model. But if a canon of albums is recognized as simply the values of a particular group perpetuated for their own reasons, then the inherent power of the canon is reduced to being simply one option in the field.

Indeed, far more so than is possible in literature and classical music, this potential canon of rock albums appears to be inherently optional. Although it is in the nature of canons that they cannot represent everything, questioning the supremacy of these albums is far easier and considerably less contentious than questioning the central role of Shakespeare in literature. Regarding these canonical values as optional seems imperative to alternative perspectives such as those of feminism or multiculturalism. This conception of the canon as inherently optional forfeits some of the power and authority associated with the entrenched canons of literature and classical music in the past, but it may also stand a greater chance of survival.

The Test of Time on an Unstable Canon

There is an element of resignation to the 'test of time' in this argument, which cannot be conclusively resolved, and at this point it is impossible to say whether a canon will crystallize or not. Bloom has described canons as the 'Art of Memory', emphasizing that canons recall the great works of otherwise forgotten times, not recent events. If wisdom through hindsight truly is the ruling logic of the canon, then we are simply not in a position to judge. Reverence is meant to accumulate with age, and it is difficult to have a canon in the moment since the very nature of canon formation demands that context be partially forgotten and other works jettisoned in favour of the honoured few. While we remain in the moment, many voices will defend the works that are apparently being forgotten and so this multitude of canonizers with a vested interest or claim of authority needs to be reduced to a smaller number with greater authority before a consensus can be achieved.

The ten albums featured in this book have the potential to become part of a canon if their value is reasserted for time to come, or if the values central to rock reception remain derivative of those values of the high arts. However, canonical works need to be interpreted by each new generation, and as long as the creators are still alive, it is more difficult to read into works qualities that were not intentionally there at their inception, without risk of the artist deriding or denying such claims. Shakespeare

---

35   Dan Silver, 'Love Will Tear Us Apart', in *From U2 to the White Stripes*, *Q* Special Edition: 50 Years of Rock 'N' Roll 1954–2004, (London: EMAP, 2004) 84–7 (85).

and Beethoven are no longer with us to dispute the claims made for their work, but rock god avatars still walk the earth; and by these criteria of value the artist/genius has some considerable canonic authority.

New rock albums are still taken seriously and a large audience remains for this music. However, increasingly it appears that new albums are not considered of comparable value to older ones until they have themselves withstood a test of (at least, say, ten year's) time; when new artists are promoted as being 'better than the Beatles', it is usually regarded as a marketing ploy rather than a genuine (supportable) claim. There is more of a certainty when dealing with the objects of the past than in judging the merits of contemporary works. It is what is remembered that becomes canonical, but currently certain artists are in a better position to be remembered.

Judging by the four *NME* lists of greatest albums that have appeared periodically over the last four decades, conventionally canonical thinking in rock, typified by the privileging of the Beatles, Dylan and the Rolling Stones, actually fluctuates over time, much as Anita Silvers has said that 'within any discourse addressing an art, the positive contributions of appeals to canons tend to wax and wane cyclically.'[36] Artists and albums can be reassessed in light of new developments and such fluctuating reception is evident in the case of *What's Going On*. For instance, Paul Gambaccini claims that 'since he was killed by his father, Marvin Gaye has been appreciated far more fully than he was even in his extraordinary career'; this new appreciation, according to Gambaccini, 'marks a major re-evaluation by the critical establishment'.[37] In the foreword to *I Just Wasn't Made For These Times*, Tony Asher recalls his sorrow that *Pet Sounds* was not better received in its day and had apparently been all but forgotten, and then his surprise upon discovering renewed interest in the album in the 1990s, which led to the album's reissue on CD.[38] Such an account depicts a very different history of the reception of these albums to the now accepted notion of their 'great' status and perpetual modernity.

Even the importance of the Beatles, who are central to the ruling logic of the canon of rock albums suggested in this book, has fluctuated. During the 1970s a stream of re-released singles failed to make any real impact on the charts. It could be argued that at this time the Beatles were not canonical but pre-canonical. Alex Petredis's article for the *Guardian* called 'A Little Help' is revealing in terms of the central notion that the Beatles have defined the rock (or 'pop') art form, since it suggests that this idea was achieved through a conscious move on the part of the music magazines to sustain this interest in the band:

> "We put the Beatles on the cover of Q in 1987 for the 20th anniversary of Sergeant Pepper, and it was seen as a real risk," remembers Mark Ellen, then editor of Q, now editor of Word. "They were just seen as an old group who had split up – and there were plenty of old groups who were still about."

---

36   Anita Silvers, 'The Canon in Aesthetics', in *The Encyclopaedia of Aesthetics*, ed. by Michael Kelly (Oxford: Oxford University Press, 1998), I, pp. 334–8 (p. 346).

37   Paul Gambaccini, *Paul Gambaccini Presents the Top 100 Albums* (GRR/Pavilion: London, 1987), p. 14.

38   Charles L. Granata, *I Just Wasn't Made for These Times: Brian Wilson and the Making of Pet Sounds* (London: Unanimous, 2003), pp. 12–18.

1

38

THE ROCK CANON

But early in the 1990s, with the rise of Britpop, musical tastes shifted again. As [*Mojo* writer Paul] Trynka says: "People just thought, pop music is always going to be about a song, with a beat and guitar we're working within a defined artform rather than moving outside the confines of it. And the Beatles had been responsible for defining a lot of that." In recent years, magazine covers have proclaimed the Beatles as everything from The World's Hottest Band (Rolling Stone) to the godfathers of garage rock (NME). Mojo puts them on their cover every 13 months without fail, while Word's Beatles coverage has been so extensive that the Mail on Sunday recently came to the conclusion that McCartney was actually working for the magazine.

Petredis notes that the future centrality of the Beatles is far from assured, since 'rock music could shift away from the Beatles' influence once more, as it did in the 1980s.' He goes on to describe some of the underlying marketing decisions that aim to perpetuate their position of value. According to Apple employee Jonathan Clyde:

> If Apple showered the market with DVDs and CD compilations and went into overdrive on merchandising, the Beatles' reputation for integrity would be compromised. Apple is here to protect a precious cultural legacy. Any short term gain would be utterly self-defeating.[39]

Such statements as these underlie the fact that such reception as has been analysed in this book is forever underpinned by the decisions of the music industry to promote their product in a certain light. They also suggest that the centrality and reputation of even the Beatles hangs in the balance, and that a distinct canon in rock does seem to happen in phases.

The mid-1990s – which saw the creation and dissemination of the *Mojo* list on which the selection of albums for this study was based, the peak of Britpop (a nostalgic celebration of the music of the 1960s), the release of the Beatles *Anthology*, and in academia the creation of the *Beatlestudies* project – appears to be the most affirmatively canonizing 'phase' in the reception of rock to date. Whether this anticipates a crystallizing canon or a fragmentation of the field will depend on the direction of rock music reception in the future. Given that this nascent canon is dependent on the values and mechanisms of established canons, then its future may be similarly intertwined; and the role of canons in our culture is a matter of ongoing debate. The question of a canon in rock music is therefore inevitably an ongoing one, for in the reception of popular music we are not simply trying to organize the past but mediate the present.

Conclusion

It has been argued that the reception of rock music albums reflects the canonical values, terms and mechanisms found in the reception of the canons of literature and classical music. Therefore, this study is a response to the call made by Philip Tagg that

> we need to be acutely aware of our own processes of institutionalisation; of our own canons (however 'subcultural', 'emergent' or 'alternative' they may currently appear to be) ... Without such self-reflection and historical awareness, popular music scholars could

---

39 Petredis, 'A Little Help From Their Friends', 15.

end up like the rearguard of the old aesthetic canon, ethnocentrically claiming universal, absolute and other supra-socially transcendent values for one set of musical practices and ignoring the real conditions, functions, contexts and structural complexities of others.[40]

This detailed analysis of both the canons of Western literature and classical music, and the reception of rock music as represented by ten albums has revealed the clear presence of canonical terms and values in the reception of these albums, but also inherent tensions that impede the formation and stability of a canon in the field. It has been shown that the value placed on originality, authenticity, seriousness, pure artistic motivation and autonomy, complexity, lack of transparency, the necessity of re-reading, the unified work, the genius/author, influence, and longevity, which are all central to narratives of established canons, are all reflected in the reception of these albums. Values more contingent to the reception of rock music albums, including rebellion, sonic originality, authenticity of performance, nihilism, hedonism, image, youth and contemporary relevance can be regarded as modern manifestations of traditional canonical values. However, underlying tensions in the field, the popular and intertextual nature of rock music and the conflict of canonic authority undermine the stability of this potential canon, and so these values are rendered at least partially optional.

The question has also been raised as to whether the creation of a canon is inevitable in any field. It would seem that the reception of rock music can be considered canonical in places, whereas the albums do not constitute a permanent canon as of yet (although this may ultimately be a matter of individual perception). A true canon is never optional since the canon constitutes the works and artists generally considered to be the greatest in their field. Such a consensus, not only of works but also of the field, remains a matter of debate.

Evidently there is a case for and against a canon in rock music. Canons exist somewhere between imagination and reality, lists and histories, and between the idea of 'the greats' and actual works that can be dissected; the canon is incorporeal and yet ever-present. It is this undefined and fluid nature of canons that ensures a future for the concept, one of varying, coexisting perceptions. The canon becomes a recognized plurality (or discourse) in which some believe in and actively support the canon, others are aware of but dispute the canon, and still others are unaware of its existence. The postmodern state of coexisting possibilities allows canons to exist but denies them a degree of their former authority.

The level to which rock music is perceived as having a canon of albums might ultimately become a matter of individual perception. This is not to say that canonic tendencies or reflections are not present, just that the level of awareness will correspond with awareness of the concept of canonicity and its related values. Any individual is far more likely to be aware of canonical tendencies in rock music if they are already highly aware of canons in other arts.

---

40   Philip Tagg, "' The Work": An Evaluative Charge' in *The Musical Work: Reality or Invention?*, ed. by Michael Talbot (Liverpool: Liverpool University Press, 2000), pp. 153–67 (pp. 166–7).

While a canon formed in today's culture might be expected to reflect the postmodern perspectives of relativism and abundant pluralities, in reality the current mechanisms of privileging of rock albums merely replicate the entrenched patterns of old canons. The values embodied by canons are likely to continue to dominate those canons that last, since these values are inherently the values of lasting relevance: complexity, influence, progress, innovation, originality, genius and enduring value. These markers of permanent modernity are also the hallmarks of artistic legitimacy.

This nascent canon of rock albums maintains a (weak) presence in the onslaught of information presented to us each day. However, it is the music that is remembered by future generations that becomes canonical. One problem revealed by this study is that despite current canon revision in literary and musicological studies, the canon in our minds always belongs to the past. The idea that the canon is still open to augmentation and change – as the lists of 'greatest' albums suggest by adding new bands like the Strokes and Radiohead to their ranks – is a far more negotiable concept than a canon can ever appear to be, and yet this may be the fate of canons of the future, given the different cultural pressures at work.

Our age, as Hugh Kenner has stated, has been canon-minded, but at the same time willing to accept many different canons. Today we meet a myriad of canons that have diluted the concept of the canon from being the elitist stronghold of high art it once was to today's more functional role of selecting the few from the many. At the same time, the traditional canons of literature and classical music continue to maintain a presence above these more recent and less substantial canons.

The structuring of the reception of popular music is a potentially exciting prospect for the opportunity it affords to abandon canons altogether, or at least to firmly reassess their relevance to today's society. As the study of popular music in academia grows, the question is raised as to whether it needs a canon in order to cement itself as a discipline, or if it will discover how to value and teach a range of musics without the limitations of a canon. It is a complex position for our understanding and interpretation of music, a double bind. Canons both limit the potential of our culture and present a common basis for discussion. An increasing number of approaches to the subject of canonicity and popular music (including this book) seem likely to lead to increased awareness of canonicity in the academic study of popular music, and a deeper and more urgent discussion of this issue in the future.

For now, however, canons are still necessary in our culture, since an alternative structure that does not exclude any works or identities is hardly a structure, and a field without categories is simply a mess. However, these canons must now negotiate a far more pluralized culture, and possibly accept a greater degree of change than has been evident in the canons of classical music and literature in the last two centuries.

Appendix

The ten albums studied in detail in this book:

Bob Dylan	*Highway 61 Revisited*	1965
The Beach Boys	*Pet Sounds*	1966
The Beatles	*Revolver*	1966
The Velvet Underground & Nico	*The Velvet Underground & Nico*	1967
Van Morrison	*Astral Weeks*	1969
Marvin Gaye	*What's Going On*	1971
The Rolling Stones	*Exile on Main St.*	1972
Patti Smith	*Horses*	1975
The Sex Pistols	*Never Mind the Bollocks: Here's the Sex Pistols*	1977
Nirvana	*Nevermind*	1991

www.acclaimedmusic.net

Henrik Franzon's amalgamated list of greatest albums based on all critics' lists up to the present day (as updated on 31st July 2007).

1. The Beach Boys, *Pet Sounds*
2. The Beatles, *Revolver*
3. Nirvana, *Nevermind*
4. The Velvet Underground & Nico, *The Velvet Underground & Nico*
5. The Beatles, *Sgt. Pepper's Lonely Hearts Club Band*
6. Bob Dylan, *Blonde on Blonde*
7. The Rolling Stones, *Exile on Main St.*
8. Marvin Gaye, *What's Going On*
9. The Sex Pistols, *Never Mind the Bollocks: Here's the Sex Pistols*
10. The Clash, *London Calling*

11. Bob Dylan, *Highway 61 Revisited*
13. Van Morrison, *Astral Weeks*
22. Patti Smith, *Horses*

The NME series of NME Writers' 'NMEs 100 Best Albums of All Time!' from 1974, 1985, 1993, & 2003:

Various contributors, 'NMEs 100 Best Albums of All Time!', NME, 1 June 1974

1. The Beatles, *Sgt. Pepper's Lonely Hearts Club Band*
2. Bob Dylan, *Blonde on Blonde*
3. The Beach Boys, *Pet Sounds*
4. The Beatles, *Revolver*
5. Bob Dylan, *Highway 61 Revisited*
6. Jimi Hendrix, *Electric Ladyland*
7. Jimi Hendrix, *Are you Experienced?*
8. The Beatles, *Abbey Road*
9. The Rolling Stones, *Sticky Fingers*
10. The Band, *Music From Big Pink*

23. The Velvet Underground & Nico, *The Velvet Underground & Nico*
38. The Rolling Stones, *Exile on Main St.*
63. Van Morrison, *Astral Weeks*

Various contributors, 'NMEs 100 Best Albums of All Time!', NME, 30 November 1985

1. Marvin Gaye, *What's Going On*
2. Van Morrison, *Astral Weeks*
3. Bob Dylan, *Highway 61 Revisited*
4. The Clash, *The Clash*
5. Television, *Marquee Moon*
6. Tom Waits, *Swordfishtrombones*
7. The Band, *The Band*
8. Bob Dylan, *Blonde on Blonde*
9. John Lennon, *John Lennon & Plastic Ono Band*
10. Joy Division, *Unknown Pleasures*

11. The Beatles, *Revolver*
13. The Sex Pistols, *Never Mind the Bollocks: Here's the Sex Pistols*
16. The Velvet Underground & Nico, *The Velvet Underground & Nico*
18. Patti Smith, *Horses*
20. The Beach Boys, *Pet Sounds*
25. The Rolling Stones, *Exile on Main St.*

Various contributors, 'NMEs 100 Best Albums of All Time!', NME, 2 October 1993

1. The Beach Boys, *Pet Sounds*
2. The Beatles, *Revolver*
3. The Sex Pistols, *Never Mind the Bollocks: Here's the Sex Pistols*
4. Marvin Gaye, *What's Going On*
5. The Stone Roses, *The Stone Roses*
6. The Velvet Underground & Nico, *The Velvet Underground & Nico*
7. The Clash, *London Calling*
8. The Beatles, *The Beatles [The White Album]*
9. Public Enemy, *It Takes A Nation Of Millions To Hold Us Back*
10. The Smiths, *The Queen is Dead*

11. The Rolling Stones, *Exile on Main St.*
12. Nirvana, *Nevermind*
14. Bob Dylan, *Highway 61 Revisited*
15. Van Morrison, *Astral Weeks*
31. Patti Smith, *Horses*

Various contributors, 'NMEs 100 Best Albums of All Time!', NME, 8 March 2003

1. The Stone Roses, *The Stone Roses*
2. The Pixies, *Doolittle*
3. The Beach Boys, *Pet Sounds*
4. Television, *Marquee Moon*
5. The Beatles, *Revolver*
6. Love, *Forever Changes*
7. The Strokes, *Is This It*
8. The Smiths, *The Queen Is Dead*
9. The Velvet Underground & Nico, *The Velvet Underground & Nico*
10. The Sex Pistols, *Never Mind the Bollocks: Here's the Sex Pistols*

19. Nirvana, *Nevermind*
27. Marvin Gaye, *What's Going On*
34. Patti Smith, *Horses*
52. The Rolling Stones, *Exile on Main St.*
83. Van Morrison, *Astral Weeks*

Paul Gambaccini, *Paul Gambaccini Presents the Top 100 Albums* (London: GRR/Pavilion, 1987)

1. The Beatles, *Sgt. Pepper's Lonely Hearts Club Band*
2. Bruce Springsteen, *Born to Run*
3. Bob Dylan, *Blonde on Blonde*
4. Marvin Gaye, *What's Going On*
5. Bruce Springsteen, *Born in the U.S.A.*
6. Elvis Presley, *The Sun Collection*
7. The Velvet Underground & Nico, *The Velvet Underground & Nico*
8. The Beach Boys, *Pet Sounds*
9. Van Morrison, *Astral Weeks*
10. The Beatles, *The Beatles [The White Album]*

11. The Rolling Stones, *Exile on Main St.*
17. The Beatles, *Revolver*
18. Bob Dylan, *Highway 61 Revisited*
19. The Sex Pistols, *Never Mind the Bollocks: Here's the Sex Pistols*
87. Patti Smith, *Horses*

'The 100 Greatest Albums of All Time According to *Time Out*', compiled by Nick Coleman and Steve Malins, *Time Out*, 21–28 June 1989

1. Prince, *Sign O The Times*
2. The Velvet Underground & Nico, *The Velvet Underground & Nico*
3. Marvin Gaye, *Let's Get It On*
4. The Clash, *London's Calling*
5. The Rolling Stones, *Exile on Main St.*
6. Bob Dylan, *Blonde on Blonde*
7. Patti Smith, *Horses*
8. Marvin Gaye, *What's Going On*
9. The Clash, *The Clash*
10. Television, *Marquee Moon*

11. The Beach Boys, *Pet Sounds*
12. Van Morrison, *Astral Weeks*
22. The Beatles, *Revolver*
35. The Sex Pistols, *Never Mind the Bollocks: Here's the Sex Pistols*
87. Bob Dylan, *Highway 61 Revisited*

Colin Larkin, *All Time Top 1000 Albums* (Enfield, Guinness, 1994)

The *All Time Top 1000 Albums* offers a series of shorter lists defined by genre, including 'The Top 250 Rock and Pop Albums', 'The Top 50 Punk Albums', and 'The Top 50 Soul Albums' etc. However, this excerpt is taken from the final 'Top 1000 Chart of Charts' that comprises an amalgamation of all the others.

1. The Beatles, *Sgt. Pepper's Lonely Hearts Club Band*
2. Bob Dylan, *Highway 61 Revisited*
3. The Beach Boys, *Pet Sounds*
4. Bob Dylan, *Blonde on Blonde*
5. The Beatles, *Revolver*
6. Pink Floyd, *Dark Side of the Moon*
7. Van Morrison, *Astral Weeks*
8. The Rolling Stones, *Let It Bleed*
9. Marvin Gaye, *What's Going On*
10. The Beatles, *Rubber Soul*

12. The Sex Pistols, *Never Mind the Bollocks: Here's the Sex Pistols*
20. The Velvet Underground & Nico, *The Velvet Underground & Nico*
57. Nirvana, *Nevermind*
114. The Rolling Stones, *Exile on Main St.*
805. Patti Smith, *Horses*

Various contributors, 'The Hundred Greatest Albums Ever Made', *Mojo*, 21 (August 1995)

1. The Beach Boys, *Pet Sounds*
2. Van Morrison, *Astral Weeks*
3. The Beatles, *Revolver*
4. The Rolling Stones, *Exile on Main St.*
5. Bob Dylan, *Highway 61 Revisited*
6. Marvin Gaye, *What's Going On*
7. The Rolling Stones, *Let It Bleed*
8. Bob Dylan, *Blonde on Blonde*
9. The Velvet Underground & Nico, *The Velvet Underground & Nico*
10. Patti Smith, *Horses*

22. The Sex Pistols, *Never Mind the Bollocks: Here's the Sex Pistols*
33. Nirvana, *Nevermind*

List discussed by Adam Sweeting, 'Ton of Joy', *The Guardian*, 19 September 1997

1. Marvin Gaye, *What's Going On*
2. The Beatles, *Revolver*
3. The Sex Pistols, *Never Mind The Bollocks: Here's the Sex Pistols*
4. Nirvana, *Nevermind*
5. The Stone Roses, *The Stone Roses*
6. The Beach Boys, *Pet Sounds*
7. David Bowie, *The Rise And Fall Of Ziggy Stardust*
8. The Velvet Underground & Nico, *The Velvet Underground & Nico*
9. The Beatles, *The Beatles [The White Album]*
10. Van Morrison, *Astral Weeks*

Colin Larkin, *All-Time Top 1,000 Albums*, *2nd edn* (London: Virgin, 1998)

[As discussed by Martin Wroe, 'Hits From the Decade That Taste Forgot' and Simon Frith, 'Our Favourite Rock Records Tend to Go Round and Round', *The Observer*, 6 September, 1998.]

1. The Beatles, *Revolver*
2. The Beatles, *Sgt. Pepper's Lonely Hearts Club Band*
3. The Beatles, *The Beatles [The White Album]*
4. Nirvana, *Nevermind*
5. The Beatles, *Abbey Road*
6. The Beach Boys, *Pet Sounds*
7. R.E.M., *Automatic For the People*
8. Pink Floyd, *Dark Side of the Moon*
9. Oasis, *What's the Story (Morning Glory)*
10. Radiohead, *The Bends*

13. The Sex Pistols, *Never Mind the Bollocks: Here's the Sex Pistols*
15. Van Morrison, *Astral Weeks*
22. The Velvet Underground & Nico, *The Velvet Underground & Nico*
26. Bob Dylan, *Highway 61 Revisited*
27. The Rolling Stones, *Exile on Main St.*
32. Marvin Gaye, *What's Going On*
88. Patti Smith, *Horses*

Various contributors, '100 Greatest Stars of the 20th Century', *Q*, 159 (August 1999)

1. John Lennon
2. Paul McCartney
3. Kurt Cobain
4. Bob Dylan
11. Keith Richards
20. Brian Wilson
22. Mick Jagger
25. Marvin Gaye
26. Ringo Starr
34. Patti Smith
36. George Harrison
48. Johnny Rotten
59. Lou Reed
82. Igor Stravinsky
92. Claude Debussy

Colin Larkin, *All-Time Top 1,000 Albums, 3rd edn* **(London: Virgin, 2000)**

This poll has taken into account greatest album lists and critics' views as well as polling over 200,000 (non-specified) people. It is international, and some interesting trends emerge from that – for instance, American bands like the Beach Boys, the Byrds and Steely Dan received less American votes than British, and likewise the British bands the Cure, Depeche Mode and Leftfield received more American than British nominations. This poll (mostly) discounts compilation or 'best-of' albums as its aim is to list albums that represent 'a showcase of songs put together by an artist at a particular time'; film soundtracks, however, are allowed, as are genres other than rock – there are a few jazz albums as well as rap, dance, reggae and soul. The introduction also points out that one label, Parlophone (part of EMI) is responsible for all of the top five albums (shared out 3/2 to the Beatles/Radiohead), suggesting a trend in labels (Colin Larkin, *All-Time Top 1000 Albums (3rd Edition)*, (London: Virgin, 2000), pp. 6–8):

1. The Beatles, *Revolver*
2. Radiohead, *The Bends*
3. The Beatles, *Sgt. Pepper's Lonely Hearts Club Band*
4. Radiohead, *OK Computer*
5. The Beatles, *The Beatles [The White Album]*
6. R.E.M., *Automatic For The People*
7. Bob Dylan, *Blood On The Tracks*
8. The Beatles, *Abbey Road*
9. Pink Floyd, *The Dark Side Of The Moon*
10. The Smiths, *The Queen Is Dead*

13. The Velvet Underground & Nico, *The Velvet Underground & Nico*
16. Van Morrison, *Astral Weeks*
17. Nirvana, *Nevermind*
18. The Beach Boys, *Pet Sounds*
26. Bob Dylan, *Highway 61 Revisited*
29. The Sex Pistols, *Never Mind the Bollocks: Here's the Sex Pistols*
35. The Rolling Stones, *Exile on Main St.*
39. Marvin Gaye, *What's Going On*
291. Patti Smith, *Horses*

Various contributors, 'The 500 Greatest Albums of All Time', *Rolling Stone*, 11 December 2003

[273 unnamed voters listed their top 50 albums, in order of preference; The Beatles have 10 entries, including 5 in the 'top 20'.]

1. The Beatles, *Sgt. Pepper's Lonely Hearts Club Band*
2. The Beach Boys, *Pet Sounds*
3. The Beatles, *Revolver*
4. Bob Dylan, *Highway 61 Revisited*
5. The Beatles, *Rubber Soul*
6. Marvin Gaye, *What's Going On*
7. The Rolling Stones, *Exile on Main St.*
8. The Clash, *London Calling*
9. Bob Dylan, *Blonde on Blonde*
10. The Beatles, *The Beatles [The White Album]*
11. Elvis Presley, *The Sun Sessions*
12. Miles Davis, *Kind of Blue*
13. The Velvet Underground & Nico, *The Velvet Underground & Nico*
14. The Beatles, *Abbey Road*
15. The Jimi Hendrix Experience, *Are You Experienced?*
16. Bob Dylan, *Blood on the Tracks*
17. Nirvana, *Nevermind*
18. Bruce Springsteen, *Born to Run*
19. Van Morrison, *Astral Weeks*
20. Michael Jackson, *Thriller*

41. The Sex Pistols, *Never Mind the Bollocks: Here's the Sex Pistols*
44. Patti Smith, *Horses*

VH1's 100 Greatest Albums, ed. by Jacob Hoye (New York and London: MTV Books/Pocket Books, 2003)

1. The Beatles, *Revolver*
2. Nirvana, *Nevermind*
3. The Beach Boys, *Pet Sounds*
4. Marvin Gaye, *What's Going On*
5. The Jimi Hendrix Experience, *Are You Experienced?*
6. The Beatles, *Rubber Soul*
7. Stevie Wonder, *Songs in the Key of Life*
8. The Beatles, *Abbey Road*
9. Bob Dylan, *Blonde on Blonde*
10. The Beatles, *Sgt. Pepper's Lonely Hearts Club Band*

12. The Rolling Stones, *Exile on Main St.*
17. The Sex Pistols, *Never Mind the Bollocks: Here's the Sex Pistols*
19. The Velvet Underground & Nico, *The Velvet Underground & Nico*
22. Bob Dylan, *Highway 61 Revisited*
28. Patti Smith, *Horses*
40. Van Morrison, *Astral Weeks*

Various contributors, 'The 100 Greatest British Albums', *Observer Music Monthly*, **10 (June 2004)**

100 critics, industry figures and pop stars polled for their top 10 British albums, not compilations.

1. The Stone Roses, *The Stone Roses*
2. The Beatles, *Revolver*
3. The Clash, *London Calling*
4. Van Morrison, *Astral Weeks*
5. The Beatles, *Sgt. Pepper's Lonely Hearts Club Band*
6. The Beatles, *The Beatles [The White Album]*
7. The Rolling Stones, *Sticky Fingers*
8. The Rolling Stones, *Exile on Main St.*
9. Massive Attack, *Blue Lines*
10. Public Image Ltd., *Metal Box*

14. The Sex Pistols. *Never Mind the Bollocks: Here's the Sex Pistols*

Various contributors, 'The 100 Greatest Albums Ever! * As Voted By You', *Q*, 235 (February 2006)

1. Radiohead, *OK Computer*
2. Radiohead, *The Bends*
3. Nirvana, *Nevermind*
4. The Beatles, *Revolver*
5. Oasis, *Definitely Maybe*
6. The Stone Roses, *The Stone Roses*
7. R.E.M., *Automatic For the People*
8. Oasis, *(What's the Story) Morning Glory*
9. U2, *Achtung Baby*
10. Radiohead, *Kid A*

18. The Beach Boys, *Pet Sounds*
28. The Sex Pistols, *Never Mind the Bollocks: Here's the Sex Pistols*
32. Marvin Gaye, *What's Going On*
34. The Rolling Stones, *Exile on Main St*
42. The Velvet Underground & Nico, *The Velvet Underground & Nico*
45. Bob Dylan, *Highway 61 Revisited*
47. Van Morrison, *Astral Weeks*

Bibliography

Abbott, Kingsley, *The Beach Boys' Pet Sounds: The Greatest Album of the Twentieth Century* (London: Helter Skelter Publishing, 2001).

Altieri, Charles, 'An Idea and Ideal of a Literary Canon', in *Canons*, ed. by Robert von Hallberg (Chicago and London: Chicago University Press, 1984), pp. 41–64.

Appen, Ralf von, and André Doehring, 'Nevermind The Beatles, Here's Exile 61 and Nico: "The Top 100 Records of All Time" – A Canon of Pop and Rock Albums From a Sociological and an Aesthetic Perspective', *Popular Music*, Special Issue on Canonisation, 25/1 (January 2006), 21–39.

Bangs, Lester, 'The British Invasion', in *The Rolling Stone Illustrated History of Rock & Roll*, ed. by Anthony DeCurtis and James Henke with Holly George-Warren, 2nd edn (London: Straight Arrow, 1992), pp. 199–208.

Beard, David, and Kenneth Gloag, *Musicology: The Key Concepts* (London and New York: Routledge, 2005).

Bergeron, Katherine, 'Prologue: Disciplining Music', in *Disciplining Music: Musicology and Its Canons*, ed. by Katherine Bergeron and Philip V. Bohlman (Chicago and London: University of Chicago Press, 1992), pp. 1–9.

Bergeron, Katherine, and Philip V. Bohlman, eds, *Disciplining Music: Musicology and Its Canons* (Chicago and London: University of Chicago Press, 1992).

Berkenstadt, Jim, and Charles Cross, *Nevermind: Nirvana*, Classic Rock Albums Series (London and New York: Schirmer Trade Books, 1998).

Bloom, Harold, *The Anxiety of Influence* (New York: Oxford University Press, 1973).

Bloom, Harold, *The Western Canon: The Books and School of the Ages* (London and New York: Harcourt Brace & Company, 1994).

Bohlman, Philip V., 'Ethnomusicology's Challenge to the Canon; The Canon's Challenge to Ethnomusicology', in *Disciplining Music: Musicology and Its Canons*, ed. by Katherine Bergeron and Philip V. Bohlman (Chicago and London: University of Chicago Press, 1992), pp. 116–36.

Bohlman, Philip V., 'Epilogue: Musics and Canons', in *Disciplining Music: Musicology and Its Canons*, ed. by Katherine Bergeron and Philip V. Bohlman (Chicago and London: University of Chicago Press, 1992), pp. 197–210.

Brocken, Michael, 'Some Other Guys! Some Theories About Signification: Beatles Cover Versions', *Popular Music & Society*, 20/4 (1996), 5–36.

Buckley, Jonathan, Orla Duane, Mark Ellingham, and Al Spicer, eds, *Rock: The Rough Guide*, 2nd edn (London: Rough Guides Ltd, 1999).

Citron, Marcia J., *Gender and the Musical Canon* (Cambridge: Cambridge University Press, 1993).

Cloonan, Martin, 'What is Popular Music Studies? Some Observations', *British Journal of Music Education*, 22/1, 1–17.

Davies, John, 'Baroque and Roll', *Times Higher*, 15 December 1995, 13–14.

DeCurtis, Anthony, and James Henke with Holly George-Warren, eds, *The Rolling Stone Illustrated History of Rock & Roll*, 2nd edn (London: Straight Arrow, 1992).

Drakakis, John, *Alternative Shakespeares* (London: Routledge 1985).

Dunne, Michael, '"Tore Down A La Rimbaud": Van Morrison's References and Allusions', *Popular Music and Society*, 24/4 (2000), 15–30.

Easthope, Anthony, *Literary into Cultural Studies* (London and New York: Routledge, 1991).

Edmonds, Ben, *What's Going On?: Marvin Gaye and the Last Days of Motown Soul* (Edinburgh: Canongate, 2002).

Egan, Sean, ed., *100 Albums That Changed Music: and 500 Songs You Need to Hear* (London: Robinson, 2006).

Erlewine, Michael, with Chris Woodstra and Vladimir Bogdanov, eds, *All Music Guide: the Best CDs, Albums & Tapes* (San Francisco: Miller Freeman Books, 1994).

Everett, Walter, *The Beatles as Musicians: Revolver Through the Anthology* (New York and Oxford: Oxford University Press, 1999).

Everett, Walter, *The Beatles as Musicians: The Quarry Men Through Rubber Soul* (New York and Oxford: Oxford University Press, 2001).

Everett, Walter, 'The Future of Beatles Research,' in *Beatlestudies 3: Proceedings of the BEATLES 2000 Conference*, ed. by Yrjö Heinonen, Markus Heuger, Sheila Whiteley, Terhi Nurmesjärvi and Jouni Koskimäki (Jyväskylä: University of Jyväskylä Press, 2001), pp. 25–44.

Fornäs, Johan, *Cultural Theory and Late Modernity* (London: Sage, 1995).

Fricke, David, 'The Velvet Underground', in *The Rolling Stone Illustrated History of Rock & Roll*, ed. by Anthony DeCurtis and James Henke with Holly George-Warren, 2nd edn (London: Straight Arrow, 1992), pp. 348–69.

Frith, Simon, *Sound Effects: Youth, Leisure, and the Politics of Rock 'n' Roll* (New York: Pantheon, 1981).

Frith, Simon, '" The Magic That Can Set You Free": The Ideology of Folk and the Myth of the Rock Community', *Popular Music*, 1 (1981), 159–68.

Frith, Simon, *Performing Rites: On the Value of Popular Music* (Oxford and New York: Oxford University Press, 1996).

Frith, Simon, 'Our Favourite Rock Records Tend to Go Round and Round', *The Observer*, 6 September 1998.

Frith, Simon, and Howard Horne, *Art Into Pop* (London and New York: Routledge, 1989).

Frith, Simon and Andrew Goodwin, eds, *On Record: Rock, Pop and the Written Word* (London: Routledge, 1990).

Fusilli, Jim, *Pet Sounds*, 33 1/3 Series (New York and London: Continuum, 2005).

Gambaccini, Paul, *Paul Gambaccini Presents the Top 100 Albums* (London: GRR/ Pavilion, 1987).

Goehr, Lydia, *The Imaginary Museum of Musical Works: An Essay in the Philosophy of Music* (Oxford and New York: Oxford University Press, 1992).

Gorak, Jan, ed., *Canon vs Culture: Reflections on the Current Debate* (New York and London: Garland, 2001).

Granata, Charles L., *I Just Wasn't Made for These Times: Brian Wilson and the Making of Pet Sounds* (London: Unanimous, 2003).

Green, Lucy, *How Popular Musicians Learn: A Way Ahead For Music Education* (Aldershot: Ashgate, 2001).

Griffiths, Dai, 'Cover Versions and the Sound of Identity in Motion', in *Popular Music Studies*, ed. by David Hesmondhalgh and Keith Negus (London: Arnold, 2002), pp. 51–64.

Grossberg, Lawrence, *We Gotta Get Out of this Place: Popular Conservatism and Postmodern Culture* (New York and London: Routledge, 1992).

Grossberg, Lawrence, 'The Media Economy of Rock Culture: Cinema, Post-Modernity and Authenticity', in *Sound and Vision: The Music Video Reader*, ed. by Simon Frith, Andrew Goodwin and Lawrence Grossberg (London: Routledge, 1993), pp. 185–209.

Grossberg, Lawrence, 'Reflections of a Disappointed Popular Music Scholar', in *Rock Over the Edge: Transformations in Popular Music Culture*, ed. by Roger Beebe, Denise Fulbrook and Ben Saunders (Durham and London: Duke University Press, 2002), pp. 25–59.

Grout, Donald J., *A History of Western Music* (New York and London: W.W. Norton & Company, 1960).

Grout, Donald J. and Claude V. Palisca, *A History of Western Music*, 6th edn (New York and London: W.W. Norton & Company, 2001).

Guillory, John, 'Canon', in *Critical Terms for Literary Study*, ed. by Frank Lentricchia and Thomas McLaughlin (Chicago: University of Chicago Press, 1990), pp. 233–49.

Guillory, John, *Cultural Capital: The Problem of Literary Canon Formation* (Chicago and London: University of Chicago Press, 1993).

Hallberg, Robert von, ed., *Canons* (Chicago and London: University of Chicago Press, 1984).

Harris, James F., *Philosophy at 33 1/3 rpm: Themes of Classic Rock Music* (Chicago and La Salle, IL: Open Court, 1993).

Harris, John, 'Out of Their Heads', in *From Elvis to the Beatles*, *Q* Special Edition: 50 Years of Rock 'N' Roll 1954–2004, (London: EMAP, 2004), 60–65.

Harvard, Joe, *The Velvet Underground & Nico*, 33 1/3 Series (New York and London: Continuum, 2004).

Heinonen, Yrjö, Tuomas Eerola, Jouni Koskimäki, Terhi Nurmesjärvi and John Richardson, eds, *Beatlestudies 1: Songwriting, Recording, and Style Change* (Jyväskylä: University of Jyväskylä Press, 1998).

Heinonen, Yrjö, Tuomas Eerola, Jouni Koskimäki, Terhi Nurmesjärvi and John Richardson, '(Being a Short Diversion to) Current Perspectives in Beatles Research', in *Beatlestudies 1: Songwriting, Recording, and Style Change*, ed. by Yrjö Heinonen, Tuomas Eerola, Jouni Koskimäki, Terhi Nurmesjärvi and John Richardson (Jyväskylä: University of Jyväskylä Press, 1998), pp. i–iv.

Heinonen, Yrjö, Jouni Koskimäki, Seppo Niemi and Terhi Nurmesjärvi, eds, *Beatlestudies 2: History, Identity, Authenticity* (Jyväskylä: University of Jyväskylä Press, 2000).

Heinonen, Yrjö, Markus Heuger, Sheila Whiteley, Terhi Nurmesjärvi and Jouni Koskimäki, eds, *Beatlestudies 3: Proceedings of the BEATLES 2000 Conference* (Jyväskylä: University of Jyväskylä Press, 2001).

Herrnstein Smith, Barbara, 'Contingencies of Value' in *Canons*, ed. by Robert von Hallberg (Chicago and London: University of Chicago Press, 1984), pp. 5–39.

Herrnstein Smith, Barbara, *Contingencies of Value: Alternative Perspectives for Critical Theory* (Cambridge, MA. and London: Harvard University Press, 1988).

Heylin, Clinton, *Never Mind the Bollocks: Here's the Sex Pistols – The Sex Pistols*, Classic Rock Albums Series (New York: Schirmer Books, 1998).

Holden, Stephen, 'The Evolution of the Singer-Songwriter' in *The Rolling Stone Illustrated History of Rock & Roll*, ed. by Anthony DeCurtis and James Henke with Holly George-Warren, 2nd edn (London: Straight Arrow, 1992), pp. 480–91.

Hornby, Nick, *High Fidelity* (London: Gollancz, 1995).

Horner, Bruce, and Thomas Swiss, eds, *Key Terms in Popular Music and Culture* (Massachusetts and Oxford: Blackwell, 1999).

Hoye, Jacob, ed., *VH1's 100 Greatest Albums* (New York and London: MTV Books/Pocket Books, 2003).

Irvin, Jim and Colin McLear, eds, *The Mojo Collection: The Ultimate Music Companion*, 3rd edn (Edinburgh and New York: Canongate, 2003).

Janovitz, Bill, *Exile on Main St.*, 33 1/3 Series (New York and London: Continuum, 2005).

Kennedy, George A., 'The Origin of the Concept of a Canon and its Application to the Greek and Latin Classics', in *Canon vs Culture: Reflections on the Current Debate*, ed. by Jan Gorak (New York and London: Garland, 2001), pp. 105–16.

Kenner, Hugh, 'The Making of the Modernist Canon', in *Canons*, ed. by Robert von Hallberg (Chicago and London: University of Chicago Press, 1984), pp. 363–75.

Kerman, Joseph, 'How We Got into Analysis, and How to Get Out', *Critical Inquiry*, 7 (Winter 1980), 311–31.

Kerman, Joseph, 'A Few Canonic Variations', in *Canons*, ed. by Robert von Hallberg (Chicago and London: University of Chicago Press, 1984), pp.177–95.

Kermode, Frank, *Forms of Attention* (Chicago and London: University of Chicago Press, 1985).

Larkin, Colin *All Time Top 1000 Albums* (Enfield, Guinness, 1994).

Larkin, Colin, *All-Time Top 1,000 Albums*, 2nd edn (London: Virgin, 1998).

Larkin, Colin, *All-Time Top 1,000 Albums*, 3rd edn (London: Virgin, 2000).

Leaf, David, 'Landmark Albums: *Pet Sounds*', in *Back to the Beach: A Brian Wilson and the Beach Boys Reader*, ed. by Kingsley Abbott (London: Helter Skelter, 1997), pp. 40–42.

Leavis, F.R., *The Great Tradition: George Eliot, Henry James, Joseph Conrad* (London: Chatto and Windus, 1948).

Light, Alan, 'Bob Dylan', in *The Rolling Stone Illustrated History of Rock & Roll*, ed. by Anthony DeCurtis and James Henke with Holly George-Warren, 2nd edn (London: Straight Arrow, 1992), pp. 299–308.

Marcus, Greil, 'Anarchy in the U.K.', in *The Rolling Stone Illustrated History of Rock & Roll*, ed. by Anthony DeCurtis and James Henke with Holly George-Warren, 2nd edn (London: Straight Arrow, 1992), pp. 594–607.

Marcus, Greil, 'The Beatles', in *The Rolling Stone Illustrated History of Rock & Roll*, ed. by Anthony DeCurtis and James Henke with Holly George-Warren, 2nd edn (London: Straight Arrow, 1992), pp. 209–22.

Marcus, Greil, 'Van Morrison', in *The Rolling Stone Illustrated History of Rock & Roll*, ed. by Anthony DeCurtis and James Henke with Holly George-Warren, 2nd edn (London: Straight Arrow, 1992), pp. 442–7.

Mazullo, Mark, 'The Man Whom the World Sold: Kurt Cobain, Rock's Progressive Aesthetic, and the Challenges of Authenticity', *The Musical Quarterly*, 84/4 (Winter 2000), 713–49.

Mellers, Wilfred, *Twilight of the Gods: The Beatles in Retrospect* (London: Faber & Faber, 1976 (1973)).

Mellers, Wilfred, 'God, Modality and Meaning in Some Recent Songs of Bob Dylan', *Popular Music*, (1981), 143–57.

Middleton, Richard, *Studying Popular Music* (Buckingham and Bristol: Open University Press, 1990).

Middleton, Richard, 'Work-in-(g) Practice: Configuration of the Popular Music Intertext', in *The Musical Work: Reality or Invention?*, ed. by Michael Talbot (Liverpool: Liverpool University Press, 2000), pp. 59–87.

Moody, Paul, 'Kurt: the Final Weeks', *New Musical Express*, 10 April 2004, 24–6.

Moore, Allan F., *The Beatles: Sgt Pepper's Lonely Heart's Club Band* (Cambridge: Cambridge University Press, 1997).

Moore, Allan F., *Rock: The Primary Text, Developing a Musicology of Rock*, 2nd edn (Aldershot: Ashgate, 2001).

Moore, Allan F., 'Authenticity as Authentication', *Popular Music*, 21/2 (2002), 209–25.

Noland, Carrie Jaurès, 'Rimbaud and Patti Smith: Style as Social Deviance', *Critical Inquiry*, 21/3 (1995), 581–610.

O'Hagan, Sean, '#4, *Astral Weeks*', in Various Contributors, 'The 100 Greatest British Albums', *Observer Music Monthly*, 10 (June 2004), 17.

Perry, John, *Exile On Main St.* (New York: Schirmer Books, 2000).

Petredis, Alex, 'A Little Help From Their Friends', The *Guardian G2*, 16 January 2004, 14–15.

Polizzotti, Mark, *Highway 61 Revisited*, 33 1/3 Series (New York and London: Continuum, 2006).

Quantick, David, '*Revolver*', in Various Contributors, 'The 100 Greatest British Albums Ever', *Q*, 165 (June 2000), 59–93.

Raphael, Amy, 'The Stone Roses: *The Stone Roses*', in Various Contributors, 'The 100 Greatest British Albums', *Observer Music Monthly*, 10 (June 2004), 8.

Regev, Motti, 'Introduction to Special Issue on Canonisation', *Popular Music*, Special Issue on Canonisation, 25/1 (January 2006), 1–2.

Reising, Russell, ed., *Every Sound There Is': The Beatles' Revolver and the Transformation of Rock and Roll* (Aldershot: Ashgate, 2002).

Reynolds, Simon, 'Walking On Thin Ice', *The Wire,* 209 (July 2001), 26–33.

Rockwell, John, 'The Emergence of Art Rock', in *The Rolling Stone Illustrated History of Rock & Roll*, ed. by Anthony DeCurtis and James Henke with Holly George-Warren, 2nd edn (London: Straight Arrow, 1992), pp. 492–9.

Rockwell, John, 'The Sound of New York City', in *The Rolling Stone Illustrated History of Rock & Roll*, ed. by Anthony DeCurtis and James Henke with Holly George-Warren, 2nd edn (London: Straight Arrow, 1992), pp. 549–60.

Ross, Stephen David, ed., *Art and Its Significance: An Anthology of Aesthetic Theory*, (Albany, NY: SUNY Press, 1994).

Sanjek, David, 'Institutions', in *Key Terms in Popular Music and Culture*, ed. by Bruce Horner and Thomas Swiss (Massachusetts and Oxford: Blackwell, 1999), pp. 46–56.

Savile, Anthony, *The Test of Time: An Essay in Philosophical Aesthetics* (Oxford: Clarendon Press, 1982).

Shaw, Philip, *Horses* 33 1/3 Series (New York and London: Continuum, 2008)

Shuker, Roy, *Key Concepts in Popular Music Studies* (London: Routledge, 1998).

Shuker, Roy, *Key Terms in Popular Music and Culture*, ed. by Bruce Horner and Thomas Swiss (Massachusetts and Oxford: Blackwell, 1999).

Silver, Dan, 'Love Will Tear Us Apart', in *From U2 to the White Stripes*, *Q* Special Edition: 50 Years of Rock 'N' Roll 1954–2004, (London: EMAP, 2004), 84–7.

Silvers, Anita, 'The Canon in Aesthetics', in *The Encyclopaedia of Aesthetics*, ed. by Michael Kelly (Oxford: Oxford University Press, 1998), I, pp. 334–8.

Stratton, John, 'Between Two Worlds: Art and Commercialism in the Record Industry', *The Sociological Review*, 30 (1982), 267–85.

Sutherland, Steve, ed., 'Bob Dylan and the Folk Rock Boom', *NME Originals*, 2/5 (2005).

Sweeting, Adam, 'Ton of Joy', *The Guardian*, 19 September 1997, 2.

Tagg, Philip, '" The Work": An Evaluative Charge', in *The Musical Work: Reality or Invention?*, ed. by Michael Talbot (Liverpool: Liverpool University Press, 2000), pp. 153–67.

Talbot, Michael, ed., *The Musical Work: Reality or Invention?* (Liverpool: Liverpool University Press, 2000).

Taruskin, Richard, *The Oxford History of Western Music* (Oxford and New York: Oxford University Press, 2005).

Tate, Joseph, ed., *The Music and Art of Radiohead* (Aldershot: Ashgate, 2005).

Tristman, Richard, 'Canon: Historical and Conceptual Overview', in *The Encyclopaedia of Aesthetics*, ed. by Michael Kelly (Oxford: Oxford University Press, 1998), I, pp. 331–4.

Various Contributors, 'The 100 Greatest Albums of All Time According to *Time Out*', compiled by Nick Coleman and Steve Malins, *Time Out*, 21–28 June 1989, 18–23.

Various Contributors, 'Set Adrift on Memory Discs: 40 Records That Captured the Moment', *New Musical Express*, 9 May 1992, 42–5.

Various Contributors, 'The Hundred Greatest Albums Ever Made', *Mojo*, 21 (August 1995), 50–87.

Various Contributors, '100 Greatest Stars of the 20th Century', *Q*, 159 (August 1999), 43–74.

Various Contributors, *The 100 Best Record Covers of All Time* (London: EMAP, 2001).

Various Contributors, 'NME's 100 Best Albums of All Time!', *New Musical Express*, 8 March 2003, 35–42.

Various Contributors, 'The 500 Greatest Albums of All Time', *Rolling Stone*, 11 December 2003, 83–178.

Various Contributors, 'The 100 Greatest British Albums', *Observer Music Monthly*, 10 (June 2004).

Various Contributors, 'Greatest Songwriters of All Time', *Q*, 219 (October 2004), 73–99.

Various Contributors, *From Elvis to the Beatles*, *Q* Special Edition: 50 Years of Rock 'N' Roll 1954–2004 (London: EMAP, 2004).

Various Contributors, *From U2 to the White Stripes*, *Q* Special Edition: 50 Years of Rock 'N' Roll 1954–2004 (London: EMAP, 2004).

Various Contributors, 'The 100 Greatest Albums Ever! * As Voted By You', *Q*, 235 (February 2006), 47–79.

Watson, Mary R., and N. Anand, 'Award Ceremony as an Arbiter of Commerce and Canon in the Popular Music Industry', *Popular Music*, Special Issue on Canonisation, 25/1 (January 2006), 41–56.

Weber, William, *The Rise of Musical Classics in Eighteenth-Century England: A Study in Canon, Ritual, and Ideology* (Oxford: Clarendon Press, 1992).

Weber, William, 'The Intellectual Origins of Musical Canon in Eighteenth-Century England', *The Journal of the American Musicological Society*, 47 (1994), 488–520.

Weber, William, 'Canon and the Traditions of Musical Culture', in *Canon vs Culture: Reflections on the Current Debate*, ed. by Jan Gorak (New York and London: Garland, 2001), pp. 135–50.

Wenner, Jann S., 'John Lennon: The Rolling Stone Interview', in *20 Years of Rolling Stone: What a Long, Strange Trip It's Been*, ed. by Jann S. Wenner (New York: Friendly Press, 1987), pp. 101–16.

Whiteley, Sheila, ed., *Sexing the Groove: Popular Music and Gender* (London and New York: Routledge, 1997).

Whiteley, Sheila, *Women and Popular Music: Sexuality, Identity and Subjectivity* (London and New York: Routledge, 2000).

Wicke, Peter, *Rock Music: Culture, Aesthetics and Sociology* (Cambridge and New York: Cambridge University Press, 1987).

Wilkinson, Christopher, 'Deforming/Reforming the Canon: Challenges of a Multicultural Music History Course', *Black Music Research Journal*, 16/2 (Fall 1996), 259–77.

Wroe, Martin, 'Hits From the Decade That Taste Forgot', *The Observer*, 6 September 1998.

Select Discography

[Recording references refer to current CD issue numbers, as listed in Jim Irvin and Colin McLear, *The Mojo Collection: The Ultimate Music Companion*, 3rd edn (Edinburgh and New York: Canongate, 2000/2003)]

Bob Dylan, *Highway 61 Revisited*. CBS. 4609532. 1965.

The Beach Boys, *Pet Sounds*. Capitol. 5212412. 1966.

The Beatles, *Revolver*. Parlophone. CDP 7 46441 2. 1966.

The Velvet Underground & Nico , *The Velvet Underground & Nico*. Verve. 5312502. 1967.

The Beatles, *Sgt. Pepper's Lonely Hearts Club Band*. Parlophone. CDP 7 46442 2. 1967.

Van Morrison, *Astral Weeks*. Warner Brothers. 7599271762. 1969.

Marvin Gaye, *What's Going On*. Tamla Motown. 5308832. 1971.

The Rolling Stones, *Exile on Main Street*. Rolling Stones Records. CDV 2731. 1972.

Patti Smith, *Horses*. Arista. 07822188272. 1975.

The Sex Pistols, *Never Mind the Bollocks: Here's the Sex Pistols*. Virgin. CDVX2086. 1977.

The Stone Roses, *The Stone Roses*. Silvertone. ORE CD 502. 1989.

Nirvana, *Nevermind*. Geffen. DGCD 24425. 1991.

The Velvet Underground, *Peel Slowly and See: The Velvet Underground Box Set*. Polydor Records. 31452 7887–2. 1995.

The Beach Boys, *The Pet Sounds Sessions [Box Set]*. Capitol Records. 7243 8 37662 2 2. 1996.

Webography

Footman, Tim, 'Gathering Moss: The Fossilisation of *Rolling Stone*' by Tim Footman, published by *Rock's Backpages*, at www.rocksbackpages.com, November 2003, accessed 09/06/07.

http://www.acclaimedmusic.net, accessed 05/08/07.

http://www.timepieces.nl, accessed 23/09/07.

http://www.rocklist.net, accessed 23/09/07.

Index

aesthetic strength 15
    portrayal of human experience 26, 60
    in the reception of rock albums 30–33
albums
    as canonical work 42–5, 66, 79, 80,
        81–2, 93, 115, 119–20, 126, 127,
        134
    as cohesive whole 42–3, 120
    compilation albums 45, 66, 138
    concept albums 43–4, 77
    cover artwork 45
All Music Guide: The Best CDs, Albums &
    Tapes (ed. by Erlewine, Woodstra &
    Bogdanov) 39, 44, 46, 51
All-Time Top 1,000 Albums (Larkin) 25, 29,
    34, 47, 60, 67, 88, 103, 105, 108,
    127, 145, 147, 148
Altieri, Charles ('An Idea and Ideal of a
    Literary Canon') 5–6, 13n40, 22,
    72, 121
analysis
    in classical music 17–18, 112
    in the reception of rock 32–3, 50n131,
        79, 112, 114, 115
antiquity 5, 11–12
    in the reception of rock albums 29–30,
        72–3, 77, 128–9
art
    ambivalence of rock towards artistic
        status 51, 52
    'art rock' 49–50, 52
    art school influence on rock music 51,
        121
    artistic ambition in rock 39–40, 48–51,
        95, 96, 106, 121
    comparison of rock music with the high
        arts 48–9, 129–30
    redefinition of art in the reception of
        rock 117
artist / genius 16, 18
    associated with works 42, 120
    collective artist / genius (the band) 39,
        61, 65, 80–81, 120

'genius' in the reception of rock albums
    29, 38, 52, 75, 97
mythologized figures 34–5, 37–8
the record producer 37, 64, 79–80,
    80n12, 130
in rock 34–5, 39, 42, 66, 80–81, 84, 122,
    126, 129, 137
Astral Weeks 40, 41, 48, 63
    album as a cohesive whole 43, 44, 46
    constant citation in lists 25, 67, 95, 102
    as expression of the self 36, 83
    mature subjects / audience 47, 93
    originality / strangeness / difference 30,
        31–2, 33, 54
    see also Morrison, Van
audience of rock 91, 105, 106, 107–9, 128,
    133, 137
    canonical audience in rock 41, 47–8,
        106, 120
aura 16, 42, 34, 67, 82, 90
authenticity 15, 16, 110
    in performance / recording 20, 81–3, 86
autonomy of vision 36–7, 67, 84
    expression of human experience 36, 95,
        106
    extremes of experience 39, 91, 109
    in the reception of rock albums 35–6,
        39, 41
    of singer-songwriter 36, 65, 82, 83–4,
        93

Bach, J.S. 5, 17, 19, 114, 131
Beach Boys, the 2, 25, 91, 112, 113
    Beach Boys' Pet Sounds: The Greatest
        Album of the Twentieth Century, The
        (Abbott) 31, 40, 44, 46, 73
    'Good Vibrations' 41, 59, 63
    secondary material 83–4, 120
    Smile 63, 63n56, 74
    see also Pet Sounds; Wilson, Brian
Beatles, the 39–40, 65, 88, 89, 98, 137–8
    academic / serious reception 1, 106,
        111, 112–14